'As the perfect complement to *Making Your Primary School E-safe*, Adrienne Katz has once again cut straight to the heart of the matter. This timely book will quickly become an indispensable and topical resource for any teacher or family member eager to keep children secure in a cyber world where it's all too easy to feel several miles behind the young people in our care. Covering all the bases, she defines just what the comprehensive issues are in lucid, readable language leaving you confident to respond appropriately to even the severest of challenges. Importantly she empowers you to put any necessary safeguards in place to make safe, whilst still great fun, all our young people's time online.'

– Jonathan Charlesworth M.Ed., Executive Director of EACH and author of That's So Gay: Challenging Homophobic Bullying, *UK*

'This book provides a complete package for secondary schools to enable them to develop and embed a whole school approach to e-safety and cyberbullying, and deliver relevant and stimulating lessons. It is full of up to date information, practical guidance and great activities for staff and students - all from a writer who is incredibly well informed by years of experience, training staff and listening to children and young people on the subject matter.'

– Paul Rigglesford, Director, Anti-Bullying Works, UK

'"If you keep doing the same things, you will get the same results." This is so apt when it comes to working with teenagers about safe online behaviours. We need to take a fresh approach to this rapidly evolving concern and this book provides just that. Bursting with useful resources and clear explanations, it is a must have.'

– Heather Jeavons, DGfL Senior Education Development Manager, Dudley Grid for Learning, Saltwells EDC, UK

'Adrienne has taken on the monumental task of bringing together all the strands of e-safety in a secondary setting in this book. The advice and resources she provides will help both staff and pupils in secondary schools to become responsible digital citizens and, importantly, to stay safe. In my work as anti-bullying coordinator, I am acutely aware of the need for this book and fully support the ideas that it promotes. I will certainly be recommending it to the schools I work with.'

– Lorna Naylor, Anti-bullying Coordinator, Children, Families and Cultural Services, Nottinghamshire County Council, UK

by the same author

Making Your Primary School E-safe
Whole School Cyberbullying and E-safety Strategies for Meeting Ofsted Requirements
Adrienne Katz
ISBN 978 1 84905 542 0
eISBN 978 0 85700 966 1

Cyberbullying and E-safety
What Educators and Other Professionals Need to Know
Adrienne Katz
ISBN 978 1 84905 276 4
eISBN 978 0 85700 575 5

of related interest

Cyberbullying
Activities to Help Children and Teens Stay Safe in a Texting,
Twittering and Social Networking World
Vanessa Rogers
ISBN 978 1 84905 105 7
eISBN 978 0 85700 228 0

Making Your
Secondary School E-safe

Whole School Cyberbullying and E-safety Strategies for Meeting Ofsted Requirements

ADRIENNE KATZ

Jessica Kingsley *Publishers*
London and Philadelphia

Cybersurvey infographics on p.8 and results throughout are reproduced with kind permission from e-Safer Suffolk.
Figure 2.1 on p.19 reproduced with kind permission from Ofcom.
BYOD list on p.82 adapted with kind permission, from a ten point guide by Lightspeed systems for NAACE.
Quote on p.131 reproduced with kind permission from Guardian News & Media Ltd.
Handout on pp.125–6 adapted from an article by Kanika Saini in Engineers' Forum, reproduced with kind permission.
Quote on pp.210–1 reproduced with kind permission from Emma Bond.
IWF logo on p.276 reproduced with kind permission from The Internet Watch Foundation.
Contains public sector information licensed under the Open Government Licence v3.0.

First published in 2016
by Jessica Kingsley Publishers
73 Collier Street
London N1 9BE, UK
and
400 Market Street, Suite 400
Philadelphia, PA 19106, USA

www.jkp.com

Library of Congress Cataloging in Publication Data
A CIP catalog record for this book is available from the Library of Congress

British Library Cataloguing in Publication Data
A CIP catalogue record for this book is available from the British Library

ISBN 978 1 84905 541 3
eISBN 978 0 85700 965 4

Printed and bound in The United States

Contents

1

Challenges When Teaching E-safety to Teenagers

All around us are young people fascinated by technology, seemingly umbilically connected to their smartphones and PlayStations. But there are also panicked adults, media hype and untested ways of keeping children safe.

Here then is a young generation, not only enthralled by the new online world they inhabit, but likely to be dependent on it for their future employment too. They should be creating, coding, inventing. They should be imagining new uses for technology. But instead of inspiring them and urging them on, the talk from adults and authorities is only of danger, risk and rules. What a turnoff! And they are turned off. Large numbers find e-safety boring. Some, especially girls, become afraid of the Internet:

'We are so bored of e-safety, they ram it down our throats all the time, I switch off.'

'I follow the e-safety advice 'cos I am scared of what could happen to me if I don't.'

Too many do not follow what they were taught. Those who are most at risk often say they did not understand the e-safety advice or did not receive it at the right age.

'I didn't think it was for me so I didn't really listen.'

'They told us too much at once and I couldn't sort of take it in.'

On the plus side, young people increasingly talk about being able to look after themselves, to find out what they need to know online to solve problems, and of knowing more than the adults who taught them:

'School doesn't understand how, so I just use common sense.'

One 15-year-old boy in the Cybersurvey, an annual online survey of young people's online lives I have undertaken since 2008, wrote:

'I just like looking it up for myself so maybe they should just tell us about good places to go and find out ourselves.'

More than a quarter of secondary students surveyed by Ofsted in March 2015 in 45 schools thought their teachers did not know enough about online safety.[1]

Do they follow our advice on e-safety and are we delivering the right advice?

In a large sample of almost 3000 young people aged 11–16 in England,[2] less than half (41%) always follow the e-safety advice. But if we break that down a little we can see that those angelic 10–11-year-olds who are our most obedient age group are also the most likely to follow the e-safety advice closely – nearly two thirds (64%) of them do so. By contrast, if we look at 14–15-year-olds, the age group at which cyberbullying and online risky behaviour peaks, only 28 per cent say they always follow the guidelines (Figure 1.1). So the question is: how can we bridge that time between age 11 and age 14 when so many cease to follow the e-safety advice? And how can we make what is taught more relevant to them?

http://bit.ly/Cybersurveyreport2014 (c) e-Safer Suffolk/Youthworks Consulting Ltd

Figure 1.1 Following e-safety guidelines

Once they are living their online teenage lives, the e-safety advice they were taught ceases to seem pertinent, or they may say it was given at the wrong age. At 14–15 years old, 18 per cent say it was given too late and 11 per cent say it was given too early. On questioning the young people further in workshops, we hear that they often think it was not age-appropriate. Or they think the warnings are overdone. A 13-year-old said:

> *'I think they overdo it by saying there are loads of restrictions on things that might not be that bad.'*

Repetition, while needed for some, can dull the message for others:

> *'They tell you OVER and OVER and OVER again how to stay safe online, and they say it so much you don't want to remember it.'*

said another 13-year-old (his upper case emphasis).

Another respondent, a 14-year-old boy, expressed the mood of self-reliance we found in so many young people who find out for themselves:

> *'Spending over 5 hours a day online kinda helps.'*

Figure 1.2 shows some of the risks experienced by 'millennials'. A few had been hacked, had had personal or credit card details stolen (6% and 2%), or had visited gambling sites (7%). Four per cent had bought goods that turned out to be fake, and 5 per cent had been tricked into paying money for something they did not want. Seventeen individuals out of 1589 had been blackmailed as a result of posting or sharing an explicit photograph of themselves (sexting). You might argue that a similar number of individuals could come to harm in the offline world, but there are unique additional risks online.

By age 14–15, 16 per cent were viewing adult content and over half had come across very violent images online. Almost one in five had been asked to meet up with a stranger they knew only online. Fourteen per cent of this age group came across nude or sexual images they did not search for. Of course, at this age they may be actively searching for material of this kind; but many are not, and those who are distressed by these images have a right to be protected from them.

Figure 1.2 Online risks of 14–15-year-old millennials

Is it the right advice?

Despite most e-safety advice focusing on high-risk situations, the difficulties more commonly encountered tended to be in the category of relationships or personal wellbeing. One in five experienced online aggression or cyberbullying, which is consistent with other figures we have collected in the Cybersurvey over the past seven years. Twelve per cent of 14–15-year-olds said that someone had pretended to be a young person interested in them, but subsequently turned out to be someone different.

More worrying findings involve issues that are not often covered in the standard e-safety education: large numbers of young people are visiting sites that urge you to be too thin, or to self-harm or even kill yourself. They come across websites urging or inciting hatred or racism and others peddling 'dangerous advice'. The impact on vulnerable or otherwise unstable young people is seen in high-profile tragic cases in which very troubled young people with multiple problems have taken their own lives.

They are often pressured to meet up with someone they know only online (10%), pressured to do something they do not want to do (10%), or learn that people are talking about them nastily online (14%).[3]

Taken together, the fact that so few young people say they always follow the e-safety advice they were taught and the evidence of vulnerable groups of young people amongst whom the highest distress levels and risk are experienced, perhaps we should re think the e-safety messages? E-safety is seldom evaluated, yet questions need to be asked: are we framing the discussion in the right way?

There are others who raise questions. David Finkelhor of the Crimes Against Children Center at the University of New Hampshire has pointed out that the current approach is based on some false assumptions that he describes as alarmist. These assumptions are the following:

- The digital environment is perilous for youth, and deviance is 'amplifying'.

- Youth problems manifesting in the digital environment are fostered by that environment and depend on its specific dynamics.

- Remedies for these problems are to be found in specialised Internet education programmes.

He suggests that a reasonable case can be made for a contrasting set of possibilities:

What if…

- The digital environment is no more perilous than other offline environments youth inhabit?

- The problems that do occur are not unique but rather extensions of social interaction or media consumption problems that cut across environments and are best conceptualised holistically rather than as unique to the digital world?

- The appropriate responses should not be specialised Internet safety training but more generic education about life skills, social interaction, emotional intelligence and media literacy?[4]

Wherever you stand on these questions, it is refreshing to think about all this without the pressure of media headlines or political grandstanding. I hope that as you read through this book you will find ideas to take you to a new position on teaching e-safety and your own inspiration and inventiveness will be triggered by my attempts at broadening the way we look at e-safety education. While I do think there are some aspects of the digital environment which foster certain behaviours and can make the impact of cyberbullying worse, I am also convinced that e-safety education needs to be shaken up and integrated with generic education on relationships, life skills and citizenship. In this new subject, which we could name RLSC, e-safety might be integrated into life skills and also appear in citizenship. Then again, it is necessary also to address it in the relationships strand. This simply illustrates how e-safety needs to be embedded more broadly in new ways.

Moral panics get in the way

There have been moral panics before – with the arrival of comics, movies and TV, and even phones. Panics tend to take the place of calm analysis and we often look back with amusement on how people reacted to comics, for example. In the late 1940s and early 1950s, US psychiatrist Fredric Wertham spearheaded the anti-comics crusade. His view was put across in articles and his book, a 1954 best seller, *Seduction of the Innocent*. He fervently believed that comic books would damage normal kids who would never be able to enjoy literature or fine art after reading comics. Furthermore, he argued, comics gave kids a taste for blood and violence and severely damaged those who were socially vulnerable. He simplistically claimed that every child who read comics would be a 'juvenile delinquent' after finding that 95 per cent of boys in a reformatory read comics. His views were picked up in the media, and Senate hearings were convened to address the 'problem'.

Nowadays there are regular moral panics about teenagers online. Media hype would have you believe that every teenager is at tremendous risk, although in fact as I write, there are several cases in the news in which adults (frequently in positions of trust) are the ones sexting, furtively filming boys in the school changing rooms and even being jailed for trolling others. We certainly cannot point to adults as role models!

Bring in the views of young people and schools

As I thought about fresh ways to deliver e-safety, I turned to young people and schools. More than 23,700 young people have answered the Cybersurvey since 2008. Workshops have also been held with young people to discuss some of the results and hear why they think people answered as they did.

In another step, the Bullying Intervention Group has worked with large numbers of schools, either when training their staff or discussing complex cases. Sometimes it is these schools that have sent us fresh and original ideas on how they are approaching this new challenge in the age of the smartphone and tablet. In other situations it is through delivering training that we learn from the problems they bring to the sessions.

Some thoughts on how to go about it in a fresh way

First: The moral panic around the behaviour of teenagers online should cease. In its place let us have a calm, practical way of addressing how to be a good digital citizen, to include real explorations of values in relationships, ethics and digital literacy. To achieve this the following needs to occur:

- The role porn might play in young people's expectations of relationships should be debated with them in an updated 21st century sex and relationships education (SRE) curriculum. It is time for a counter-narrative on genuine relationships, romance and respect.

- Rights and responsibilities on and offline must be agreed, both for pupils and for professionals, who should of course adhere to a code of conduct. (That applies to all professionals in positions of trust. It also applies to parents who set up online pages to criticise their child's teacher.)

- Teach (actually demonstrate on computers or phones) the *practical* digital skills required to protect your personal privacy and photos on a range of platforms.

- Teach what to do if something unpleasant or deeply distressing occurs. (Too many teachers and social workers say they do not know what to do if a student reports a case to them.)

- Teach where to look online for *reliable advice and support* when you might need it.

Second: Rescue e-safety from the shores of ICT where many kids who are not into computing, so much as what they can do with computers, will ignore it. E-safety should not be delivered only by ICT specialists or the police, as so often happens, but also needs to be delivered by pastoral leads, in drama classes, PSHE classes, literature classes and history classes, through classroom debates, pupil-led campaigns, flashmob events in school playgrounds and innovative graphic design. To do this, more teachers need training. Nearly a third of teachers say they do not feel confident teaching online safety, while two in five say they have never attempted any lessons in the subject, according to a new study commissioned for e-safety provider Point2Point described by Josie Gurney-Read in the *Telegraph Online*.[5] On top of that, 43 per cent said they don't understand the digital content and apps that pupils are accessing on their personal devices whilst in school.

Third: E-safety should be embedded into every aspect of the curriculum – and the policies around it should be shaken out of their 'silos' and integrated. I am thinking of policies on behaviour, equality and anti-bullying in particular; and, of course, safeguarding and child protection. Written by different senior leaders, these policies are often not singing from the same song sheet nor are they integrated. Prevention of bullying should include e-safety and discussions about how to behave online, what is a digital citizen and what is acceptable in a relationship.

Fourth: Focus on emotional wellbeing. It is now widely recognised that there are increasingly high levels of anxiety, depression and suicidal intent among many young people, some of which stems from bullying-related issues, while some is related to online content and contact.

Fifth: Involve the mental health professionals. Research from both Warwick University[6] and the Institute of Psychiatry, King's College,[7] has demonstrated that bullying leaves a long-term impact well into adulthood, affecting mental health, relationships and the ability to hold down work. Being bullied at age 11 was found to be a predictor of self-harm at age 17.[8]

Mental health among young people appears to be a growing concern. ChildLine reported in its annual review of 2013/14[9] that counselling sessions on mental health conditions were up 34 per cent and sessions on online sexual abuse soared 168 per cent year on year. While it is good that young people are seeking help for their problems, it is also true that self-harm is currently startlingly higher in the teenage population, and many visit websites encouraging this.

In August 2014 the NHS stated that the number of children aged between 10 and 14 treated in hospital after deliberately hurting themselves had risen by more than 2700 since 2012. It also revealed that teenagers between 15 and 19 treated for self-harm over the same period showed an increase of 23 per cent. In 2014 the London School of Economics EU Kids Online programme issued the *Net Children Go Mobile* report[10] that showed a significant increase since 2010 in young people being exposed to potentially negative forms of user-generated content online, including self-harm websites. The report showed that in 2013, 17 per cent of 11–16-year-olds in the UK had seen self-harm content online, up from 6 per cent in 2010. Self-harm among children and young people has risen by more than 70 per cent in the past two years to record levels, according to the Health and Social Care Information Centre.[11]

The year 2013 saw a raft of dreadful tragic deaths allegedly linked to the Internet. ChildLine also reported in January 2014 that, in the previous 12 months, contacts received by the charity about cyberbullying had increased by 87 per cent on the previous year. In 2013/14 some very high profile tragedies hit the headlines – the majority involving girls – and cyberbullying was allegedly a factor in several of these cases that ended in suicide.

Greater understanding of the tragic cases mentioned above has revealed the complex web of factors in the lives of some of those who took their lives. Cyberbullying was only one of many factors, but its impact is deep, cruel and long lasting. It may be the last straw in a complex web of other factors which include depressive illness. But online goading, mocking or encouragement can and does amplify problems. There is much 'shaming' and rumour-spreading that causes excruciating pain to vulnerable teenagers. There is also appalling 'advice' available, and some young people discover how to take steps to harm themselves via online sites.

Sixth: Get parents up to speed. Navigating the online and mobile phone world is like other dangerous environments – roads, for example – for which we carefully prepare our children, giving them different levels of protection as they grow older. You could get killed if you stepped off the kerb into oncoming traffic, but somehow most parents handle the transition from holding a child's hand when crossing the road to waving their child goodbye on a bike or first car. But despite the media headlines and moral panics, parents are simply not utilising the parental controls now being routinely offered them, as we learned in a report by Ofcom in July 2014.[12] Take-up is in low single figures for three of the four major broadband providers, despite all new customers being forced to make an active decision on take-up. While parents are increasingly talking to their children about e-safety, as the Cybersurvey shows, nevertheless they tend to talk to their daughters more than their sons about how to stay safe online, and they seldom check age ratings on games or movie downloads. There remain about one third who do not discuss e-safety with their children. Schools need to engage with parents on e-safety messages, despite the difficulties of doing so, and to aim for a coherent message to be delivered by parents to support the work of the school.

Seventh: Train social workers and carers. Social and care workers, counsellors and mental health professionals all require training in the digital lives of teenagers. Too often we find that the policies in care settings are wholly inadequate to deal with the online dimension. Staff like to believe that because Internet access is controlled within the care home setting, controlling relationships, grooming or inappropriate contact will not occur. But this overlooks the times when the young person is out and about with others who may have online access in the palm of their hand. It also overlooks gifts of mobile phones that are kept secret and secondary Social Networking Service (SNS) accounts in other names. These social workers and carers need to work more coherently with educators to protect the young people in their care.

A report from the British Association of Social Workers and NSPCC[13] highlighted the lack of knowledge among social workers on how to spot the warning signs that a child is being targeted for sexual abuse online. Half of all social workers surveyed said they felt concerned about dealing with online sexual abuse or behaviour, yet their clients are among our most vulnerable children.

Other findings

Almost half of social workers questioned said that a quarter of their sexual abuse cases now involve some form of online abuse. In all, 47 per cent said they were not knowledgeable about how young people communicate on social networking sites, 36 per cent felt they did not know the right questions to ask to identify and assess online sexual abuse, and 30 per cent said they did not feel confident dealing with child protection sexual abuse cases using the Internet. As many as half said they didn't know how to recognise the signs of online sexual abuse in children. Some joint training with school safeguarding staff, social workers and care providers might be a really useful strategy when you have vulnerable young children in your care. I find that training a variety of professionals together can yield the most fruitful discussions about cases, the most innovative solutions and a diversity of views which can add creativity to the learning.

Keep asking: Are the e-safety messages the right ones?

E-safety messages may work well for 10–11-year-olds, but do they engage the 14-year-olds?

When I first began to collect young people's views via the Cybersurvey, fewer than half of the pupils said they followed the e-safety guidelines they were taught, and at age 14–15 adherence was as low as 26 per cent in 2009. This was despite pupils saying the e-safety education was good. This situation has improved only slightly over time and in only some local authority areas. In other locations it is almost static. Five years later adherence was still painfully low in the mid-teens and among vulnerable groups of young people everywhere. Many profess to be 'totally bored with e-safety'.

We should keep in mind that cyberbullying peaks in the mid-teen years, as does experimental risk-taking, sexting and other exploratory or indeed rebellious behaviour. Add a dash of that sense of invincibility we all remember and you can imagine why young people do not generally want to listen to another assembly on e-safety. When we asked young people in workshops what could improve the teaching of e-safety, they volunteered that there should never be another assembly on the subject! Instead they wanted lively practical demonstrations and videos in groups.

Too many warnings can make young people fear the Internet

There is such an emphasis on stranger danger and abuse, with media stories exaggerating the idea of abduction or suicide, that many girls fear the Internet. In truth they are far more likely to experience cyberbullying from classmates or embarrassing photo incidents online than child sexual exploitation, horrific though that is. More work is needed on how we behave towards one another, what being a digital citizen means and how to conduct our lives safely online. Fear of using the Internet may paradoxically make these girls less safe as they do not develop the skills they need. Our young people need a new code of behaviour towards one another, and there are small signs that they are beginning to develop this themselves.

Positive steps are coming

At the 'We Protect Children' Summit held in London in December 2014 a new package of measures was put in place to address child abuse images online. For the first time it seems that there is a coherent co-ordinated approach that has the potential to address the ugly side of the net. David Cameron, the UK prime minister, announced:

- a new unit to tackle paedophiles on the 'dark net'

- the unveiling of new technical solutions by Google, Facebook, Yahoo, Microsoft and Twitter to block and remove illegal child abuse material online

- a new UK database enabling swifter identification and investigation by law enforcement agencies of child abuse images

- new global action to build law enforcement networks and improve child protection in over 30 countries.

In the UK, new legislation addresses so-called 'revenge porn' and also assists police and prosecutors to act in cases where someone is 'fishing' for child abuse images and it cannot be proved that they are in possession of them.

YouTube, one of the most beloved sites for children and young people, has launched YouTube Kids, a safer environment for young children.

The iRights initiative brings industry and government together to improve iRights for young people when using the Internet. Included in these rights is the right to delete content that a young person may be ashamed of in later years.

Concluding remarks

In this book I hope to move away from a view in which e-safety is classed as the preserve of digital experts, a subject which has some simple rules that, once delivered mechanically, will be expected to deal with e-safety among teenagers. Of course some simple clear messages need to be distilled to help pupils remember them, and there are some digital skills that are essential. But the big conversations, debates and relationships lessons are needed even more. I want to broaden out the ways in which e-safety can be addressed within so many other subjects. This is an argument for e-safety to be seen as an essential component of modern life, to be embedded in the lives of our young people in ways that seem relevant, engaging and real. Above all, we have to tackle the 'e-safety is boring' attitude expressed by teenagers.

The work described in this book relates to the PSHE curriculum or the Social, Cultural, Moral and Spiritual development of learners, whichever you are following. It also relates to the new Computing curriculum of course and, most importantly, to Safeguarding and Child Protection within the school. It has a role within Citizenship. For inspection purposes, bullying generally falls under personal development and welfare. E-safety will be inspected as part of safeguarding. Do not overlook the importance of a modernised SRE curriculum for the age of the Internet.

There are differences in gender patterns when we explore cyberbullying. Girls are twice as likely as boys to report that they are being cyberbullied. Bullying amongst girls particularly can be pernicious, covert in nature, and difficult to identify and resolve. Mobile phones and the Internet have added a new complexity to the picture. In such a febrile environment we need a combination of calm, tried and tested approaches that have been shown to work in cases of real-world bullying, along with the addition of some specific new tools to address cyberbullying.

12 points for e-safety educators

- These points can make a vital difference: Model positive and exciting use of technology.
- Involve students as co-researchers in finding solutions to problems online.
- Involve students as peer-teachers and encourage a sense of autonomy.
- Chunk the information into digestible bites.
- Consider age and gender, plus abilities of your audience.
- Ask for feedback on what they have learned, to check for understanding.
- Poll students to keep up with trends in youth culture and their view of risk.[14]
- Monitor the effectiveness of what you do.
- Engage with parents and ensure they are up-to-date.
- Update yourself regularly on safety advice for hand-held devices, SNS sites and all other available safety advice which often changes.
- Training is needed in partnership with mental health professionals and social and care workers.
- Liaise with other agencies.

2

The New Context for Schools

Radicalisation: new risks and inspection targets

The new context for teachers, non-teaching staff and social/care workers contains a challenge never encountered before. The UK is concerned about radicalisation of young people as war rages in Syria, Iraq, Yemen and Libya, and the Internet is very often the arena in which this plays out. One well-known outstanding school was downgraded at inspection because sixth-formers were active online with a page said to be linked to various 'extremists'. Some of the pupils had already left the school, but an online search by Ofsted before an inspection revealed that this Facebook page had the school's name on it. The school was shocked to find itself reduced to 'inadequate' despite its good results.

Inspectors do an online search before visiting a school. How often does your school do an online search for everything linked to your school? What are parents saying about your school and what are pupils doing online that could be linked to your school? A regular search is vital. Why not set up an alert for your school so that you are alerted to any mentions of the school name online?

Other current preoccupations with identity are reflected in inspections, which seek to find out if 'students are prepared for life in a modern, diverse, British society', although schools can be unclear what this means.

There is evidence that young people are becoming 'radicalised' or enticed to go to Syria, for example, via social media. In response, the new guidance 'Promoting fundamental British values as part of SMSC in schools' was issued late in 2014 and Ofsted will now include this aspect in inspections.[15]

Grooming and sexual exploitation

At the same time, the country is convulsed in shock at the extent of child sexual exploitation that has been revealed through both historic and current cases. Young people in care and in other unstable situations are especially vulnerable to being targeted and controlled via mobile phones given as a 'gift' or become blackmailed over explicit images. A few care workers still believe it is enough to restrict Internet access in the care setting, failing to grasp how easy it is to get online by other means nowadays – in the shopping centre, in the street and on a train, or on your friend's phone. This approach to teaching e-safety also overlooks cases where young people are given mobile phones by someone wishing to control them – phones that are kept secret from caring adults. But grooming can also occur in the most caring of homes and in all backgrounds, and child sexual exploitation is a serious threat at all times in all situations.

Sophisticated grooming attempts

At the extremes, vulnerable children can be lured into agreeing to meet someone who might promise to teach them how to win at their favourite online game, or find themselves manipulated by clever adults claiming to love and protect them when they need it most, then grooming them for their own purpose over many months of apparent friendship. Groomers tend to hang around online where young people congregate, talk their language and study their likes and dislikes, the better to be able to interact with them convincingly on various platforms.

Groomers can be very plausible, as we saw in the tragic case of Breck Bednar,[16] whose mother was rightly suspicious about just such a player in a small 'exclusive' gaming group. Her conscientious attempts to report her concerns to the police, and to talk to her son as she noticed changes in his behaviour over the months of contact with the groomer, were sadly not enough to prevent him secretly going off to meet this man where he was murdered, after telling his mother he was going to a friend's house. It was reported that the groomer had given him another phone to use in order to avoid being monitored by Breck's mother.

These cases are not common, but are so appalling that we as adults need to be on a high state of alert to anything that gives a suggestion that this could be taking place. Any complacency is misplaced.

E-safety is a tool to keep young people safe in all aspects of their lives. It should not be seen as an add-on or a separate subject that is tacked on to ICT or Computing. It is not simply another tool in the Prevent strategy. Above all it is not enough to have an occasional session on e-safety and leave it at that. Young people need to be able to return to an issue with questions after a session, re-visit certain aspects of e-safety and have it continually evolving along with their online experiences. They need to be able to raise new issues for discussion within the group as youth culture changes.

Teens born in the broadband age

Teens born around the year 2000 are unlikely to have known 'dial-up' Internet and are the first generation to benefit from broadband and digital communications while growing up. An Ofcom report in 2014 defined this group as 'millennials'.[17] In the autumn 2014 Cybersurvey there were 918 respondents aged 14–15, offering a detailed glimpse of the experiences of our millennials – a cohort who have never known life without broadband. Over the past seven years our Cybersurvey data has consistently shown that the mid-teen years are a peak time for cyberbullying and online risky behaviour. The millennials conform to this pattern, but new behaviours appear each year as technology changes.

High risk and low adherence to e-safety advice

The millennials are now at the age when we see a peak in cyberbullying and high-risk online behaviour alongside a startling drop in the number who follow e-safety advice.

The 14–15-year-olds are less likely to say that the e-safety education they received was very good (only 28%) and also less likely to say that they always follow what they have been taught. One in five does not follow it at all. Thirty per cent say they were taught either too early or too late. At the same time we know that they take greater risks, and experience more unpleasantness, aggression, cyberbullying and pressure in their online lives than other youth age groups, so it could be argued that we need to develop a new approach to the delivery of online safety education to them. This contributes to the rationale for age-appropriate e-safety teaching.

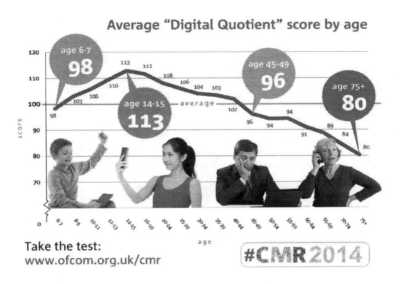

Figure 2.1 Ofcom digital quotient

Self-reliant and problem-solving

A significant segment of this age group wants a degree of autonomy and to be helped to know how to sort out problems for themselves or where to get help. They feel competent, dislike having a rigid set of rules imposed on them and enjoy discussions and practical demonstrations. This first became evident in the 2009 Cybersurvey, and the patterns in the data on e-safety adherence have remained similar every year since and in all other locations where the Cybersurvey has been run. So the challenge remains: how do educators meet their needs in new ways?

Life online for mid-teens

- 87% spend their time messaging.

- 83% watch videos and films online.

- 74% search for information for homework, studies or research.

- 68% of them are gamers.

- 56% are shopping online.

- 47% post photos.

- 47% have downloaded music or film without paying for it.

- 37% spend five or more hours online per day.

- 30% post about what they are doing.

Experience of online risks

There are 918 respondents in the age group 14–15. Some have not experienced any of the following. However:

- 53% have seen 'very violent pictures or videos that they did not want to see'.

- 53% have come across nude pictures or videos 'that they did not search for'.

- 40% have seen websites promoting advice they think could be dangerous.

- 39% have seen sites promoting hatred and racist views at least once or twice.

- 29% of all 14–15-year-olds have been cyberbullied.

- 24% often visit 'sites urging you to be very thin' and a further 24% have done so once or twice.

- 23% often visit sites encouraging self-harm and/or suicide while 24% have done so once or twice.

- 22% have experienced 'some online aggression or cyberbullying, including homophobic or racist bullying'.

- 20% have had their social networking site account hacked.

- 19% have been contacted by someone pretending to be a young person interested in them, but who later turns out to be someone quite different.

- 16% look at adult content online.

- 44% of all young people involved in sexting are aged 14–15.

Once upon a time there was a watershed

Once, not so long ago, there was an official 'watershed' and TV programmers were obliged to adhere to it, not scheduling programmes for adults until after the 9pm cut-off time. There was a concern about material that children and young people might see.

But today we have a merging of content as it can be streamed, saved and re-played at any time, or found online and viewed at any time of the day or night. TV and downloadable content are merged in the minds of young people and they can access it all from their phone or tablet. This throws down new challenges to e-safety educators and parents, as there is little control over content once it can be accessed outside of the broadcast schedules. There is no control at all over downloaded content usually generated by others on YouTube or shared between people. This change has come about so fast, and relatively recently, that the idea that content is not locked up safely inside the TV schedules only to be viewed when broadcast has not really entered the world of e-safety. This may be because there is relatively little that can be done about it other than to urge parents to use filters, to select which TV channels their children can view, to sign their child up to YouTube Kids, or to educate.

A lack of training persists among staff

Schools are finding that pupils' online life intrudes into the life of the school. Their safeguarding and e-safety obligations are rapidly changing, yet staff training appears to be one of the weakest elements of their practice, according to Ofsted (Inspecting E-safety in Schools, April 2014).[18] A year later another Ofsted survey of 45 secondary schools found that staff training was inconsistent and only 63 per cent of staff members strongly agreed that they had received e-safety training in the last 12 months.[19] Try surveying your staff on their training needs to help identify what training sessions to design. In Chapter 7 there is a sample staff training needs survey.

A fragmented environment

Schools are also working in a new, more fragmented context, as the academies and free schools programme means that large numbers of schools are outside the local authority family and responsibility for safeguarding and e-safety now lies with the school's proprietors or Trust.

Services that used to be available to schools are now reduced, or offer a lesser or traded service, and some schools or chains are buying in the support services they require individually. This increased independence from local authorities and the loss of considerable amounts of funding and guidance means a wider variation in threshold levels, varying support and, in many areas, too few places in child and adolescent mental health services, educational psychology, speech therapy and dwindling youth services alongside over-stretched social care services. Even the Child Exploitation and Online Protection Centre (CEOP), the police agency working on the extreme issue of online child sexual exploitation, claims to be overwhelmed with cases.

This environment can make referral difficult, but schools must be tenacious in taking a case to the local authority designated officer where required. Safeguarding remains everyone's responsibility.

Helping staff feel more confident

If your staff feel unsure or anxious about the rapid pace of change in the digital world, a discussion of the changes they see can help them to reduce this feeling of being out of their depth. By naming these changes, they will soon realise they already have many skills to help guide the young people and do not have to 'leave it all to the ICT manager or the geeks'. There is an example of this type of discussion in Chapter 7.

Many are reassured to realise that their counselling skills and empathy are just as needed to help children navigate in cyberspace as they are in the real world. Indeed, being someone to trust is an essential role, as long as you know what to do if you receive a disclosure. That is why every single member of staff should be trained. Nobody knows which person will seem right to a desperate child – they will choose a person they have decided to trust not on the basis of their knowledge, but on their warmth, decency, kindness and general friendliness. The challenge is not to fail them by not knowing what to do and how to preserve evidence.

Protecting staff from abuse

Another emerging trend has seen teachers report a significant increase of online abuse targeted at them by parents between 2014 and 2015. Forty per cent of teachers reported that parents were being abusive about their children's teachers compared with 27 per cent the previous year. Two thirds of teachers had experienced insulting comments from parents and this appeared to be giving pupils the green light to do the same.

One teacher reported being sworn at by a parent online over a PE lesson, while a female dance teacher said she had been called a 'paedophile' for simply wanting to film a performance by her students.

Teachers had been the target of insults from parents about their appearance and weight (even when pregnant), while others report comments and insults of a sexual nature.

The poll by teachers' union NASUWT[20] also showed that the proportion of teachers suffering abuse from both parents and pupils has more than doubled over the past year. Around 8 per cent saw allegations of inappropriate behaviour with students, 6 per cent saw videos or photos taken without consent and 3 per cent were told they had behaved inappropriately towards parents. These allegations, if malicious, can be career-destroying and they cloud the work of those who genuinely want to root out any abuse of children.

This demonstrates how vital it is to consider your school's policy on acceptable use of ICT and any other relevant documents such as home/school agreements to make clear that this behaviour is unacceptable. Chapter 5's discussion on policy explores this further. It is against this backdrop that the work to deliver a relevant, practical, sensitive e-safety education and school approach is undertaken.

3

What Do Young People Need to Know?

The tools are always changing

As I sat down to write this paragraph I had a quick check on who could see my social network page. Had I really set it so that only friends could view it? What photos were out there? Was there anything someone else had posted which included a photo of me that I had not noticed before? To do this I had to Google a 'how to' question. But the answer popped up in seconds and it was plain sailing from there on. Was it a nuisance having to do this? Yes, but pretty essential. You see, Facebook, like many other providers, change their settings all the time. Handing out rigid instructions to young people is therefore a mistake. Teaching them how to find out what to do would be more use to them.

Problem-solving tools and the will to use them

It would be unlikely that any of us could hold in our heads the latest 'how to' for every site or app we use, let alone our changing phones and tablets. But we need to know that we have to protect ourselves and to know that we can easily check this out because the information is at our fingertips. But we also need to have the motivation to do this. Although many teenagers are concerned with their image and reputation, they are conflicted over privacy. They hate the idea of their photos being humiliatingly misused but they often don't think before they upload a shot they feel makes them look popular, sexy, cool, having a great time, or all of the above. After all, they are at the age at which young humans feel invincible. They also might believe that they know more about the online youth world than the teacher or their parents.

Get them to actively use e-safety advice

In over seven years of collecting their views and experiences in the Cybersurvey, we have found that adherence to e-safety rules is at its lowest in the mid-teens and that this remains unchanged even after all these years of headlines about the dangers and widespread e-safety teaching. So the first challenge is to make e-safety meaningful and also to give learners the skills they will need when they do decide to use them. Furthermore, the majority say the e-safety education was quite or very good, but do not put it into action. A second challenge

23

therefore is to galvanise knowledge into action so that they use what they have been taught and become safe participants in the digital world. This is the hard bit.

Navigating a safe path through our digital lives has become more complex and difficult with both moral and practical dilemmas facing us several times each day. So the question of what young people need to know is constantly changing. I think they need to know how and where to find out about the e-safety basics, such as blocking someone or turning off the GPS setting on their camera. They also need to explore the moral issues of behaviour towards one another with a mature, trained adult facilitating this. The digital literacy curriculum is more than a range of skills, it is also about relationships – how we treat one another. I call these situations 'digi-dilemmas' and there are many in this book. But you can create your own examples from real life any day of the week, I am certain. These discussions might have more impact on teenagers than do dry instructions and rules.

So to begin, I have provided an activity to define what e-safety actually is. How do they understand the term? You might find they add a few thoughts to your plan. Students may have an entirely different idea of what e-safety should include. Defining what we mean by e-safety is so useful, rather than assuming they know what we mean. This is because we hope that when they realise the breadth of what it covers they may take it more seriously and because young people with learning difficulties might need to be led step by step into this subject. In addition, because it calls on pupils' own personal online experience, the resulting list is more likely to be relevant to them.

WHAT IS E-SAFETY?

This is an activity that suits year 7 and should be done again in year 8 or 9 because their needs will have changed markedly.

Aims

- To ensure everyone is clear about the purpose and goals of e-safety lessons.
- To reveal their priorities and concerns.
- To clarify all aspects of e-safety.
- To illustrate to you what they know and where the gaps are.
- To make your teaching relevant to the lives they live online.

In pairs, ask students to do the activity. Then once they have completed this, move on to colour code the themes, as explained below. This will set the scene for wall displays and illustrative material on or offline.

1. WHAT IS E-SAFETY?

Do you think it is A, B or C? Circle the one you think it is.

A. It teaches you how electric gadgets can be safely used

B. It teaches you about health and safety when using an electronic tablet, laptop or mobile

C. It teaches you how to be safe online or on your smartphone

2. WHO SHOULD BE RESPONSIBLE FOR E-SAFETY?

A. Parents

B. My school

C. Me

D. My older brother or sister

E. All of us together

3. WHICH OF THESE DO YOU THINK IS TRUE?

A. I only play games online so I don't have to worry about e-safety

B. I keep all my documents and photos in a cloud so I don't need e-safety

C. My parents trust me so I don't need e-safety

D. I never use a credit card online so I don't need e-safety

E. I do not have a Facebook page so I don't need e-safety

If you did not think any of the statements above are true, please explain in your groups why you thought this.

4. ONLINE THERE ARE WONDERFUL THINGS WE CAN DO, BUT THERE ARE ALSO SOME RISKS. PLEASE THINK ABOUT THIS AND PREPARE TO EXPLAIN YOUR IDEAS ABOUT THE RISKS TO THE GROUP OR CLASS.

A. There are risks from other people

B. There are risks from hackers who use software to find out passwords

C. Everything you post online could hang around forever or get shared

D. I might meet someone online who is not who they say they are

WHAT OTHER RISKS CAN YOU SUGGEST?

How can you protect yourself from harm? You learn to cross the road safely, so what do you think you need to learn to use the Internet safely?

Share your ideas with the group.

List them and put them into order, with the most important ones at the top.

Give them to your teacher.

Colour coding the themes

Breaking down the confusing mass of information about e-safety into themes, and then into bite-sized 'chunks' which young people suggest, will make it easier for them to absorb.

Taking into account the students' lists of risks from the 'What is e-safety?' activity above, ask them to also consider what e-safety education should include. Ask the students to sort the e-safety messages into key themes, then try using colour to 'brand' the different themes or issues.

Learning outcomes

- Students will understand the different themes that e-safety covers.

- Students will find it easier to recognise messages about e-safety when they are in clear colour codes.

Rationale

Too many young people say '*it [e-safety education] is confusing, they tell us too much at once*'. They ask if we could explore how to deliver 'bite-sized' chunks of knowledge in ways that hang together. Why not pick a colour which will be used on everything to do with social networking advice? Every time you (or the students) do a wall display or a presentation or an advice card on SNS matters, it will always be branded with one colour. Everything to do with GPS could be a different colour. Basic, I know! But over time you will have clear colour branded strands of information which do not jostle in the mind of the pupils quite so much as when a guest speaker arrives to 'do e-safety' and tells them everything in one session in one afternoon. Besides, these young people live in a world of brands so it seems natural to them. Try making logos for strands too if that helps with recognition.

Preparation

Draw up the themes identified in this activity. Allocate colours to each theme and show this in a key like the one illustrated below. These colours can be used in all materials and displays from now on. The simple use of colour helps some students make sense of the material and feel less swamped by all that they need to know about e-safety. Students can be invited to add to the display as they come across good tips or advice so that they have a sense of ownership.

COLOUR CODE THE E-SAFETY MESSAGES

Students complain they are told too much at once!

To

- separate them out into strands of activity
- help students remember where to find the advice they seek
- assist students with special needs,

displays should be clear, uncluttered and in the same colours you have used in the table.

This table allows for 5 top tips for each section; please adjust your table as you choose. Add or change questions. Use the colour codes to get students to fill in a matrix or create colour themed displays of advice.

	How do I know it is safe?	What should I watch out for?	How can I protect myself?	How can I be sure I do not harm others?	Where do I go for help if things go wrong?
Green = Safe search					
Yellow = Safe talk					
Purple = Safe posts					
Pink = Safe shopping					
Light blue = Safe relationships					
Dark blue = Safe gaming					
Orange = Safe downloads					

What to include

The new computing curriculum says the following:

- *Key stage 3* pupils should be taught to 'understand a range of ways to use technology safely, respectfully, responsibly and securely, including protecting their online identity and privacy; recognise inappropriate content, contact and conduct and know how to report concerns'.

- *Key stage 4* pupils should be able to 'understand how changes in technology affect safety, including new ways to protect their online privacy and identity, and how to identify and report a range of concerns'.[21]

Types of risk online				
	Commercial	**Aggressive**	**Sexual**	**Values**
Content	Adverts Spam So-called 'free' content Personal info	Violent/hateful content Misused images	Pornographic/ unwelcome sexual content	Prejudice: linked to race/disability/ sexual orientation Misleading info/advice, manipulation
Contact	Tracking Harvesting Personal info	Being bullied, harassed, stalked	Meeting strangers Being groomed	Self-harm Unwelcome Coersion/pressure to do things or meet up
Conduct	Illegal downloading Hacking Gambling/financial scams	Bullying or harassing another Threats Rumours Terrorism	Creating and uploading inappropriate/ abusive material 'Sexting' Blackmail over images	Providing misleading info/advice Uploading pro-ana photos urging thinness Promoting self-harm

Figure 3.1 Types of risk online

Components of E-safety for Secondary-age Young People

E-safety

Young people learn that to enjoy and explore what the Internet can offer, and to collaborate with others, they need some more advanced advice to stay safe. They build on the SMART rules to help them do this. Their understanding and recognition of risk grows and develops with age.

Privacy

Young people learn several ways to keep their privacy protected, they understand what constitutes personal information and they learn about usernames and strong passwords. They understand why they need to take these steps and how to refuse requests to provide personal information.

Safe search

Young people learn to search for information and to question the credibility and accuracy of search results and information they obtain online. They evaluate and compare material. They are able to be more discerning. They know there are inappropriate and harmful websites.

Copyright

Young people know they must acknowledge the owner of the work and not copy and paste information as if it is their own work. They learn to interpret what they find in their own words and credit the original where needed. They understand that the creator of the work has ownership.

Digital footprint

Young people learn to be careful about what they upload or say online and respect their own and others' privacy. They understand that material they post or upload can be around for others to find, leaving a permanent digital footprint. They learn to protect photos they do decide to upload or post and to show judgement about acceptable use of new technology.

Cyberbullying

Young people learn to treat one another with respect, they understand what to do if they experience aggression or cyberbullying online and they help their friends if they experience this. They work to prevent bullying in their setting.

Safe relationships

Young people learn to make safe relationships and understand that friendship online can be very different to real friends offline. They learn to edit 'friends' lists on social networks and to behave safely as good digital citizens. They understand the risks of unsafe contact. They use the appropriate language for the circumstance. They know how to get help if anything worries them or makes them uncomfortable online. They can report abuse.

Downloads

Young people learn about download risks and how to beware of scams, phishing, viruses and unsafe attachments. They can recognise and distinguish adverts from content. They can successfully download legitimate material and work with it using different software programs.

Uploads

Young people learn to post photos and comments online selectively and with care and to take steps to ensure photos are protected. They understand privacy settings and tags. They do not use photos of other people disrespectfully.

Safe play

Young people understand the risks when playing online games, they are aware of the risk when in contact with players they have never met and can confidently take themselves out of a game or chat room and report any problems to an adult. They play games appropriate to their age.

Safe shopping

Young people look for trusted online retailers, checking security symbols and the URL before using a family credit card. They can use PayPal. They learn that apps and games could have hidden costs despite being free to download at first.

Safe phones

Young people learn to use their mobile phones safely. They understand location services. They use messaging apps, and services but know they should not pass on bullying, rumours about other people, inappropriate images or threatening messages. If they are contacted by anyone they do not know or feel uncomfortable about anything, they know how to seek help. Phones should not be used for cyberbullying.

Safe talk

Safe talk covers all forms of communication including text, messaging, emailing, chat and apps, as well as chat in games and phone calls. Young people learn to communicate and collaborate safely and appropriately with others online. They learn to recognise risky situations and know how to block a sender, save evidence and get help. Safe talk includes safe social networking and groups.

Secure users

All these components contribute to young people becoming secure, competent and confident web users, taking on new devices, new software and apps and conducting themselves safely.

A new journey of learning together

When working with an age group who often think they know more about the digital world than you do, it helps to 'seemingly' relinquish control and go on a journey of learning together. Unless we can explore their online world with them, we are going to struggle to find out what they need to know in order to navigate it. A few rigid rules thought up by adults, though useful as an essential basic starter, are not enough to cope with the tangle of emotions, hormones and highly developed photographic and digital skills that teens encounter or deploy.

So start from the proposition that you are unlikely to know everything. When you do not know the answer to a problem, why not find out together and teach them to weigh up the value or integrity of the different solutions that you find. This approach can draw a contribution from students that will greatly enhance everyone's experience.

They should be encouraged to share their skills, discuss problems and help one another. In this open dialogue-style learning you can find out *what they know* and design your lessons to *fill the gaps* without boring them to death with endless repetition of the same basics that they say turn them off. You should not abandon efforts to recapitulate and reinforce the learning of basics – but the challenge is to keep it fresh and interesting alongside the more complex situations. That is why a quiz, a problem of the week, a debate or a digi-dilemma to solve may be a good way to keep the basics of e-safety alive. Examples of all of these are given in this book.

Chapter 6 contains classroom posters, checklists and activities, many of which are photocopiable. Some items are useful for wall displays. There are ideas for lessons, debates and group work, along with essay writing, design, drama and quick quiz or short-bite sessions. By coming at e-safety from a wide range of angles, I hope that young people become more involved as partners, more engaged and able to help one another. They will create their own artwork and videos.

Essentially this is about living alongside and in relationships with each other. It is also about becoming competent and resilient. Tried and tested anti-bullying activities are used because we know they work successfully in prevention work and in situations where relationships have fallen apart. They work when resolving conflict. E-safety education has not been widely evaluated as yet. Other ideas are included because they work well in schools or have been tested out with young people.

Re-visit basics and build upon them

As you start this journey together, it is helpful to be clear on what e-safety is and to invite young people to add their ideas to the e-safety framework.

First use the SMART rules to recap on basics which they should have learned in primary school, then move on to the rather more sophisticated SMARTER rules which are intended for secondary school students.

SMART RULES!

1. **Safe:** Keep safe by being careful not to give out personal information when you're chatting or posting online. Personal information includes your email address, phone number and password.

2. **Meet:** Meeting someone you have only been in touch with online can be dangerous. Only do so with your parents' or carers' permission and even then only when they can be present. Remember, online friends are still strangers even if you have been talking to them for a long time.

3. **Accepting:** Accepting emails and messages or opening files, images or texts from people you don't know or trust can lead to problems – they may contain viruses or nasty messages!

4. **Reliable:** Someone online might lie about who they are, and information on the Internet may not be true. Always check information by looking at other websites, in books, or with someone who knows. If you like chatting online it's best only to chat to your real-world friends and family.

5. **Tell:** Tell a parent, carer or a trusted adult if someone, or something, makes you feel uncomfortable or worried, or if you or someone you know is being bullied online.

These rules are the basics of staying safe online for young children. As you get older there is more to think about, so make sure you are clear on these 5 basics before moving on to new steps.

SMARTER rules

If students were writing their own set of SMARTER rules, what would they add?

Introduction

Use the 'What is E-safety?' activity from earlier in the chapter to get started on exploring the bigger question of what e-safety is or should be if you have not already done this. Always welcome suggestions and encourage students to prepare units to deliver to the class for the next session. Discuss why you might need to add certain elements to the e-safety discussion. The 'What to include' section above sets out what the current thinking is on the teaching of e-safety, so that you can be sure to cover all these elements.

Activity

The SMART rules are basics that every child in primary school is taught. The SMARTER rules are ideas for making the rules more useful to teenagers. If you were writing a set of SMARTER rules, to be suitable for your year group, what would you put into them?

SMARTER rules for older students

The Digital Literacy handout below covers different areas of digital literacy that should be covered. It can be used by teachers as a framework from which to plan lessons and by students to give them an outline of the e-safety content that they need to know. They can suggest additional areas to include. To follow through with the colour code theme suggested earlier in this chapter, it would be useful to keep it colour coded to match the colours you have chosen.

SMARTER RULES for older students

Think of cyberspace as a great big highway – you can go to exciting places, near and far, but there are also lots of risks like speeding cars and bad drivers. But you learn to cross roads safely as you grow up and also, in time, to drive yourself. That is what you are doing on the Internet Highway. We do not suggest that you avoid the highway – this would cut down on your opportunities and fun.

S Safe and Secure

Shopping: If you need to register on websites or shop – why not consider another email address that all the family can use for buying stuff online or registering on websites? When using personal details and credit card details look for signs it is a secure website.

Settings: Have you checked your privacy settings lately? The options change often and you may not have done yours for ages. Set location features on cameras to off.

Your photos: Think about the photos you upload. Would you be happy for your parents to see them?

Sending photos: It is so easy to be cruel to seem witty in front of friends. It is only a joke if the person being tagged also finds it funny. Snapchat images do not really disappear – hackers can get at them.

Secure passwords: From time to time change your passwords and avoid the ones anyone could easily guess. Use numbers and letters for a stronger password. Don't use the same password for everything either. Run scans regularly to protect against viruses on a laptop. Make sure your phone locks or has a security pin or pattern and don't lend it to others. Say it's out of battery.

M Meeting up

Agreeing to meet someone in the real world if you have first met online is downright dangerous.

If you absolutely must, make arrangements: in case they are not who they say they are, please tell a parent where you are going and why, and take someone with you if you are determined to meet up.

Choose a public place where there are lots of people – never meet alone where nobody can see you. Even if you have done this before without any problems – don't relax your guard. There are people who want to attract young people for the wrong reasons.

A — Accepting messages from people you don't know and trust is not a good idea

Learn to recognise and ignore messages that are trying to sell you something unwanted, weird names, threats and chain letters.

Abusive or funny? Don't ping messages thoughtlessly to other people if they contain hurtful stuff. This accelerates bullying.

Aggression: If you receive a nasty or threatening message block the sender and save the evidence – you might have to report this and will need evidence. Some incoming messages can contain a virus or try to steal your personal details. Use your junk or trash box and send unwanted messages into them.

Find the 'report abuse' button on the websites you use most. This might be useful if you ever have to report some material or a message that is offensive or goes against the rules of the website or service.

Make sure you know what the CEOP report abuse button looks like in case you should ever need to report something serious or very threatening.

You can copy (munch) a screen and save it as evidence.

R — Reliable! Are they who they say they are?

Many people create another identity online and a message or invitation could be from someone who is not who they say they are. Their age and name could be entirely different.

Replies – try to check this out without replying. Can you do a search online or on an SNS site and find out a bit more? Can you trust the information you find? Be alert, be sceptical.

Respect others.

T — Tell someone if you are upset or bothered by a message or someone's behaviour online or via your phone – get help

Tracing callers: Phone providers and websites offer support. Callers can sometimes be traced.

Harassment, incitement of hatred and other malicious behaviour is against the law.

Take screengrabs – you will need to keep evidence.

Taking down requests can take quite a time. You may be able to have a cruel or nasty photo or message taken down but it is slow. In that time, many people might see it. That is one of the many reasons why we all have to behave respectfully to others online.

E — Exploited

Please tell someone if you are upset by people or websites urging you to do something harmful. If you once visit these sites, the Internet will keep providing adverts for these kinds of sites on your screen. This may make you feel that everyone is using these sites. This is not true and could be really dangerous. The way Google works is that it calculates what you have been looking at in the past and will then offer you lots more of the same. Don't get stuck – there is all of cyberspace out there, do not get stuck on hate or harm sites. Report them and move on. (Pro-anorexia or pro-suicide sites, and those inciting racial hatred, for example.)

R — Report abuse

If the incident or situation does not need police help, report abuse to the site or service.

If you are in danger, or being pressured to do something, threatened or blackmailed, it is a matter for the police.

Learn about the CEOP report abuse button or talk to local police.

WHAT DO YOU KNOW?

NOT EVERYTHING ONLINE IS TRUE

You are doing a big assignment or project.

How would you assess a page you were thinking of taking some facts from for your work?

> Does the URL end in .edu or .ac or .gov? What does this tell you?
>
> Are there typos on the page and careless grammar errors that suggest the writer may not be who they say they are?
>
> Compare more than one source.
>
> When was the page last updated?
>
> Does it use facts that you can check? Or are they simply giving opinions? Do they use experts? Can you look those people up and find out who they are?
>
> Academics have their pages at their universities and list their publications.
>
> References are given that you can check or follow up.

EXAMPLES

> Are sensational claims being made? Are personal opinions expressed?
> **'Why I think Scotland should take over the Arctic.'**
>
> Is there a whiff of gossip about well-known celebrities?
> **'Kim Kardashian runs off with husband of 81-year-old comedian.'**

INAPPROPRIATE

You see a web page that is really racist. What do you do?

> Report it to the website using their report button in the first instance. Get free advice from Citizens Advice about the law on this issue. They will help you decide if it is a police matter and how you can take it further. Save a screenshot and copy the URL as evidence with the date and time. Tweet about it if you like.

What sorts of websites try to influence young people?

> Answers should include: pro-anorexic websites, sites about suicide or self-harm, pornography sites, sites showing violence.

What would you do if you saw a page that was shocking and upsetting involving some of the material you have described in question 2?

> Report it to the website or service provider. If it involves child sexual exploitation, report it at once to CEOP using the button you can find on their site and many others.
>
> You can talk to someone at ChildLine via phone, text, email or chat.
>
> You can call Samaritans to talk in confidence.
>
> Talk to parents or someone you trust.

WHAT DO YOU KNOW?

NOTHING IS REALLY PRIVATE ONLINE

Susie posted an invitation to a beach picnic on her SNS page thinking only her friends would see it, but all sorts of other people she did not know turned up. She has been hoping for a romantic time with Jason but her plans were wrecked by all sorts of people arriving that she did not know.

1. Can you explain what might have happened?

> Susie's privacy settings may be set to public.
>
> One of her friends might have shared this invitation with her friends list.

2. Can you suggest ways to improve Susie's privacy online?

> Don't post personal addresses or where you go to school – even look at photos for what they reveal about your school or clubs you attend.
>
> Don't publicise parties, or at least where they are being held through SNS. Check and reset privacy settings often – they can revert when websites update their software or you may have old settings.
>
> Make sure all the people in your friends list are people you actually know. It does not make you look more popular to have so many people on your list.

3. I have set up a blog/a YouTube account and I want people's views.

> If you want to get people's opinions on a blog, photo or any item, how should you do this?
>
> Ask people to put their opinion in the comment box – do not give your email address.

GAMES AND GROOMING

Jamaine is really good at online games and he talks to lots of other players all the time and often late at night.

One has become a friend and is suggesting they meet up. Gamers are not really your friends. They might want to get to know kids for the wrong reasons.

1. What are some signs that might make you think twice about someone you were talking to in games online?

> They get annoyed if you leave the game.
> They try to befriend you, saying they like the same music or football team.
> They send you gifts or offer to lend you a mobile phone.
> They suggest meeting in real life.
> They ask where you live and which school you go to.
> They turn you against your family and friends.
> They make you feel guilty and ashamed.
> They talk about adult things or suggestions.
> They ask to share intimate photos (Your avatar is so cool – I'd like to see what you look like; send me a pic').
> *This could be grooming.*

2. What should you do?

> Tell a grown-up you trust.
> Close chat channels.
> Activate the 'Ignore' setting.
> Report this to the game site.
> Keep evidence – take a screenshot.
> Never give out your name, address, contact details like phone number, messaging information, Twitter name or email.
> Set up guilds or chats with friends you know in real life so that you are not alone.

WHAT DO YOU KNOW?

CYBERBULLYING

Tara broke up with Keir. She felt bad but she did not want to lose face among her friends. She sent a text to the biggest gossip in her class saying Keir was useless at sex and could never make any girl happy. She knew this girl would share it and she did.

Soon everyone was pointing and laughing at Keir, and Tara felt excited and powerful. She added a new message to the conversation with an intimate photo of Keir they had shared when they were together. It went viral among her friends.

Then it spread beyond her class. Keir had been feeling depressed that he and Tara had broken up and then his granddad had become desperately ill. He relied on him a lot and felt stunned and lonely. When he realised he could not turn to his friends and saw the ugly message and cruel things people were saying about him, he was in despair.

1. What would you tell Tara?

2. How would you help Keir?

3. What should teachers do when they learn of this?

4. What should pupils do when they learn of this?

This is a chance for some reflection, and the students' answers can reveal how well they have taken on board the e-safety and anti-bullying messages. Teachers can assess what needs to be addressed from these replies and share the best advice with the class. Domestic digital dramas are happening every day. The moral and ethical aspects of handling relationships will need to be discussed alongside the e-safety.

SRE in the age of the smartphone

It has always been a challenge to prepare children for positive and healthy relationships in a gradual and appropriate way. But whereas it once meant the dreaded talk from a parent on the birds and bees, or the school lesson on STDs, in today's world it is all this and far more. Now this task must include paying attention to relationship etiquette online too. The issues of easily available porn, the safe use of new technology and issues of sexual consent, violence and exploitation must be taught to enable our young people to stay safe.

Children's physical, moral and social development needs to be supported so that they can understand themselves, respect others and eventually sustain healthy adult relationships. But along the way they will be negotiating friendships and relationships online and via their mobiles – first love, friendship breakdowns, rejection, revenge and prejudice are today all played out in cyberspace.

Most children and young people are engaged in managing and tweaking their reputation as they present to the world the sunlit or rose-tinted image of themselves they choose to display – usually showing them to be popular, having a stunning time, always at the heart of things and most certainly not bored and lonely at home.

But here lies risk. Witness the girl who listed 'lover' among her hobbies and love of fluffy kittens, or the boy who felt his opening move in a relationship with a girl would be aided by sending a photo of his penis. These examples demonstrate how immaturity can lead to long-term risk and problems that could hang around in a digital footprint until the day a prospective employer or partner finds it in a search.

In a sexualised era when even adverts or pop videos reveal more than would have been deemed OK in the swinging sixties, we learn of young people seeking or sharing porn at a rate never before researched. Headlines tell us that this will affect their view of relationships and be extremely damaging to their future relationships.

Against this backdrop children and young people need to be prepared for life in a digital future we cannot even imagine. So where do you start? For one thing PSHE is not a statutorily required subject. For another, the SRE curriculum has been thought to be outdated for years. But there is a glimmer of light. The PSHE Association offers a sample PSHE curriculum and there is new SRE guidance that takes account of the Internet. Neither, though, is currently statutory.

Whilst I recommend that you explore these, I would also say it is necessary to integrate the e-safety advice into every area of the curriculum, especially into anti-bullying work and work on relationships and friendships, in a natural way. It should also be used intensively with foster parents, care workers and social workers.

- Boys in care are twice as likely as girls to say they 'never' follow e-safety rules.
- 35% of these boys had received threatening homophobic messages or insults.
- 63% of boys did not tell anyone they were being cyberbullied.
- Almost half of boys said they had a learning or physical disability.

The PSHE Association, Sex Education Forum and Brook have collaborated to create new SRE Guidance which takes account of the Internet. It is supported by the DfE. This can be found online for a free download.[22]

Gaming online – advice for young people
Upper Key stage 2

Introduce the subject – elicit what they are playing and share the sheet 'Five things to look out for when gaming'. They can do further research on the weblink given there. Use the following to address the young people.

Introduction

You have probably found that when you are playing online games you meet up with other players who could be anywhere. Even in other countries. When playing these games such as *World of Warcraft* and *Clash of the Clans* or using a gaming portal such as Miniclip it is exciting to be able to 'chat' and 'meet' other people when you play with them.

But of course, just like in the offline world, you need to be careful when playing with people you do not actually know. They may be dodgy or be trying to make friends with kids for bad reasons.

Five things to look out for when gaming

It's easy to lie online or hide your real identity and age. Some of these people, who want you to think they are 'friends' in your online game, may actually want to harm you in some way. So be on your guard – what should you watch for?

1. *They will try to gain your trust and 'make friends' with you.* They build this trust by making you think they like the same things as you do – such as hobbies or the game that you're playing with them.

2. *They might try to get you to do things that make you uncomfortable.* They might ask you to add them as a friend on a social network, give them your phone number, send them photos or chat on a webcam. This can get very difficult if they talk about things which make you uncomfortable or ask you to do things you don't want to do. They might threaten you.

3. *They might offer to tell you 'cheats' to help you out with a game.* Think about why they are doing this. Are they a 'real' friend or trying to build your trust? What do they want to get out of this? Be alert!

4. *Remember, if they share a link with you it could be a computer virus or spyware.* This tells the person your personal information without you knowing – be careful and don't click on links from people you don't know!

5. *They may encourage you to tell them personal information.* This may be where you live and what school you go to. This is part of their attempt to get your trust and will tell them how to find you in the real world. Never give out your phone number or address.

Where can you find out more about this?

Find out more about cybercrime on ThinkuKnow: www.thinkuknow.co.uk/11_13/ Need-advice/Staying-secure-online.

Public Wi-Fi presents new security challenges
Upper Key stage 2 and Key stage 3
Learning objective

- To understand how to protect personal information when using public Wi-Fi.

- Introduction, discussion and activity on how to stay in control as far as possible.

Use the following to address the young people.

Introduction

For those of us who use public Wi-Fi, there are some key things we should be aware of. Does anyone know what Firesheep is? Firesheep is called a 'sniffer'. It was originally created to prove how easy it would be to get accounts and identities of people using Wi-Fi hotspots. It can intercept sessions on popular websites, sniff out and steal cookies and then pretend to be you from the same Wi-Fi spot!

What Firesheep showed was that popular websites we all use only encrypt your login – but then they use an unsecured connection once they have checked your cookies. So it seems that anyone from your IP address (i.e. the public Wi-Fi hotspot) with that cookie could appear to be you. The lesson we should take from this is that, when using a public hotspot, be very careful to only send essential messages and not handle sensitive, personal or otherwise important confidential information as your connection is not secure! Public Wi-Fi in the UK with the Friendly Wi-Fi logo is filtering content to be suitable for children and young people. But that does not mean you should relax all your other security actions or use it to buy things with a credit card.

Discussion

Who can explain the security differences between your private network at home and a public Wi-Fi network?

Answers

Ensure the answers cover all the following points.

The number of free public Wi-Fi hotspots is growing, but not every hotspot can be as safe as your private home network. Your notebook, tablet or smartphone's default settings and firewalls may not be enough to keep you safe from prying eyes while you are out and about. If you want to keep your information and files secure, here are a few steps you might take especially if you often use public hotspots.

Activity: List at least five things you should do to stay in control

Ask students to work in pairs and compare their lists with others in a plenary.

Hand out the sheet 'Before you connect to a public network' and ask students to check how many of these suggestions they know. They may come up with further ideas on staying safe on public Wi-Fi which could be added to this list and displayed.

Before you connect to a public network

Take a moment to consider your settings:

1. If you usually share your music or a printer in your own Wi-Fi network, turn off sharing.

2. Is your Firewall enabled?

3. Is your anti-virus software up-to-date?

4. Does your device always ask you before connecting to a public network?

5. Look for sites that use HTTPS to secure the transfer of data or use a browser extension 'HTTPS Everywhere' if you regularly use public Wi-Fi when working.

6. Use two-step authentication. This simply means you need two pieces of information to log into an account. One of these is usually something you know, such as your first school, while the other is a password and code – this could be a code sent to your mobile phone that you then tap in.

7. If you are in a café or library, make sure you check the actual name of the network so that you avoid networks set up to look very similar to the real one, but which are fakes. The Wi-Fi details are often displayed in a hotel or library, but if not, ask a person who works there.

8. Don't do banking or send very private messages on a public Wi-Fi network.

4

Cyberbullying and Its Relationship to E-safety

The interactions and communications, the images and videos, the public shaming and the revenge or reputation damage we see online often have their roots in a culture of cyberbullying, and vice versa. What is more, we have found that people who are badly bullied or cyberbullied often go on to take risks online as they search for friendship or intimacy to compensate for their isolation or despair.

Cyberbullying can be associated with young people at high risk online

Among a recent sample of 113 young people involved in sexting, 68 per cent had been cyberbullied.[23] While we cannot claim cause and effect, we can see that this is a particularly high percentage in comparison with 23 per cent of their peers – about three times higher. This suggests that we might provide different support to those who are cyberbullied, especially if they are vulnerable in other ways, or known to be depressed.

Sixty-five per cent of these young people involved in sexting had also visited websites talking about people hurting themselves or trying to kill themselves and 61 per cent had visited websites encouraging anorexia. They may not talk about this at first, but may choose to share with you that they are being cyberbullied. So it can be treated as a presenting issue and a way in to a supportive dialogue where more might emerge if you know the questions to ask.

In addition to all the usual ways one would tackle a cyberbullying case, help can be given to those who report being cyberbullied by exploring their online lives with them and helping them towards a safer approach. It is also useful to be alert when screening or assessing a case – severe or persistent cyberbullying may be present when there are problematic behaviours or further victimisation. Another thing – it is a lot easier to begin by asking about the cyberbullying someone has experienced than to immediately address the more serious issues you may suspect around child sexual exploitation (CSE) or sexting. That is why there is an emphasis here on cyberbullying. It is so entwined with e-safety.

About cyberbullying

Some people think cyberbullying is simply bullying with new tools. It is true that the intent is the same. But there are some features of cyberbullying that make it markedly different:

1. It can reach the target 24/7.

2. Nowhere is safe; there is no refuge, even in the bedroom.

3. Cameras on mobiles and tablets allow humiliating photos to be taken and shared.

4. Smartphones allow young people to be constantly connected as never before.

5. Social networking and messaging is an essential part of social life for young people.

6. Isolating someone and talking about them behind their back is easier online.

7. Managing one's reputation and image with an elaborate PR effort becomes essential for young people who post pictures and messages to show they are popular and having a great time. This can be easily sabotaged by others.

8. Children and young people admit people they do not know to their inner circle as a 'friend' in order to look popular; this brings inherent risks as these people may say or do cruel or jealous things. They may have the intention to harm.

9. A person's identity can be stolen, misused or exploited online.

10. Bullies can enlist large groups of people to attack someone chosen as a target and it is all very public; for example, they can set up a webpage 'We hate Jack' and invite others to post hateful messages about this boy for all to see.

11. Prejudice and hatreds can thrive as people flock together with like-minded individuals; for example, homophobic bullying is rife online in chat rooms, spreading rumours and images. This can reinforce their existing prejudices.

12. Attacks on girls and women include 'slut shaming'; threats of rape and other group-bullying or trolling of women and girls are now sadly common online as some very misogynistic spaces and behaviours have developed.

The types of cyberbullying we commonly see

Threats	Stolen passwords
Insults	Rumours and gossip
Hacking	Abusive comments
Blackmail	Inciting hatred and prejudice
Extortion	Unwanted sexual jokes, threats or pressure
Chain letters	
Stolen identity	Humiliating photos of the victim shared or altered
Nasty pictures	
Name-calling	Sexting – self-generated content that can often be misused

Although name-calling is the most common, it is not the form of cyberbullying that apparently causes the most hurt. Young people tell us that rumour-spreading and misuse of their photos hurt most. They rate as very hurtful bullying that tries to isolate someone, to embarrass and humiliate them and to socially exclude them. They also tell us that being humiliated in front of people you know is more hurtful than being bullied online in front of an audience you have never met and do not have to meet at school tomorrow.

Prejudice thrives online because people with the same views tend to flock together and reinforce these attitudes. A young person can come to believe that most other people think like they do. This can make tackling prejudice-driven behaviour difficult.

Age patterns

There are two 'peaks' of cyberbullying.

The first occurs at age 10–11 when many children get their first mobile phone. Chain letters with threats, scary messages and insults are commonly reported at this age. It would help to tell nine-year-olds to expect chain letters but simply to recognise them as rubbish, and save them and tell someone they trust. They memorise their friends' passwords and often use the same one for everything. They play games online and hack each other's games account quite often. They leave their phones logged on to SNS or messaging apps and friends pick them up and send messages in their name.

The second peak occurs in the mid-teens when sexual jealousy is rife. It is also at precisely this age that teenagers tell us that they do not follow the e-safety education advice they have had! This can put them at greater risk in a number of ways:

- They might agree to meet people they only know online.

- They search for intimacy and friendship online if they are isolated, bullied or lonely in real life.

- They have relationships that break up and then photos they had shared consensually are suddenly shared with the wider group. This can lead to 'slut shaming' for girls and rumours about boys' sexual prowess (poor) being circulated in a moment of revenge.

- Above all they want to look popular, and this leads them to admit all sorts of people as friends even though they may know it is risky.

- More girls than boys are cyberbullied and girls are more likely to report it. But this does not mean that boys are not suffering. Extreme cases of cyberhomophobia are sadly seen and boys report extortion.

Some young people are far more vulnerable than others

The groups listed below are often more vulnerable generally and this means that online they may need extra support and some reinforcing of their e-safety education. This is not an exclusive list and young people can move in and out of a state of vulnerability at different times in their lives:

- Young people in care (be alert to flashy gifts of new phones – these may be used to control someone).

- Those who are young carers (they report little parental advice and some do not have Wi-Fi at home, they may use their phone to make social contacts if they feel they are stuck at home when everyone else is out having fun, or they may go online via their phone with little parental advice and help).

- Those who have special needs (they need to be given e-safety demonstrations often, in short bursts).

- Those who have experienced recent losses (they may seek groups online for comfort, or they may visit pro-suicide sites).

- Those for whom English is not their first language (they may not understand the e-safety advice).

- Those who have moved school several times or joined the school in the middle of the school year (they may have missed out on e-safety education).

- Young people bullied in school (they may try to retaliate online or seek new friends, validation or intimacy).

Lonely, isolated young people are often the very people groomers prey on. They may be grateful for the attention and flattered at first. They might be giving clues about this neediness in their online profile, choosing a sexy name, or posing provocatively. This can be a desperate bid to fit in or to show peers they are popular, having a good time and have lots of friends, although they may not know three quarters of them. It is too painful to appear to be the one who is left out. To effect change, this has to be understood. Rules will not override emotions.

More support is also needed by people who are known to have emotional and mental health difficulties, and in particular those who self-harm. Don't overlook the online lives of very thin young people who are anorexic.

Our research with young people shows that most are pretty resilient and they do help each other out. But the groups discussed here are in need of intensive support. They may lack resilience, resources and parental or professional support. All too often their emotional needs lead them to take risks. Their histories are often complex and professional services may be required.

Is cyberbullying different for boys and girls?

Although much of the online experience of our young people is universal, there are some differences between boys and girls when it comes to cyberbullying and online aggression. These are of course generalisations, but they do serve to give you a guide or a 'heads up' to the sort of behaviour to watch out for or prepare to counter. They are developed from large samples of our pupil surveys in the Cybersurvey.

Access

Whether the setting was rural or urban, we found little difference in the way young people accessed the Internet and their experiences once on it. Smartphone use is very high in the UK and this is the key to these universal experiences.

Naming the behaviour

Giving the name to the type of behaviour can help both staff and students recognise what is happening. This is discussed later in the chapter.

Understand the impact of the behaviour

Although boys were often unwilling to say they were very distressed by what was happening to them online, they took refuge in answers such as 'I'm not bothered', but this often concealed their pain. Girls were more willing to report what had happened to them and also rated many of the types of cyberbullying as 'really awful' and said they were 'very distressed and angry'.

In this book there is advice on preserving evidence, on how to address relationships and friendships, plus a description of what the law says. If the behaviour contravenes the terms and conditions of the site, such as a social networking site, it is possible to report it as a contravention immediately. However, if the site is based in another country, the law may be different or the UK may have no legal arrangements with that country. In the USA, for example, the first amendment right to free speech is often used to trump efforts to tackle offensive speech.

Cyberbullying by boys

Figure 4.1 Boys' 'wordle'

Ten ways in which boys cyberbully

Anonymous sender

Messages, threats and even friendly encounters can all have in common the fact that they are often anonymous online. Boys may receive a barrage of anonymous messages, leaving them bewildered and unsure if it is coming from someone they sit next to in school. This can taint their relationships as they become suspicious and anxious.

When gaming online, many players chat, and this can lead to anonymous messages, threats and insults.

Service providers can trace senders on phones. If the messages constitute harassment or stalking, it is a matter for the police. But if the person is on the other side of the world or the website is based in a country outside of our jurisdiction, there will be little that can be done unless the messages are seeking to sexually exploit a child. In such a case, contact CEOP.

Banter

This is the most common form of cyberbullying we see with boys, but it is also the most frequently heard defence when their behaviour is questioned. On the other hand, being able to 'take' a certain amount of banter is the key to being accepted, which is why it is important to discuss with boys the following: 'What would be going too far?', 'What does friendship look like?' and 'When is it banter and when is it bullying?'.

Coercion

Pressurising someone to do something, such as steal from a shop, is one way in which a pack of boys can exert power over a weaker boy or even one with learning difficulties. Younger boys report receiving chain letters which say 'If you don't do X your mum will die'. They need to be prepared before age ten when chain letters on mobiles proliferate, so that they recognise these as harmless and avoid sleepless nights.

False identity

Boys report being approached by someone who tries to pass themselves off as a person of their own age, but when they agree to meet they might find they are nothing of the sort. Older men turn up at meeting points, or someone who pretended to be a girl turns out to be a man.

Extortion

Some boys are forced to give up dinner money or do things they do not want to do. There are also rare reports of blackmail and extortion. If once tricked into sending a nude photo of themselves to someone who may have pretended they were a girl interested in him, a boy can be blackmailed into sending further photos or the blackmailer will tell his friends and family about the photos.

These cases require police intervention.

Hacks

Hacking is more common among boys who hack each other's passwords, accounts and computers, but of course hackers may target anyone, male or female. Careless talk, guessable passwords and other security casualties all contribute to the ease with which they can hack each other, but some young people are very sophisticated with high levels of skill. A pupil once hacked into his school's staff password system.

Work on strong passwords is essential. Why not invite a local police community safety officer to come in and discuss cybercrime?

Humiliating photos shared

If drunk at a party, boys can find humiliating photos of themselves shared around the class before they sober up. These images can hang around in cyberspace forever, causing them problems in new relationships and job interviews.

Other photos are engineered by a bully with the express intention to trap his or her target in an embarrassing situation. Alternatively, photos can be deliberately altered for the same purpose. In some cases these humiliating photos are then used for blackmail and the situation escalates dramatically. Former girlfriends might share intimate photos of their former boyfriend with hurtful comments.

Both boys and girls have rated 'humiliating photos deliberately shared in order to hurt someone' as the most hurtful of all types of cyberbullying.

The speed with which a photo can be snapped and posted can often mean that no thought was given to the impact or outcome. But all too often there is intent proven. In these cases some restorative justice work may help to reduce the distress but can never bring back the image, copies of which are by now shared on numerous sites. The perpetrator can be asked to take down any photos he has control of.

Boys are prone to impulsive steps when they discover that photos of them have been used in this way or indeed when they are subjected to any form of cyberbullying. They tend to bottle up their distress until it is unbearable, then do something dangerous. Believing they must deal with it themselves or stand on their own two feet can lead them to stay quiet and avoid telling someone who could help.

Rating girls

Boys are always commenting on girls online. 'She's fit' can turn into 'She's a slag' if the girl rejects the boy's advances, or she could be described as frigid to the whole school in a massive text share. If a boy does not join in with this 'fun' he could be subjected to rumours that he is gay.

Intensive work on SRE is needed, but in a modern form that addresses the impact of the Internet and the easily available sexual imagery and porn that has so influenced young people. Even pop videos are very revealing, as are adverts on every billboard or truck.

Adults need to break through this hard shell of attitude and offer help without presenting the boy with an image of himself as needy, weak or vulnerable.

Revenge porn

Intimate personal photos are often shared within a relationship, but when that breaks up these images can be 'leaked' by one of the pair as revenge.

Sometimes a boy shows his best mate photos of his girlfriend and the best mate shares the pictures widely in a fit of jealousy that she turned him down and went with his friend.

Sharing this type of image of anyone under 18 is a crime. Revenge porn, as it is known, is now illegal under the Criminal Justice and Courts Bill.

Rumour-spreading

Homophobic bullying is markedly reduced in some schools where they have tackled difference and bullying with great success. But this is not the case everywhere. There are still tragic cases of boys being subjected to rumours about their sexual orientation, whether true or perceived. This can quickly isolate them in harmful ways such as the boy who was photographed while changing for swimming and a photo sent round with a message saying 'Avoid X, he's gay'. This resulted in a series of attacks on the innocent target who was held under the water in swimming and thrown in a ditch between the school and the pool.

Boys are often subjected to rumours by girls. These might be because a boy rejected the girl's advances, or from a former girlfriend who spreads a rumour that he is no good at sex and that is the reason they broke up.

Ugly rumours are often shocking to adults, especially when written down. Teenagers maintain that this language is the currency of their everyday lives and boys especially will try to say 'I'm not bothered' even when very distressed. It is essential to see through this outer shell or shield. The support should be given in a way that the young boy has a sense of agency – power to make decisions over next steps – or given useful help on solutions he can take himself, for example to make his accounts more secure. He will not want to break down or be seen as weak.

Are boys without empathy?

It is often thought that boys who bully are cruel, friendless and lacking in empathy. But they are significantly more likely than their peers to report parenting that is often neglectful, punitive or overbearing.[24] A boy who enjoys leadership and likes the admiration of his followers may be looking to this group for affirmation. He does understand others. In fact he reads them like a book. He uses his knowledge of how they tick to impose his power and dominate. He also uses it to home in on the most suitable targets to bully because he can see how they might make easy prey and help him to look powerful. So turning his behaviour around does not involve crushing him in front of his acolytes. It means giving him (and them) a new way to exert his leadership qualities in positive ways because this role and the admiration of his 'friends' is such a vital need of his. Work with the friends to help them move away from supporting this negative behaviour at the same time.

Many of these bullying teenagers may smoke, drink and take risks online and in the neighbourhood as part of a bid to be seen as afraid of nothing.[25] His own e-safety is likely to be poor. He may instigate cyber-abuse and ask his henchmen to circulate it or even execute it. He may get into fights easily. If parents are largely absent through work or separation this can contribute to a feeling of neglect, which is compensated for by the devotion of his friends or pack. If parents cannot stop arguing, and life seems very uncertain or threatening, he may be unable to control his own emotions or anger.

Helping boys who bully

One option is to have 'boys who bully...work with a caring adult who can help them uncover the roots of their anger and find new ways to achieve the high status they're getting from bullying', according to Dorothy Espelage. She suggests they might need someone to give them 'a different vision of power and leadership'.[26]

Summary

In the work we have done in schools and in the research *Bullying in Britain* we found the following:

- Some boys internalised their dad's behaviour.

- Boys often believed you have to stand on your own two feet and shoulder problems yourself. This meant they did not seek help until things got out of hand and they were kicking off, acting out or extremely depressed.

- Boys who bullied others were more likely than non-bullying boys to smoke, drink or make use of other substances and to be in trouble with rules/laws/police.

- Boys who bullied were significantly more likely to report punitive harsh parenting.

- Boys who bullied were significantly more likely to report neglectful parenting.

- Boys who bullied responded well when new ways were found to show their leadership skills in a more prosocial way.

Useful strategies for dealing with boys who bully include the following:

- Remove and challenge the audience of admiring students.

- Explore what people think of bullies without naming names in some group work so that the bully hears the unpopularity of this behaviour.

- Do not push the bully into a virtual corner, as with his 'back to the wall' he is likely to come out fighting. Always leave open a path to change that does not lose him face.

- Give praise for positive behaviour and leadership.

- Try to change the bully's image from Feared Aggressor to Fireman: strong, admired and caring.

Cyberbullying by girls

Figure 4.2 Girls' 'wordle'

Ten ways in which girls cyberbully
Whispering

Almost invisible to a teacher's eye, girls talk, message or whisper amongst one another about another girl in her presence. The intent behind this act is to cause a feeling of alienation. They want her to feel as though she isn't a part of their circle. They want to make her feel miserable or destroy her confidence. Mobile phones make it possible to do this even while physically in a group with the target girl and even in class with the teacher present.

The desire to fit in is very strong, but never more than in the teenage years. Girls can feel that they are not good enough, even repulsive, and that they 'deserve' this ostracism. Some will internalise these criticisms.

Others react differently and become aggressive and angry. They can behave totally out of character at home and at school as they struggle to do battle with this insidious behaviour.

Alliance building

The bigger the group, the more power the Queen Bee wields. She and her henchwomen control the pack. They may group message their followers about social plans and ensure they leave out the target girl. On social networks they gossip and laugh at their target while telling each other how great they look and how popular they are. They scoop up as many followers as they can and display them as 'friends' online and in school.

This is more like a boys' pack with a hierarchy. The target girl is entirely outnumbered, and many people in the pack, especially the lowly ones, are too scared to defend her.

This intimidation can, but luckily rarely does, lead to physical attacks by the pack.

In this situation it is easier for the Queen Bee to force her target to act, to manipulate her and coerce her to do things she would never otherwise do. The target girl may become desperate and try to retaliate online.

When faced with a timid girl who is isolated and has suddenly done something entirely out of character, consider the social patterns around her. What made her do this?

The alliance can only be dissolved by working with individual girls at first and then the wider group to encourage open disapproval of cruel behaviour to be voiced in a safe way which does not talk about the actual group and leader but discusses scenarios. Pupils can discuss cruel behaviour in fiction, enact scenarios created to illustrate points you want to explore with them, or have debates and discussions. 'Include Alliance Building' is explicitly mentioned in your Anti-Bullying Policy.

Alienating

Yes, friends do fall out, but along with the loss of the one special friend, some girls also experience the loss of former friends who are quickly claimed by the girl with whom she is falling out.

Bullying emerges when one of the dyad wants to build a new clique around her and make sure her former friend is excluded. She wields her power forensically and pressures any timid girl who might be sympathetic to her former friend. In fear, the girls cluster round her even though they may feel guilt and shame in doing so.

Like a divorce, people take sides. The former friend will find herself being shunned and turned away. She is likely to be left out of group activities like shopping trips, skating or bowling outings or parties. The group will gossip about her behind her back and online, and tease and taunt her when they are with her.

Being alienated from a group of former friends in this way can lead to depression in some young girls. This wholesale rejection is devastating. But the size of the group is the key to working to change the situation as you can select individuals to begin the process.

The target may be magnetically drawn to watch the others on SNS where they display their 'popularity' all the time. They want to see and be seen, manage their reputations and make the target feel worse. Her own online behaviour may change and she might look for friendships online. This is a high-risk time for her. Help her check her friends list and her privacy settings. Support her and give additional e-safety advice at this time.

Mock friendship followed by ostracism

A girl who arrives mid-year or is in other ways a bit of a loner can be singled out for a planned strategy of isolation and ostracism. The intent is clear: this person is being targeted for humiliation almost as a sport or for entertainment by a ringleader for her audience.

They might even let her think at first that she has been accepted into their circle. Then when they know more about her (more intimate secrets shared = weaknesses to target) they turn on her. The turning point is often very public when the ringleader displays the fact that this 'friendship' was all a ploy planned from the start and the betrayal is a public shaming of the target.

Vigilance is needed for girls likely to be in this situation, and preparation of the class before a newcomer arrives can be helpful. In this instance, the more popular girls accept the other girl into their circle. After inviting her in and making her feel as though she is a part of their group, they turn against her. Admitting that it was all an act is usually something that the bully takes pride in and will be sure that it all unfolds in front of an audience or, better still, online for all to see. The actual moment may be like a flashmob, in which others are alerted about the time and place by text or messaging service. Investigating the trail of messages may reveal the entire plot.

Name the violation – it is 'relational aggression with intent'. This makes it easier when talking to parents and easier to include in policy in a clear and succinct way.

Inciting others

Powerful ringleaders have willing henchwomen to do their dirty work for them, eager to prove their worth. These girls eagerly intimidate the chosen target and often other girls in the pack on behalf of their leader. They work hard on social media, or in person, isolating and making fun of their target and policing the other girls in the pack – even encouraging them to post messages on a 'hate page' especially set up for this purpose. They might post humiliating images of the girl in question and they do the 'admin' for the Queen Bee, enlisting others into the project.

Screengrabs of evidence are vital when dealing with cases of this kind. Inciting hatred is, in some instances, against the law if it is aimed at people because of a disability or race, religion or culture, or sexual orientation.

Work on digital footprint lessons: how your actions and online behaviour will be there forever and likely to turn up in a search one day when someone you care about does a quick search on you. Work to break up the power of this group and have the henchwomen acknowledge the harm they have caused. Then work on the leader last when her power is diminished.

Joking to humiliate

Girls play pranks on one another in a deadly cruel 'game' to humiliate and embarrass the target. The intention is harm. The tools vary. Jealousy may play a part, as a girl who is jealous of her former boyfriend showing an interest in her friend may post him a humiliating photo of her friend. One girl found that an image of her had been posted on a public forum advertising her as 'ready for sex'.

Jokes that are racist or homophobic may be clothed as humour in order to get away with what is not acceptable. People with special needs are often the butt of jokes in order to humiliate them, especially if they do not understand the joke.

You cannot accept the defence that 'it was just a joke'. Work via restorative justice approaches to try to get the perpetrators to acknowledge the harm caused. 'It does not matter how you meant it – what you said is not OK in this school.'

Threatening online

Messaging, texting, chat and social networking offer tools to coerce someone in so many ways. Some argue that the Internet has proved to be a misogynistic environment. Trolls single out women in the public eye and young girls are often targeted both by people they know and strangers. Anonymous messaging can lead people to post cruel judgements on someone's photo, encourage them towards anorexia or self-harm, or simply send threats about what will happen next. Blackmail and extortion are not unknown. In some cases girls are urged to send revealing images of themselves with threats outlining what will happen to them if they do not comply.

Ensuring a girl will feel safe enough to come forward is a major but essential task. Making it clear that they will be supported even if you do not like their behaviour is a must. This can be a matter of life and death in some very tragic situations. Full safeguarding procedures must be triggered.

Prank calls

Mobiles are often used to make prank calls and threats. They can make the victim think the caller is someone else, or that she has won a prize. Repeated calls over time may be seen as stalking or harassment. If there is a pattern of repeated calls it is sometimes simple to have a teacher or parent answer that phone for a day. Callers will deny the harassment and targets should keep a note of the date and time of the calls.

Take a snapshot of the screen or save texts. If the caller is blocked they may get other people to continue on other numbers.

Service providers log calls and the caller can be identified. It is often someone in the contacts list of the target girl's mobile. In most cases the instigator is known to the target. Report any abuse to the service provider.

Full-blown cyberbullying

Every app, service or new device can be pressed into service by bullies. Some people argue that cyberbullying is no different to real-world bullying – only the tools differ. But I don't agree. The anonymous and 24/7 nature of cyberbullying is relentless, and the way the new media amplify the hurt and pain in front of an audience girls often know is excessively cruel. Girls are so communicative, they love to chat and message one another, and mostly this can be fun and safe. But the ways in which new media can be used for bullying, harassing or stalking someone are legion.

Girls and boys need to be taught from a young age about being a good digital citizen and about acceptable behaviour in cyberspace. Your school should have an active and living Acceptable Use Policy (AUP) in ICT which is signed and agreed to by everyone. E-safety and SRE should be integrated as we prepare students for the world they inhabit. Asking them not to use social media or taking away the mobile phone of a targeted pupil is a step so isolating that it will not protect anyone, least of all a teenage girl.

Rumour-spreading

All around girls today are gossip magazines, newspapers that spread rumours and websites that specialise in gossip and rumour. Everything celebrities wear, every bit of weight they put on or lose, is commented upon. They could be forgiven for thinking this is OK. Girls love to dissect everyone amongst their friends. Judging what people wear, how they have their hair and what music they like is the least of it. Rumours are spread about girls to damage their reputations, and sexual jealousy is a major driver. Thus girls are labelled sluts or slags, or labelled frigid or heartless and maybe gay. It is not only girls who comment on other girls but boys too. In turn, many girls are very cruel to boys as well as girls.

Group work on ethical behaviour within relationships can lead to valuable discussions among young people who can express their real views in the safety of a group with pre-arranged rules such as no names mentioned. Work on what you look for in friendships can be useful to trigger the conversations needed to work together to navigate some agreement on what is acceptable within the group: How do we want to treat one another?

Drama, poetry, art and graphic design as well as song can be harnessed to explore and express feelings.

It can be that someone who was happy and popular, with seemingly no problems, suddenly finds themselves in a changed environment and, within a short period, things begin to spiral into difficulties. We can hear the undertones of this possibility in the case below.

A mother reports

The anonymous case below can be used in staff training sessions to explore what steps could be taken in cases of this type:

> 'My 13-year-old daughter has always been pretty and popular at school and we have never had any problems with friendships until now. She fell out with one of her best friends a few weeks ago as another friend showed her evidence that this girl had been bitching about her in private messages on Facebook. When confronted with this the "friend" refused to admit she'd done anything wrong and defected to another group of notoriously bitchy girls who she is now apparently best friends with.

> Ex-friend is now making up code names for my daughter and posting horrible statuses about her on Facebook and Twitter using these codewords. The other two bitchy girls have also become involved and it seems to be spiralling out of control. My daughter still has friends on her side but she spends hours online checking who is talking about her. She is looking sadder and much thinner and I am worried that these two very powerful girls are going to turn others against her. How should I deal with this?'

What would you do?

Ask the mother and daughter to retain evidence such as screengrabs and note dates and pattern of behaviour.

Develop group work on friendship and loyalty.

Discuss: Is jealousy common when one girl is pretty and popular? Bullying will not really bring anyone real friends but only people who are either afraid of the person or get a real kick out of being nasty.

Use literature (depending on age) for example, *Cat's Eye* by Margaret Atwood.

Drama is another method: Have pupils act out a scene illustrating this behaviour, then allocate sections of the audience and have them advise the actors on what to do next.

With the class

Discuss the case without mentioning any names:

Why is this behaviour totally unacceptable?

Does it contravene the rules of the website/service?

Should the perpetrator take down all this material and post an apology on her page?

How can we support each other?

What behaviour is acceptable online?

How can you report something to a website, SNS or Q&A site?

How do you keep evidence and track what is happening?

With the ex-friend

Attempt to address the behaviour directly. Ask:

How do you really feel now?

Who do you think has been harmed by your behaviour?

How were you feeling when you first started this attack on your former friend?

How do you think your former friend might be feeling?

What do you suggest you might do to put things right?

When will you have removed the offensive material?

With the mother

Explore the mother's fears with her and try to engage her as a partner in the work the school will be doing. Ask her to reinforce her daughter's confidence. Help her keep a diary of events and preserve evidence. Arrange to see her or report back to one another regularly.

With the victim

Try to put the victim into another group either via lunchtime clubs or using a nurture group or peer support group. Having a friend is protective against bullying.

Provide one-to-one support via a counsellor and explore this girl's online life. Is the cyberbullying continuing? Is it more subtle or indirect behind her back? Is there discussion of her appearance? What is leading her to lose so much weight – is she visiting sites that encourage the 'thigh gap' and comparing herself with images of extremely thin girls? Is there a filter on her phone? She might like to join some lunchtime clubs so as not to be alone at that time. Sensitive discussion may elicit other online situations in which this girl finds herself. It is always a possibility that the bullying arises out of an image this girl may have shared or posted. Girls are very cruel to one another, being quick to 'slut shame'.

Work on helping her to feel more positive about herself and call in professional help if required to look at her emotional state. Are other girls in the group focusing strongly on body shape? If so, tackle this with group work on appearance.

If it is possible to work with the two girls in some mediation process, this can be the opportunity to have them work towards an agreement of sorts. These questions can be tried:

What has this been like for you?

May I share with you how I have felt?

How do you think I contributed to this situation?

Can you illustrate this with an example?

How do you think you contributed to this situation?

Do you want to know how I have felt?

Why were you so affected by what I said?

For me the worst aspect of this was when…

It is my right to be different – can you accept that?

Is it worth trying to find a way forward now?

What can we agree?

What the research tells us

Several studies have linked being a victim to peer rejection,[27] whereas in contrast having friends,[28,29] and especially a best friend (if reciprocated),[30] can be protective against being singled out for victimisation.

Evidence has also been found for the importance of the quality of friendships.[31] Both peer rejection and lack of friends have been identified as risk factors.[32] A longitudinal study[33] found that, in middle childhood, internalising problems, physical weakness and peer rejection all contributed to gains in victimisation over time. This might have an impact on a pupil during transition to secondary school if the social interactions are not improved in the new school.

It may not be straightforward or easy for a victimised young person to be assimilated into friendship groups. That is why some trained peer supporters are often seen as useful to help integrate this student. Sadly, research on pupil attitudes finds older pupils are generally less sympathetic than younger pupils.[34] It has been found that girls were more likely to show an increase in empathy for both male and female victims once these girls reached the age of 10 years, but boys showed the opposite pattern.[35] Among boys, empathic concern decreased, especially towards other boy victims. However, boys may be influenced by the presence of girls as to whether they actively support peers in distress or feel the pressure to conform to 'macho' values in their peer group by expressing derision for vulnerable boys.[36,37] Victims may 'blame themselves' for their experience and internalise the problem.[38,39]

By reflecting on this information, it is clear that by managing the dynamic of the classroom, peer working, team selection and training of peer supporters, there is much that can be done to ease a victim into a less weakened position in the hierarchy of the group. Using lunchtime clubs to integrate a bullied young person into a small but different group can also be fruitful. If having a friend is protective, then efforts should be made to help the young person into a new group where they might develop social skills and relax a little.

Why language matters

> Negative words:
>
> ## Anti-bullying
> ### Stamp out bullying
> ## Beat bullying

Turn the emphasis from negative to positive for a compassionate environment

A lot of what you will deal with on a Monday morning is cyberbullying or online aggression that has taken place over the weekend, off the school premises, out of your control. One of the messages of this book is to involve young people in thinking about how we treat one another and to promote and reward positive behaviour. If they only behave when they are at school because there is a threat of punishment, and then rush online at the weekend to cyberbully or troll other people, this message has not got through. You hope these values and principles will be taken into their lives and relationships wherever they are, whether in school or out. To give it the greatest chance of success, it pays to consider the words you use to convey the message.

Why talk about what we are against instead of what we promote?

Why is bullying intervention always described in negative words? Anti-bullying is the term commonly used in the UK. But if we stop to think about it, this word 'anti' sets up what we are against, not what we are for. It is negative language.

We hear that we must 'stamp out' or 'beat' cyberbullying. Both 'stamp out' and 'beat' are surely bullying terms? The hard truth is that you cannot bully young people into stopping bullying, nor can you simply command them not to bully others. Sternly saying bullying and cyberbullying 'will not be tolerated' is an empty threat. In fact it is just the sort of threat that bullies issue. It might make the behaviour go underground, become anonymous or more secretive than it already is. Of course no-one would tolerate bullying on or offline. The question is, not whether your school would tolerate it, but what is your vision for the school and what is your strategy to achieve that?

Language matters because it frames the debate. In the work of the Bullying Intervention Group we have taken a different approach: recognising the work of schools where positive prosocial behaviour is rewarded; where young people are fully engaged and participating in shaping the ethos of the school; and where peer mentors or supporters are trained to help address the problems that their peers face.

Most people do not bully or troll others. We should highlight them more than the few who do behave aggressively. The majority can be mobilised to assert the new normal – that is, giving the message that this is how we behave on and offline in this school and most of us disapprove of bullying, aggression, cyber-humiliation and shaming as well as rumour-spreading and cruel behaviour.

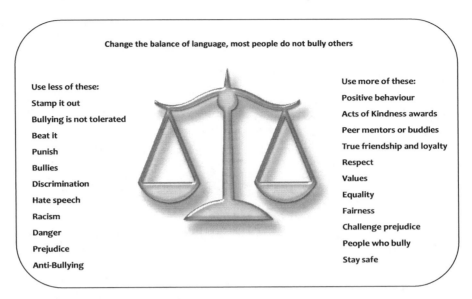

Figure 4.3 Change the balance of language

Schools 'where all belong'

Positive words:

Respect _____ Equality
Compassion _____ Inclusive
Empathy _____ Support

Many successful schools begin their policies with an inspiring vision statement about respect and equality rather than a flat 'Bullying is not tolerated in X school' statement. These schools 'where all belong' go on to set up inspirational committees, focus groups and peer support programmes in which young people play a lead role and 'own' the bullying intervention work. This is a compassionate environment. Burnham Grammar School calls its policy a 'Freedom from Bullying Policy'.

We hear of a Catholic school that states on the front of their policy on bullying intervention:

We believe that God has created each person to celebrate life to the full.

And the vision statement from an academy in Tyne and Wear states:

Value Diversity, Strive for Excellence.

Here are the names of some student groups or teams who are trained and working to support their peers:

The Peace League

The Peace Patrol

The BIG group (named after the Bullying Intervention Group)

The Digital Leaders

The Cybercitizens

The Cyber Care group

The Respect group

The FAST group (Families and Staff Together)

The FAT group (the Focus Action Team; the name is meant as a joke and makes it easy to remember, using the word 'fat' in a positive way)

The FAB group (the Focus Against Bullying group).

Banter or bullying? Who finds it funny?

Unless it is discussed and named, people may not be clear about where boundaries are. Teachers so often hear the defence 'It was a joke, sir' when someone is accused of racism, for example. It has to be crystal clear what is not seen as an acceptable joke. Some words are never acceptable:

- Set a tone of respect in the classroom and control the seating arrangement and the dynamics. Well-managed classrooms reduce the likelihood of bullying of all types.

- Create ground rules:

  ○ Develop rules and agreements with students so they set their own environment of respect and responsibility.

  ○ Use positive terms – what to do, rather than what not to do.

  ○ Celebrate difference and promote equality.

  ○ Support school rules and policy. Ensure all staff are consistent.

  ○ Name the behaviour explicitly in policy and strategy.

- Reward positive behaviour. Try to affirm prosocial behaviour four to five times for every one criticism of bad behaviour.

- Monitor student body language and reactions. If a topic seems to be affecting a student, follow up discreetly.

- Be informed about the support that you can call on for students affected by cyberbullying. It is everyone's responsibility to challenge it.

Images can speak louder than words, and even louder with words!

This Roots of Equality poster was created by Middlesbrough College[40] where I saw many other inspiring posters, artwork and plasma screen displays making every student feel welcome.

Figure 4.4 The Roots of Equality

Naming the problem enables victims to report it

Bullying and cyber-aggression always loves an audience, and the first step is to reduce or remove that audience and the henchmen, bystanders and other players that reinforce the bullying behaviour.

Online there is a huge audience potential, but what young people often tell us is that they are more humiliated and embarrassed by cyberbullying that is viewed by people they know than by an unseen audience all over the world. To be humiliated online in front of everyone you know or have your whole class sniggering over excruciating or intimate photos of you is to feel the depths of despair. Young people say that to be threatened online by someone who has power over you and who inhabits the same space with you for six hours a day is more terrifying than a threat from someone in a chat room whom you have never met. Of course I am excluding here very serious cases of grooming, threatening, blackmail or sexting, which are in another league.

But bullying in school often migrates to cyberbullying as targets become polyvictimised. This intense experience of being targeted and ostracised can lead to people taking risks online they would be unlikely to if their lives were happy and fulfilled. Bullies will use any tool available to crush their victims. Technology adds a range of new tools that have the power to hurt and humiliate and terrify in new ways anywhere you go.

Human beings can challenge the way technology is used, and what some young people call 'electronic embarrassment' or 'drama' can be reduced. Language can play a part. The way we define the different forms of cyberbullying and cyber-aggression really matters. Something identified and explicitly mentioned in a policy or in bullying intervention work is easier to report. So if you actually describe the different types of cyber-aggression, it enables someone not only to recognise that they are experiencing this and it is wrong, but it gives them the words to use to report it. This is particularly true in the case of prejudice-driven behaviour. Unless you explicitly mention homophobic behaviour alongside racist behaviour, it can get swept under the carpet and staff do not address it either.

By naming it you can reduce the audience – students stop sharing the offensive message and disengage with it, or they report it. Better still, they might get a few like-minded students to join in with them on social media saying they don't like racism or homophobia. The audience can turn into a support group when positive behaviour is celebrated and highlighted in your strategy with strong ideals of respect and inclusion.

Girls are twice as likely to report cyberbullying as boys. But it can be as intangible as simply ignoring someone's messages or rolling their eyes and messaging their supporters every time the target girl puts a foot wrong. Bullying among girls includes relational aggression: alliance-building, alienating friends, social exclusion and manipulative friendships. If these are named as forms of bullying then students will feel free to report it if they see it or it happens to them. Staff are more likely to take appropriate action than if a narrow definition of bullying is used. After all, how can you take action over eye-rolling or ignoring messages? (Just imagine justifying this to parents.)

But on the other hand, if this forms a pattern of relational aggression you can call it that, by looking not at one or two eye-rolling incidents but at a whole pattern of behaviour which might include online and offline behaviour over a period of time.

Pupils with special needs report a form of exploitative bullying in which their tormentors take advantage of their difficulties or inability to recognise that they are being manipulated for others to laugh at. Name it! Talk about it, ensure that everyone admires positive caring behaviour, and they push out the cruelty, stereotyping and power play.

When enabling young people to come forward to report problems they are having online, we need to adopt their language. Very few really talk about cyberbullying, but they do say 'I'm having a drama' or a 'digital drama', or more often 'a situation'. It can be humiliating to admit one is the victim of bullying, and many will not want to use that language and put themselves into a weak, powerless role. One way of tapping into their language is to use it in cards they can use to report incidents. This can help them to find the words to report a problem. This language allows the 'victim' to take charge and take action, rather than be pushed around in the situation. It can be empowering for the person reporting a problem – to them it can feel like problem-solving. And it is also helpful because you get a better idea of what the problem is. Very few will tell you they have a problem with sexting. They might say 'I have a problem with a photo'.

Here are some cards that might be useful to enable students to raise problems they are having with bullying.

I have a problem with a photo

This photo is   Private ☐

                Offensive ☐

                Hurtful ☐

Other ....

I need help to have it taken down ☐

I need other hekp over a photo ☐

Talkback card

I would like to talk to someone

Contact me this way: email ☐

                      Text ☐

                      Note ☐

talk

....

Talk Back Card

Gunnarswanson.com

My online issue

I have a problem with:

A person ☐   A group of people ☐   A hack ☐   My privacy settings ☐

A photo ☐   A troll ☐   A bully ☐   A mistake ☐

Other...

I have raised this before ☐   **I have not reported this before** ☐

Things got better for a while but..

Things have not got better...

Things have just happened now ....

I would like to: Talk to someone ☐ **Get help on email** ☐ **Get help by text** ☐

How can we get back to you? Please choose to say who you are, or give a number to text or an email address.

....

5

What Do Schools Need to Have in Place?

Leadership and management

Behaviour and safety

Staff training

Coherent practice relies on stepping back and taking an overview of all the policies and strategies your school has in place and somehow linking the pieces of the jigsaw into one picture. Even then the 'picture' needs to be refreshed and evaluated to stay alive. It also needs to be communicated. In this chapter we look at what schools need to have in place for effective e-safety. Schools should provide:

- leadership and management

- behaviour and safety

- staff training.

Schools should also consider how to address:

- policy and procedure

- e-safety training and infrastructure

- cross-policy links

- communications strategy

- serious incident management – safeguarding and child protection

- law – is your school compliant?

- new ways of doing things, such as with BYOD (bring your own device)

- general anti-discrimination and cyberbullying work:

  o recognising bullying or harassment of all types

  o raising awareness

- o prevention, including teaching e-safety

- o response when incidents occur

- o recording and monitoring of incidents

- o staff training to prevent and respond to incidents and to follow school procedures

- o pupil peer support training

- o engaging parents

- o complaints procedure for parents.

Take a moment to think: what would your school do in any of these situations?

- Did we have permission to upload that photo of Susie Smith?
- Is cheating going on with students using their phones?
- Has the teachers' area of the website been hacked?
- Did someone access porn on one of the school's computers?
- Is a student being cyberbullied?
- Are parents defaming teachers on social networks?
- Has a fake media webpage of the school appeared online?
- Can our teachers respond effectively if a student reports a cyberspace problem?
- Has an inappropriate video clip of a teacher appeared on YouTube?
- Has personal data about students or staff left the premises on a USB stick and got lost?
- Are sixth form students forming a political group with links to sites/blogs or videos we are worried about?
- Are teachers' school-issue laptops secure when at home/on the bus or train?

The infrastructure and policies, systems and procedures that a school sets up are there to counter exactly these sorts of situations and many more. Think of them as practical solutions rather than as a tick-box exercise of things you must do. One way to do this is to run a cycle of reflective practice.

A cycle of reflective practice

Keeping the strategy alive involves a cycle of consultation, implementation and review that is continuous – there is no end point! With each new term and intake, awareness-raising begins anew. Policy planning and strategy has to be responsive to what is happening and what your data tells you. Do your teachers find the procedures too time-consuming and tedious or do they feel they work well? Is the policy actually useful in helping the school with the incidents that occur? Do all pupils know of and understand the relevant policies?

Mindlessly repeating what you did last year may be acceptable on the surface, but does not take into account new devices, apps and message services. It overlooks new behaviours that have popped up and national or international trends that have come to dominate since last year – witness the selfie craze! Who could have imagined in 2012 that the president of the most powerful country in the West would be in on the trend within 12 months?

Reflective practice demands that we evaluate. The ongoing process of collecting data and the views of the 'clients' – your pupils and their parents – will lead you to tweak your strategy, update your information and re-think your communication plans. You feed this through into a refreshed policy and the cycle begins anew (Figure 5.1).

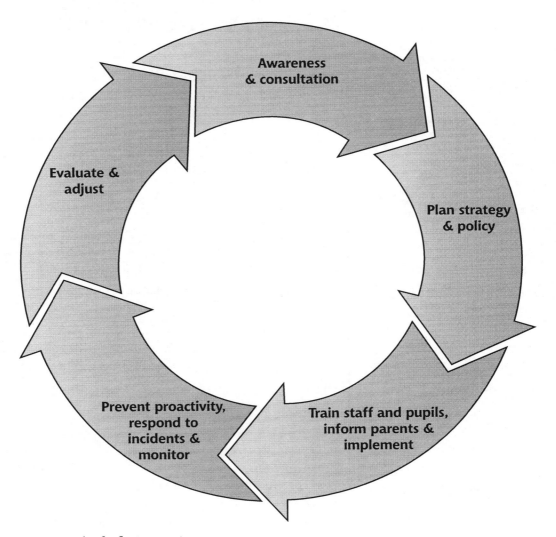

Figure 5.1 Cycle of reflective practice

At the same time, everyone has one eye on best-practice guidance and what the inspection process requires. The rise of rather militant parents who lay the blame for out of hours cyberbullying at the school's door, the 24/7 character of cyberbullying and the powers schools have to discipline pupils for behaviour that takes place off premises – all combine to bring schools into the front line of intervention. This can mean that accurate record-keeping is a vital part of the process, so that referrals are effective, professional standards are maintained and, if a case needs to be escalated, best-practice records are in place.

Policy and procedure

There are five essentials for effective policies (Figure 5.2).

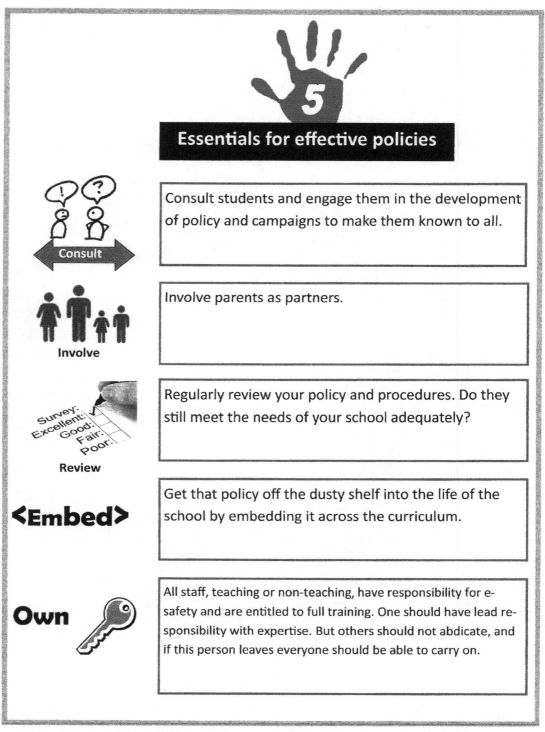

Figure 5.2 Five essentials for effective policies

To get anywhere with policy that relates to teenagers, it is vital to consult and empower them in the policy drafting or review process. Anything that will get them to feel they are full and valued participants is positive. In this process they will take some ownership of the policy rather than have it planted upon them from on high. Student representatives can help prepare a student-friendly version.

Engaging parents is the second essential, for they need to work with the school – or at the least agree to support the school's approach.

Regular reviews keep policies up-to-date and refreshed. This is a fast-changing environment, and any policy that relates to the online world becomes out-of-date fast.

Embedding something as intangible as a policy is harder than it sounds. It needs to be a living document, perhaps with various versions such as a student-friendly version and a public-facing version on the website. Alongside this can sit an internal version for staff which has more detail on how to implement the policy. Communication proves to be key.

All staff, both teaching and non-teaching, should be trained in policies that could be part of a child protection or safeguarding incident. They should also be able to feed back their thoughts on the efficacy of the policies.

Only a policy?

Policies are an expression of your vision and values; they can be a living document, regularly reviewed or a dry dusty file on a top shelf. Today schools should have their policies on their website. This is a showcase for the ethos of your school. Parents thinking of sending their child to your school can learn a great deal about your attitudes to diversity, the way you deal with bullying behaviour and the approaches you advocate on behaviour management. They can learn how you approach safeguarding and the care you take of the wellbeing of pupils and staff. They should be able to access your advice to them on e-safety, too.

When one deputy headteacher was going through an assessment of the school's policy and was given careful feedback on what was lacking, he said with a slight tone of exasperation: 'But it's only a policy!' This told me all I needed to know. You should be proud of your school's policies as a true reflection of the school. A policy is so much more than a bit of paper or an online document that is merely compliant. It should express what your school stands for and guide your staff to the approach your school takes. It is indispensable for supply staff and those going through induction. It should inspire the school community.

There are those who find a good policy on a local authority or charity website and simply add their school's name to the top and with a tweak or two they feel they have 'ticked the box'. The truth is that the process by which you develop your policies, the consultations and the communications around them, serve you well. Without buy-in from everyone in the school community you might as well not have a policy.

One more general point about policy: I frequently come across schools where the policy and the practice do not tally at all. Day-to-day practice may be influenced by an inspired senior leader – totally integrated, modernised and effective – while the policy may have been written by someone else, and this was years ago. There can be a fundamental difference of approach between the two in how cases are dealt with. The practice approach might be strong on prevention, mediation, restorative justice, making amends and challenging prejudice. The policy on the other hand could begin with phrases about zero tolerance and be purely punitive. This is not likely to be successful! Be consistent – it really is an essential.

Policies are no longer stand-alone documents

Your Anti-Bullying Policy should have a pupil-friendly version, and your internal version for staff can contain instructions on how you want them to handle cases if they occur. If it is to be at all effective in today's world it should cover cyberbullying and refer to e-safety in the work to prevent bullying. This is a perfect example of how policies nowadays need to interact. No longer can they be isolated documents that are not linked.

After a moment's thought you will see that there is a need to link safeguarding and Acceptable Use of ICT with the Behaviour Policy and with the Anti-Bullying Policy. There is a need to link, say, child protection with e-safety and Acceptable Use of ICT when serious incidents are addressed. Then of course there is inclusion, and what about SRE? Many cases involving teenagers involve relationships and self-generated images. Where does the staff code of conduct fit in? Together they all form a jigsaw of pieces that form a coherent picture of how the school addresses the wellbeing and safety of everyone in the school community. Try filling in the range of policies you see as interlinked. Take a moment to think about how your other strategies, such as 'Prevent', relate to this group. Perhaps you would like to add others? The handout sheet gives you a blank jigsaw for you to add your policies. Figure 5.3 is an example of some policies that might be included in the jigsaw.

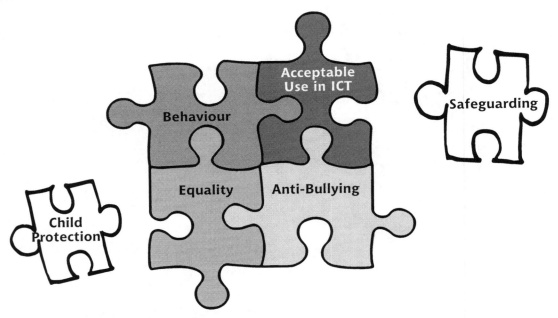

Figure 5.3 Anti-bullying policies in the jigsaw

The elements below should all connect up in your finished jigsaw:

Keeping children safe in education (safeguarding)

Behaviour principles (including bullying of all kinds)

Child Protection Policy and procedures

Special Educational Needs/inclusion

Data Security Policy

Complaints procedure

Home–school agreement

Equality Policy and Public Sector Duty goals

ICT Acceptable Use Policy

E-safety Policy

SRE Policy

PSHE Policy

Inclusion Policy

Anti-Bullying Policy

Dealing with allegations against staff

Serious incident procedures

Staff code of conduct.

In Chapter 8 I discuss how to deal with serious incidents.

Additional points to convey to all staff, teaching and non-teaching

- *Ofsted:* Understand how Ofsted will inspect e-safety and safeguarding within your organisation (see Chapter 9).

- *Infrastructure and safe systems:* Ensure that these are up-to-date and effective. The responsibility for safeguarding cannot be delegated – Academy owners and boards are responsible, not the company or consultant supplying the internal system.

- *Mobile devices:* Know your legal rights to confiscate, search and delete evidence on mobile devices to help tackle cases of cyberbullying and sexting in your school.

- *Staff conduct:* Implement robust policies and procedures to ensure that staff exhibit professional conduct online and offline.

- *Outside the school gates:* Clarify your responsibilities for safeguarding students beyond the school gates so you can be sure when you should intervene, for example in cyberbullying cases.

- *Allegations:* Make clear how you should appropriately handle and manage allegations against staff to protect both the child and adult.

- *Any record keeping and incident forms:* Ofsted will want to see documentary evidence relating to bullying both on and offline. All staff should know about your systems, including:

  ○ records of bullying incidents, pupils being removed from lessons and the use of rewards and sanctions, and information about exclusion and 'internal exclusion'

  ○ records and analysis of bullying, discriminatory and prejudicial behaviour, either directly or indirectly, including racist, disability and homophobic bullying, use of derogatory language and racist incidents.

Relevant and alive

Policy should be reviewed at least every two years, and preferably annually, to keep it up-to-date and to make any changes that the consultation reveals as necessary.

By reviewing your incident, truancy and absenteeism records for cases linked to bullying/cyberbullying, you will see how well your strategy has served the school in the past 12 months. Anonymous pupil surveys and consultations with peer supporters/peer mentors and the governors will give a picture of how well they see it working. You can also test how many of them know about the relevant policies – an important indicator. If staff find the recording or management systems too time-consuming, then perhaps they need to be simplified? Without this it could mean that many cases are not entered into the system simply because it takes so long to do it that busy staff will tend to minimise cases.

A vision statement can be the central focus around which a policy is constructed. This should represent the institution's character and ethos and be kept consistently in the frame during preparation of policy documents.

Communicating your policy

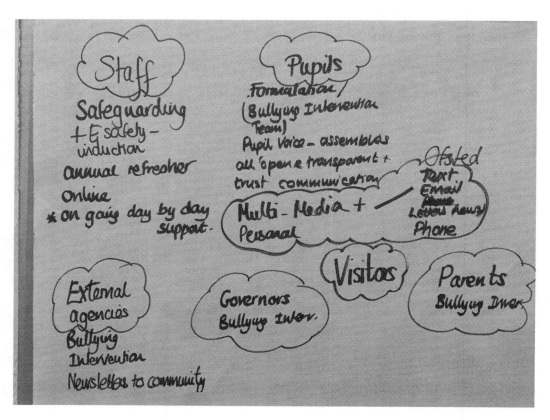

Figure 5.4 Communications plan

Plan your communication strategy with key staff. How will we make our Anti-Bullying Policy and e-safety strategy known? Who are our different audiences? What do they need? How should we reach them?

Staff issues scenario

A teacher took home a laptop issued to her by the school. On it she prepared lesson plans, presentations and undertook marking and recording students' work.

One day she came into school with it and the IT manager asked if she would drop it off with him for an hour or so as he was updating everyone's laptops with new safeguarding software. While working on the laptop he found that the teacher's daughter had been using this laptop to send intimate images to her boyfriend.

- How would you handle this?
- What are the steps to be taken?
- What are the risks evident here?
- What support should be put in place for the teacher's daughter?
- What would you include in staff training?
- Would you update the professional code of conduct in your school?
- Would you review your AUP in ICT Policy?

If pupils perpetrate inappropriate actions against staff

Follow the appropriate steps below:

1. Screengrab the evidence.

2. Identify who is involved.

3. Discuss the incident with the pupil(s) and aim to get them to acknowledge the harm caused.

4. Remind them of the school's acceptable use agreement signed by all students.

5. Find out if they have shared the offensive material with others and try to get all versions of it removed if it was shared within the school.

6. Ask them to remove the offending material.

7. If it is taking a long time to get the material removed, contact the professionals' helpline to get it taken down.

8. If the perpetrator(s) are under the age of 13 years, and the material is on a social network, contact the social network and have the account closed if they do not cooperate.

9. If the insults contravene the Equality Act 2010, inform them and their parents that this is against the law.

10. If the insults involve altered images or sexual content, refer to your serious incident protocol.

11. Inform parents/carers if the incidents are serious and persistent.

12. In serious cases, inform the police.

13. If the students' behaviour suggests to you that they might be behaving this way because they are at risk, contact your school child protection lead who may decide to contact the LADO.

14. Bear in mind some young people display aggressive behaviour because of problems in their own lives.

15. Refer to a counsellor if required.

16. Reinforce the Acceptable Use of ICT Policy with all students.

17. If the offensive material has been widely circulated among many students, write to all parents and insist all versions are withdrawn and removed. Remind them of the Acceptable Use of ICT Policy and the home–school agreement.

Contact the professionals' helpline for advice or to have material removed faster: 0844 381 4772

Unions can advise staff members

Reinforce your Acceptable Use of ICT Policy among all students

Provide support to your staff member

Notify parents as needed

COMMUNICATIONS PLAN

Audience	Media	Frequency
External		
Website		
Parents and new pupils		
All pupils in child-friendly format and language		
Prospective parents		
Promote reporting systems		
Promote peer supporters' service		
Prizes/awards for anti-bullying work		
Internal		
Staff induction process		
All staff and training updates		
Processes and incident-reporting systems		
Monitoring and review systems, data, survey		
Action plans		
Reporting to governors and senior leadership team		
Policy and strategy review consultation		

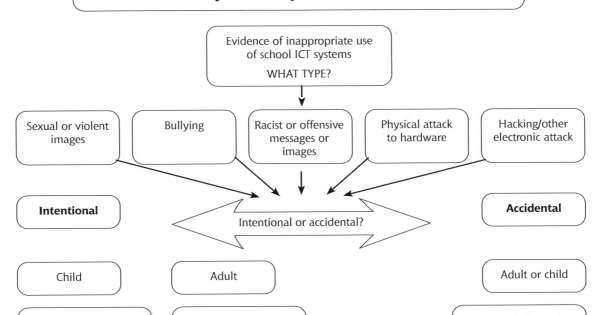

E-safety incident procedures for staff

Evidence of inappropriate use of school ICT systems
WHAT TYPE?

| Sexual or violent images | Bullying | Racist or offensive messages or images | Physical attack to hardware | Hacking/other electronic attack |

Intentional or accidental?

Intentional   **Accidental**

| Child | Adult | | Adult or child |

Child

Quarantine computer or confiscate mobile device

Provide effective listening.

Is the child at risk? If yes, contact CP lead or Safeguarding lead who will contact appropriate agencies and apply the CP procedures.

Is an adult involved? If yes, such as in cases of sexual images and CSE, contact police.

Is a child the perpetrator? If yes, contact SMT and assess the case; take screengrabs of evidence unless it is of illegal images.

Identify victims and make them safe.

Plan approach to be used. Apply sanctions and check back with victims to ensure actions have stopped.

Adult

Quarantine computer/device

Contact HR or SMT Safeguarding lead for advice. If a child is involved, your Child Protection lead should contact the police.

Treat this case as confidential.

Retain detailed notes of report and actions taken. Screengrabs if available.

ICT manager should check school filters and e-safety settings used on devices by this staff member and re-visit good practice for staff.

Follow advice from police.

HR and SMT to take appropriate steps when investigation is complete.

Re-train staff.

Adult or child

Quarantine computer/device

Contact ICT manager and report URL if known. Inform SMT.

Fill out incident record.

Carry out any technical steps or advice.

Inform parents of children who may be affected by witnessing the accident.

Advise all staff to update their systems and practice.

Remind staff to view all clips and searches in advance of using them in the classroom.

Group work with class to counter offensive messages and to discuss the Internet and risk.

Extra support for those with SEN or emotional difficulties, to ensure they understand.

BYOD – preparing for 'Bring Your Own Device' into the classroom

BYOD can be used in a new style of teaching often described as blended learning: a formal education programme in which a student learns at least partly through online delivery of content and teaching, with some aspect of student control over time, place, path or pace.

If it feels like a whirlwind of choices and responsibilities against a rapidly changing backdrop – it is! But others have done it with great success and it is clearly the way of the future. It offers exciting pathways to take advantage of the opportunities technology offers. Do check commercially available content for classroom use with care. BYOD also gives you the chance to create new content.

Here we are concerned with the type of policy and procedural changes you may need if you are considering bringing in this approach. In your planning you will want to explore and weigh up the advantages and disadvantages – then plan for the change. Here are a few points to consider.

What are the advantages?

- Budget impact is low.

- Encourages and develops anywhere, anytime learning.

- Students can access any web-based functions or learning platforms and network resources.

- Empowers students with the choice of their own device when working together, alone or on homework.

- Prepares students for the modern world of work.

- Promotes independent learning as they can access and edit their own files.

- Gives shy students the opportunities to shine in a collaborative platform.

- Slow students are helped by the collaborative platform.

- Students develop self-discipline using devices in the allotted time.

- The load of your ICT manager is lessened through individual troubleshooting.

- Students find it easy to use the devices they are already familiar with when they do their school work – it can therefore seem natural.

- A broader range of functions are available to students in the classroom and outside it, such as video capture for field trips; dedicated apps can be downloaded onto all devices for specific purposes.

- It can ease the pressure on shared resources in the classroom.

What challenges should be considered?

- Digital equity for all students.

- The high risk of distraction among students.

- Teacher management of all the devices in the room.

- Setting up the networking infrastructure for the new demands.

- A bigger range of devices to know for troubleshooting – a load on your ICT manager!

- Network safety – keeping your primary network safe.

- There is the need to re-think your Acceptable Use Policy (AUP). Does it cover software licensing, virus protection and software updates, as well as turning off a phone's 3G/4G capability while it is being used in the classroom?

- Training teachers and staff.

- Obtaining the right new solutions – for example, Windows and Mac computers can both run agents such as RM Tutor on CC4 which would allow the teacher to view the student's desktop remotely. There are mobile solutions which vary in quality.

- Parental agreements.

- The risk of introducing viruses into the school's network.

Infrastructure and technology

All organisations providing services to young people and which also provide access to ICT should:

- identify all systems and devices used within the organisation and carry out full e-safety risk assessments

- consider and select the most appropriate additional software and/or settings to limit the e-safety risk

- use up-to-date security software/solutions including firewalls within the school's infrastructure to prevent students with devices from accessing the main site.

Web content filtering products or services must as a minimum:

- subscribe to the Internet Watch Foundation Child Abuse Images and Content (CAIC) URL List

- block 100 per cent of illegal material identified by the Internet Watch Foundation (IWF)

- be capable of blocking 90 per cent of inappropriate content in each of the following categories:

    o   pornographic, adult, tasteless or offensive material

    o   violence (including weapons and bombs)

    o   racist, extremist and hate material

    o   illegal drug-taking and promotion

    o   criminal skills and software piracy.

BYOD: Ten things to address

Schools may issue tablets to students or they may consider having them bring their own devices into class. If you are weighing up these options, here are some points to consider:

1. Think through why you need this option and list the benefits – what educational goals are being met by BYOD?

2. Prepare a thorough plan before you try to get approval from senior management and parents. Be ready to answer questions.

3. Decide on a list of devices to be allowed on site. Determine whether you will allow Wi-Fi connectivity or 3G/4G connectivity.

4. Review and update your AUP for ICT so that staff, pupils and parents are aware of the changes and how new rules apply. Ensure buy-in from everyone.

5. You will need to limit the times when IT support will be offered, and outline what IT support will or won't do. (They won't fix personal devices.) Have people sign to show that they have understood this.

6. Train your teachers to deliver lessons across multiple platforms.

7. Make provision for those who do not have their own device and draw up terms and conditions for using devices that belong to the school. Work out how many supplementary devices you will need to purchase and store.

8. Prepare your network. Is your wireless infrastructure ready for the new demands that will be made on it?

9. Ensure your primary network is secure – divert personally owned devices onto a separate LAN and ensure filtered access through the LAN. Security walls can separate this area from your main system.

10. Provide a platform for this new 'anywhere, anytime learning' – it will need to be compatible with any device students and teachers can access for schoolwork or group discussions, assignments, resources and submissions.

Be well prepared but remain flexible. Try to visit schools that have adopted this approach and learn about the challenges you might face while looking for bright ideas.

Percolate

Your e-safety education will need to become embedded in every part of the curriculum. This is a far more effective approach than single-event sessions with a guest speaker who leaves and then is not in school to provide any follow-up discussions or answer questions. So blended learning ideas need to percolate through the curriculum.

Further information on BYOD can be obtained from Lightspeed systems for NAACE: www.naace.co.uk/2086.

Professional conduct

DfE Guidance for Safer Working Practice for Adults Who Work with Young People states:

Communication between children and adults by whatever method should take place within clear and explicit professional boundaries. This includes the wider use of technology such as mobile phones, text messaging, emails, digital cameras, videos, webcams, websites and blogs.

Adults should not share any personal information with a child or young person. They should not request, or respond to, any personal information from the child or young person other than that which might be appropriate as part of their professional role.

Adults should ensure that all communications are transparent and open to scrutiny.

- To maintain professional boundaries at all times, all forms of digital communication between staff and pupils or staff and parents/carers must be professional in tone and content. Official (monitored) school systems are the only route permitted for communication. No personal email addresses, text messaging or public chat applications or services may be used.

- It is not acceptable for any member of staff to befriend students online in any forum or social network or via any application or messaging service or chat room.

- No personal images should be shared with, or requested from, a young person. Personal information will not be posted on the school website and only official email addresses should be used to identify members of staff.

- As part of this policy, children are not to be named on social networks or tagged into posts or photographs on school Facebook and Twitter pages – any posts that name children must be deleted.

Unsuitable/inappropriate activities

All members of the school must agree to use the school ICT for appropriate and suitable work-related activities. Any Internet activity considered unsuitable or inappropriate will be deleted and will lead to disciplinary action. Internet activity which is illegal will be reported and could lead to criminal prosecution.

Responding to incidents of misuse

It is hoped that all members of the school community will be responsible users of ICT, who take this policy seriously and are aware of their professional responsibilities. However, infringements of the policy could take place accidentally, through careless, irresponsible use or through failure to manage data. It is of the utmost importance that every member of the school community takes advice from the IT manager if they are in doubt about anything. The school's incident procedures will be followed in all cases.

Safeguarding is everyone's responsibility

Safeguarding describes everything an organisation can do to keep children and young people safe. It covers preventing accidents, using safer recruitment procedures and action when children suffer or are at risk of significant harm. Your organisation has a responsibility to have the right policies, procedures and training in place

Child Protection: Protecting Children from Abuse and Neglect	Safeguarding: Promoting the Welfare and Safety of All Children	Worried About a Young Person?
Child abuse is the term used when an adult harms a child or a young person under the age of 18.	Safeguarding is about everything an organisation does to keep children and young people safe:	If you're worried about any child and think they may be a victim of neglect, abuse or cruelty, contact your Designated Safeguarding Lead in school or the local Social Care Office or the Police.
Most types of child abuse can take one or several forms. For example bullying and domestic violence often take both physical and emotional forms.	Minimising the risk of harm and accidents Having safe recruitment practice Having a code of conduct for staff and volunteers Having the right policies and procedures in place to deal with issues if they occur	For online child sexual exploitation contact CEOP
There are different levels of abuse and harm. You can learn to recognise them by getting information from your local Safeguarding Children Board or from the NSPCC.	Reviewing these policies and procedures to ensure they are up to date, working well and suit your needs. • Bullying Prevention • Preventing and responding to Domestic Violence • Teaching e-safety • Recruiting Safely • Avoiding accidents	The Internet Watch Foundation is the UK hotline for reporting criminal online content - Child sexual abuse content hosted anywhere in the world Criminally obscene adult content hosted in the UK Non-photographic child sexual abuse images hosted in the UK
Abuse includes: Child Sexual Exploitation Domestic Abuse FGM Neglect		Report it to the right place. Secure evidence or device. Ensure the child's safety

Figure 5.5 Safeguarding

A new focus

Along with the changes of the key judgement on Behaviour and Safety to the section 'Personal Development, Behaviour and Welfare', under which bullying intervention will be inspected, other recent changes in the *School Inspection Handbook* underline the importance of safeguarding and pupils' spiritual, moral, social and cultural development:

The judgement on overall effectiveness is likely to be inadequate where any one of the key judgements is inadequate and/or safeguarding is ineffective and/or there are any serious weaknesses in the overall promotion of pupils' spiritual, moral, social and cultural development.

But, before making the final judgement on overall effectiveness, inspectors must also evaluate the effectiveness and impact of the provision for pupils' spiritual, moral, social and cultural (SMSC) development. If this is deemed to require improvement or be inadequate it may impact negatively on the judgements for leadership and management, personal development, behaviour and welfare and overall effectiveness. This refers to paragraphs 159 and 160.

Paragraphs 132 to 135 of the *School Inspection Handbook* outline what evidence inspectors should look for when making a judgement about pupils' SMSC development.

Inspectors will also make a judgement on Equality:

…how leaders promote all forms of equality and foster greater understanding of and respect for people of all faiths (and those of no faith), races, genders, ages, disability and sexual orientations (and other groups with protected characteristics as defined by the Equality Act 2010), through their words, actions and influence within the school and more widely in the community.

The uses of filtering

Interestingly, Ofsted reported that schools that heavily block access to content find it to the detriment of their e-safety practice.[41] In contrast, those professionals who see filtering as only one piece of the puzzle can find that filtering:

- can provide report logs on content accessed, potentially tracing back to an individual

- when used effectively, can form a positive part of e-safety practice and policy

- can be used as an effective review tool to help give the establishment intelligence about the content that is being accessed on site

- can help, but not entirely prevent, searches landing on offensive material.

With all this in mind, let us explore some of the common misconceptions that people have about filtering.

Filtering stops children and young people accessing graphic images on search engines – FALSE

Parents worry that their children will inadvertently land on violent or sexual images and schools obviously scramble to protect their pupils. The problem can be prevented, to some extent, by using a moderated search engine. But the results are only as good as the filter dictionary. The problem is that the web addresses (URLs) of the images don't always contain anything offensive. This is what the filter reads, so it is not really surprising that graphic thumbnails may appear. If we think about the URL as a code and this code contains a 'trigger' word or string of letters/numbers, for example 'porn' or 'xxx', then it is likely that it will be picked up by the setting's filter. However, if this code is just a random string of letters and/or numbers, the filter won't necessarily recognise it, resulting in the graphic content being shown.

Filtering stops cyberbullying – *FALSE*

This is a common misunderstanding. Cyberbullying is carried out by people, not by websites! It is the behaviour we need to address. The websites or apps are only tools to communicate. They might make certain types of behaviour easier or even encourage it, but only people can actually choose a target and be a bully. By trying to block access to the sites where people are being abusive, the intervention is temporarily useful but does not address the real problem. Furthermore, if a young person wants to access something, they will simply find a work-around or get it from a friend. It is worth noting that the much-relied-upon Internet Watch Foundation's CAIC filtering list prevents access to illegal content only.

What they can't see online won't hurt them – *FALSE*

Knowledge is power. To let young people enter the unchartered online world without good guidance is to set them up to have bad experiences. Simply blocking and banning will not make them safe. This is not to suggest that good filters should not be in place, but to argue that more is needed in addition.

Experts are agreed that children and young people need to understand the different areas of risk online before facing these, in order to learn resilience. Some points you may wish to think about that can help you encourage resilience are:

- considering the steps your school has in place should a young person come across something inappropriate online

- how well young people are trained in what to do if they come across unsuitable material inadvertently

- how well aware your students are of the ways in which they can report any problems they encounter.

Filtering protects childhood innocence – *FALSE*

Filtering is a vital tool but it is not a substitute for parenting or teaching. While it can help prevent access to the most extreme content it is only part of the solution – education is key. Below are some key strands of work that are needed to build a web of e-safety.

If you need further advice or support with any incident relating to exposure of extreme content online in your setting, you can call the Professionals Online Safety Helpline on 0844 381 4772 or email them at helpline@saferInternet.org.uk. You can also follow them on Twitter @UK_SIChelpline.

The strands of work that build a web of e-safety

Teachers' support

Another element in the coherent approach is good e-safety support for teachers when using internal systems for staff. Both management and staff are involved in this process.

Encryption

If you carry around any important documents on a USB stick, these could so easily be lost. Should this material ever leave school premises? If yes, have you encrypted the information? Always check the school's procedures for keeping data secure.

Archive it and retain access

You may need to have access to this data when working at home or at another site or campus. Would a dedicated cloud service be the answer? There are also services where you can securely store large files. You are advised to use these on Internet-connected drives that you own and control. Any cloud service or public Wi-Fi system is not secure.

Long-term storage

Storage of data is always an issue, as the data grows exponentially. Consider using a secure file-archiving service.

Browsing

Every search is tracked and filtered to provide you with more adverts for 'blue toddler shorts' or 'man with van' ads after you have ever once searched for these. This targeted advertising is worth millions of pounds and becomes more sophisticated all the time. But this system also keeps throwing up suggestions to a vulnerable young person who has once searched for websites on self-harm, for example. It will keep offering them links to such sites as they search generally. As they begin to see more and more of these suggested sites, a young person can come to believe everyone is visiting these sites, or simply be tempted back to one. If you are worried about safeguarding a young person, suggest to their parents or carers that filters are adjusted at home and on their mobile device to block these sites being promoted.

As far as teachers and other professionals go, remember that your search history or clickstream can be examined – so act professionally at all times.

Regularly update your browser and configure it for maximum security. You can search online for the latest advice.

Agree a set of values

Use participative discussion to mutually agree the values we want for digital citizenship Explore the meaning of Respect, Equality and Rights.

Build Skills

Practical demonstrations, share solutions to common problems, learn from one another. Pupils can rate websites with e-safety advice and support

Modernise SRE

Teach about relationships in the era of the Smartphone. Include ethical behaviour towards partners and ex-partners

Teach e-safety in small units

Do no to overwhelm and confuse people by giving too much information in one session Recap and refresh often. Make it relevant to their lives now.

Embed e-safety across the curriculum and life of the school. Don't isolate it in ICT but use n every aspect of life

Cater for those who need extra help

Those with SEN and other vulnerable groups need top ups of e-safety advice geared to their needs plus extra support.

Explore all aspects of images online

Figure 5.6 Strands of work for e-safety

1. Often the browser is not set up in a secure default setting. This can allow spyware to be installed and create a number of computer problems.

2. Check all new devices to see what has been pre-installed.

3. Don't simply click on sites you have searched for without checking it is not a fake site first.

4. Updates are important as they fix weaknesses that could have become apparent since the software was first developed or sold to you – you will not be able to get these updates if your software is not genuine or original. This is relevant to staff who may work from home with school data. How up-to-date is the software they are using? Are they only using work-issued devices? What happens if they take work home on a USB stick to use on their own device?

5. When downloading software on your individual laptop, perhaps at home, beware of additional programs piggy-backing onto the download. These can be disabling or cause problems to your computer. It is all too easy to blindly click 'OK' or 'Allow' when installing a program you planned to download, but in fact it may be asking you if you want a new browser or adding some search feature you did not ask for.

6. Hackers often use weaknesses in a browser set-up to try to compromise a system.

7. Get help from your school's ICT manager if you are not sure how to configure your browser settings at home, and get advice on which settings can weaken your security. Attackers can use these vulnerabilities to take control of your computer, steal your information, destroy your files, and attack other computers by using yours. Exploiting vulnerabilities in web browsers represents an easy low-cost route for attackers to do this. An attacker can create a malicious webpage that will install Trojan software or spyware that will steal your information.

8. Visit the website of the browser seller to learn more about your browser settings.

9. Consider setting the security level for Trusted sites to Medium high and Internet sites to High.

10. If you have multiple browsers you could select one to be used for sensitive functions, such as banking or handling secure school data, that you wish to remain very secure. This can lessen the chance that your sensitive information is compromised.

11. Using Tools and Internet Options in Explorer you can adjust settings by visiting Microsoft's Setting Up Security Zones advice. Google similarly has online advice for using Chrome.

What is a cookie?

Are cookies benign with their cute name? Or are they an intrusive form of spying tracker? Cookies are files placed on your system to store data for websites. Cookies may contain information about the sites you visited, or details that enable access to the site. They help the site to recognise you when you return, perhaps as a member or account holder and open your personal account.

Cookies are designed to be read only by the website that created them, so you will encounter them in many locations, usually when a pop-up warning flashes asking whether or not you accept the use of cookies, as sites are obliged to do. They are not a program! Usually they contain the site name and your unique user ID. So, when you visit a site, a cookie is downloaded and at the next visit your computer checks out whether it has a cookie for this site. If it does, it then sends the information contained in the cookie back to the site so that it recognises that you have visited before. Cookies can help show what items you have bought or what is on your wish list, for example. Cookies are a solution to online shopping and membership websites that need to recognise you, and these sites are obliged to notify you that they are using cookies.

Are there risks to cookies?

Cookies can be used to uniquely identify visitors of a web site, which some people consider a violation of privacy, so sites are obliged to tell you about the use of cookies. If a website uses cookies for authentication, then an attacker may be able to acquire unauthorised access to that site by obtaining the cookie. Persistent cookies pose a higher risk than session cookies because they remain on the computer longer. So the cookies have asked your permission to store and retrieve data about your browsing history. In most cases you check that the website is genuine and say yes and carry on as normal.

- You can change how cookies are stored on your computer by using the Tools menu in your browser.

- Session cookies carry less risk than persistent cookies.

- You can set your system to alert you to every cookie request so that you can decide whether to accept the cookie if it comes from a reliable website.

- You can also specify which websites are permitted to use cookies.

Ensure all IDNs (Internationalised Domain Names) are displayed and check whether it is the actual address of the site you intended. This means you want any encoded address to be shown. There is a setting for this. BT.com may be the name of the site, but a convincing fake could be set up on BT.co.uk and pose as the genuine site asking for your details. Stay alert!

QUICK AUDIT ON E-SAFETY FOR SCHOOLS

Policies

	Yes	No
Does the school have an E-safety Policy?		
Does the school have an Acceptable Use of ICT Policy?		
These policies were last reviewed on: _____		
The policies were agreed by the governors on: _____		
The school has a serious incident protocol/flowchart easily accessed by all staff		
The policies are available online		
Do all staff sign an Acceptable Use Policy upon induction?		
Do all pupils agree to a pupil version of the Acceptable Use Policy?		
Do parents/carers sign an agreement on compliance with the school policy on acceptable use of school systems and safe respectful conduct online?		
Do parents agree to safe respectful conduct online themselves?		

Training and skills

	Yes	No
Is training regularly provided for all staff and governors, including CPD options for key staff?		
Are all staff provided with regular updates and advice on e-safety procedures?		
Are parents engaged through regular e-safety events and notifications?		
Are pupil surveys and consultations carried out regularly to explore their experiences and concerns?		
Are incident records used to inform training and policy reviews?		

Leadership

	Yes	No
Does the school have a nominated e-safety leader/champion?		
The e-safety co-ordinator is: _____		
The designated safeguarding lead is: _____		
The responsible member of the governing body is: _____		

Education

	Yes	No
Has e-safety been embedded across the curriculum at all stages?		
When was the e-safety curriculum updated?		
Have e-safety materials been obtained for use in school (e.g. Thinkuknow, Knowitall or Childnet International)?		
Is e-safety education age-appropriate?		
Are vulnerable students identified and given assistance with e-safety education?		
Are resources available for those with special educational needs?		
Are all pupils, parents and staff aware of how to report an incident or concern?		

Response

	Yes	No
Is there a clear, consistent procedure for responding to incidents of concern?		
Is there a consistent approach to preserving evidence where required?		
Are there links with appropriate outside agencies for referral where necessary?		
Are incidents logged and monitored?		
Is the whole school community made aware that all Internet use is monitored and activity can be traced?		
Is there a protocol for handling serious incidents?		

Data protection

	Yes	No
To comply with the Data Protection Act, is permission requested from parents/carers of children if photographs or videos of under 18s are used online or for any activity by the school?		
Are rules in place about identifying children online?		
Are consent forms always used when gaining permission to use images or videos?		
Is all personal data encrypted if leaving the site?		

What does an Acceptable Use of ICT Policy need to cover?

It is not good practice to use a generic policy – but far more effective to develop your own. That is why this is merely a skeleton onto which you can build your own policy:

- *School name.* It also needs to state who is responsible for the policy – for example, a named staff member and a designated governor; the date it was last reviewed and the next planned review date.

- *Who does this policy apply to?* The policy applies to all students, staff, governors and volunteers associated with the school.

- *What does the policy relate to?* The use of ICT in all forms, current and emerging. It is part of the school development plan and relates to other policies, including those for behaviour, anti-bullying, safeguarding and child protection. It has been written by the school and approved by staff and governors with pupils' participation. It works in conjunction with the school's E-safety Policy.

- *The school's vision.* Every member of the school community should be using the opportunities offered by digital technology safely. Everyone has a right to be free of bullying and discrimination, exploitation and harassment.

- *The school's objectives.* To inform every member of the school community about how they can be safe on the Internet and when using mobile phones and hand-held devices; to set up clear boundaries and agreement on the acceptable use of ICT, the school's systems and those used by every individual, both staff and pupils; and to make staff, pupils, parents and governors partners in the delivery of an e-safe school.

- *The five main areas of the policy:* current digital technologies; teaching and learning; e-safety risks; strategies to minimise risks; and how concerns about e-safety will be handled. There are often two agreements: one for staff and another for pupils.

  o *Current digital technologies:* ICT in the 21st century has an enabling, creative and essential role in the lives of children and adults. New technologies are rapidly enhancing communication and the sharing of information, images, music and film. The school's students and staff should benefit from the opportunities this represents but everyone acknowledges there are risks. Current and emerging technologies used in school and outside school include: the Internet accessed by a wide and growing range of devices; intranets; virtual learning environments (VLEs – e.g. Moodle); mobile phone texts, messaging, email, apps, cameras and video; instant messaging services; social networking sites; video-sharing sites; chat rooms, webcams, blogs and podcasting; Twitter; gaming; image-sharing sites; virtual worlds; and music and film downloading sites.

  o *Teaching and learning:* The Internet is an essential tool for learning in 21st century life and is integral to education, work and social life; the school has a duty to provide pupils with quality Internet access as part of their learning experience; Internet use is part of the statutory curriculum and a necessary tool for staff and students; the school infrastructure will be designed specifically for pupils' use and will include safety features and filters that are up-to-date and well monitored; pupils will be given clear guidance on acceptable behaviour, use of ICT and how to stay safe; pupils will be taught how to search for information safely and effectively and to cross-check information to ensure accuracy; pupils will be taught how to publish and present information to a wide audience; pupils will be shown how to evaluate content and respect other people's ownership rights; pupils will be taught to be responsible digital citizens and respect others; and pupils will be taught how to report abusive or offensive content.

o   *E-safety risks:* These include content – exposure to inappropriate material for their age and stage, inaccurate and misleading information, socially unacceptable material such as inciting violence or hatred or urging unsafe behaviour, and coercive websites such as those promoting anorexia or self-harm; contact – grooming, harassment or stalking, and unwanted contact of any kind; e-commerce – spam and phishing emails, exposure to advertising that is not suitable for children, online gambling, and pressurised selling and hidden selling such as free apps or games that have hidden costs; and conduct – cyberbullying, cyber-aggression or abuse, child sexual exploitation, rumour-spreading, unwanted image sharing, illegal downloading of music and films, and plagiarism.

o   *Strategies to minimise risks:* All staff, students and parents will sign the Acceptable Use Policy (AUP) for ICT; staff will receive training in effective strategies and how to respond to incidents; parents and pupils will be asked for consent before photographs are used on school websites; parents will be sent regular briefings on e-safety; pupils will receive e-safety education embedded in the curriculum; e-safety advice will be displayed throughout the school; all pupils will log in through a screen which asks for acceptance of this policy; filtering systems will be in place and will be regularly updated, although smartphones, games consoles and other devices can bypass the school's system and access the Internet directly – this represents a risk for the management of content; good infrastructure will be in place and regularly reviewed; staff will use safe searches and vet video clips before showing them to pupils; and mobile phone use within school is limited to certain times and lessons.

o   *Concerns about e-safety:* Child protection concerns should be reported to the designated safeguarding lead. The school will take steps to protect data and keep personal information about pupils private and securely encrypted; no data will be permitted to leave the school site unless encrypted; pupils' names will not be used with any photograph on the school's websites; pictures and work will only be shown where consent has been given by parents; parents will be clearly informed of the policy on taking and posting photographs; the use of social networking sites in school or for school use will not be allowed unless by agreement with all parties; pupils will be taught never to give personal details online, and will be encouraged to use moderated SNS sites and to use avatars or nicknames on SNS; no member of staff will contact any pupil on matters of a personal nature, using mobile phone, messaging or any other form of direct contact unless it is expressly agreed by senior management or the pupil is a member of their direct family; webcams will not be used unless specific reasons demand it and consent is sought; and sending abusive or aggressive messages, jokes, images or videos is unacceptable and any incidents must be reported to staff who are trained to support students. If any member of staff is aware of or concerned about any safeguarding matter involving anyone in the school community, they should come forward and, as a whistleblower, will be protected.

Pupil participation

A statement is needed that sets out how pupils will be partners in carrying out this policy and it is good practice to show that they will be consulted when it is reviewed. Make it clear once again here that pupils will also be asked to sign up to the school's agreement on acceptable use of ICT as a condition of use.

Provide for change in a fast-developing field

A sentence of this type could be a useful addition to your policy: *As we develop the use of devices such as tablets for learning, we reserve the right to amend this policy and we will undertake regular pupil surveys to consult with them.*

Common questions teachers ask
Must I close down my social networking site now that I am teaching?

No, you can maintain an SNS page, but as a professional person there are clear rules. Set your privacy settings carefully so that your pages cannot be accessed by students. Ensure you are careful to only upload appropriate images. Be aware that friends can re-share your images and comments, so be circumspect about what you post. Do not 'friend' students or admit them as friends. Use secure passwords to access your profile and change them often. Posting or blogging about your school can lead to disciplinary action. Regularly search for pages where you are tagged in other people's pictures and monitor your online footprint. Avoid suggestive online names and do not over-share.

If a student has evidence online of an incident, can I save it to my phone or school laptop?

No, you should only use a school laptop or phone for this purpose with the express permission of the ICT manager or the designated safeguarding lead. This should then be securely stored as evidence. Never use your personal devices. Alternatively, ask the student to save the evidence on their device and then make it secure until the incident is investigated. Do not view the material but hand it to your designated safeguarding lead.

How do you define inappropriate material?

Material may be legal but still inappropriate to have in a professional situation or around children and young people. If material is both inappropriate and illegal this is likely to be a criminal offence which would lead to the loss of your job and being barred from working with young people. It is illegal to possess or share/distribute indecent images of a person aged under 18 years. Viewing such material, even if not stored, can be identified by police and prosecuted. The different laws described in Chapter 12 show that inciting hatred or sending malicious communications are offences. The Equality Act 2010 covers instances of discrimination. Very violent images are inappropriate.

Behaviour that may bring your school into disrepute is inappropriate. If your behaviour breaches the trust and confidence placed in you as an educator and in a position of trust and authority over children and young people, the most serious consequences will follow. Examples include:

- sharing violent or offensive images

- posting insulting comments about fellow staff members

- accessing images of pornography on school computers or on your own device during school hours

- misusing or Photoshopping photos of staff or students

- communicating with students via SNS or in chat rooms, text or other means other than for school purposes and sanctioned by senior management, such as to organise a school trip. (Use a school phone or device. Use the school VLE where possible – never give out your personal number or email address.)

Am I permitted to take photos of students on a school project outing?

Permission forms must be signed by parents and students aged 16+ before photos are taken. These should only be taken on a school device that is accessible to managers. No images can be used or uploaded onto the school website or newsletter with the student's full name. Some students should never be photographed for protection reasons. Photographs must be stored securely within the school network or destroyed after use. Do not leave photos on phones, USB sticks or tablets.

If take my school laptop home to do work in the evening what do I need to know?

If any confidential personal data is taken home on a portable device such as a laptop, USB stick or tablet for work reasons, it should be encrypted and secure. There is a high risk of loss or forgetfulness endangering the security of this data, with the consequence of severe disciplinary action. Speak to your ICT manager about how this can be managed, including via the use of cloud storage systems. Make certain that you are fully informed of the school's data protection systems.

Establishing a peer support programme

First decide on the aims and anticipated outcomes of the support scheme you plan to set up. There are many different forms of peer support:

- friendship or buddy schemes

- mediation between pupils or groups of pupils

- mentoring (cyber, academic and social)

- listening

- problem pals

- nurture groups

- trained cybermentors.

All seek to provide children or young people with some form of support from their own peers. Many schools look for peer support schemes to reduce bullying and the time spent by teachers sorting out minor fall-outs. Others aim to improve reading grades or other academic success.

Training peer supporters and staff

Can children really be trusted to counsel other children? What happens if bullies are amongst the peer supporters? What if they say the wrong thing and make things worse? What if they spread other people's secrets?

Providing that children undergo good-quality training and that appropriate safety measures are put in place, these concerns are unfounded if the approach is thorough and well supported.

Four elements hold the key to success:

- careful selection of the peer supporters

- thorough training

- ownership of the system

- support from a teacher responsible for the scheme.

Selection

Peer supporters or mentors need to be carefully auditioned and selected. Avoid appointing a clique of powerful friends. Equally, avoid choosing all the peer supporters from people who have been bullied themselves or who are seen as weak. You want the group to be seen as credible with a good mix of strong, sociable, popular people and those who have been bullied and have true empathy with potential victims. Many victims would like to be protected by someone strong, while others simply want someone who understands their situation. Ask potential peer supporters to give reasons why they would like to be a peer supporter and what they will bring to the role. Look to appoint people from different year groups.

In some schools a few from each year group are chosen, while in other schools pupils from the higher years only are used.

The peer supporters will be dealing with sensitive issues and a lot of emotion! They will need to be committed (no dropping out halfway through the term), discreet and level-headed.

Training

The thorough and thoughtful training should include effective listening, training on confidentiality matters, and some scenarios in which they explore real-life cases and work out what they should do in these circumstances. Some clear rules or protocols need to be in place. They cannot promise total confidentiality to those they help – in cases where the client is at risk, the peer supporter must share this with the teacher in charge even if they are implored not to tell anyone. This can be very hard.

Mediation approaches do not tell the person what to do, but explore the possible options with them, they identify the harm they feel has been caused, and also work with the perpetrator to try to have them recognise the harm they have caused and make amends. Mediation is only suitable in some types of cases. In other situations a victim simply needs someone to walk with them at play time, sit with them at lunch or simply to be there for them to talk to for advice now and then. The presence of peer supporters in a school is known to make many pupils feel safer even if they have never been personally bullied or cyberbullied. Peer supporters are not only reactive, but they run awareness campaigns, design logos and wear a badge or uniform – cap, sweatshirt or tabard. It is something that should be on their record as a contribution to the life of the school. Peer supporters can feed back to the teacher or the focus group any new trends they are spotting. For example, if they pick up a trend which suggests pupils are moving to a new social networking site or app and problems are occurring, this can be vital information for the school.

When someone tells a peer supporter something very upsetting, it may affect their judgement. It can be hard to be objective. Also, the problem presented to the peer supporter is very often not the real problem at all. Peer support training will include teaching the young people a series of questions to ask. Though these provide a framework for the supporters to work from, peer supporters cannot know what to expect and should be prepared and supported thoroughly.

Training usually includes:

- active listening

- presentation skills

- conflict management

- facilitation

- problem-solving

- summarising

- building rapport

- assertiveness

- managing mediation

- confidentiality and reporting to staff

- e-safety skills.

Ownership

The peer supporters are likely to have greater ownership of the system if they help to plan how it will run on a daily basis. They will need to consider:

- a catchy name and logo

- how to advertise their service – mine enjoyed using an assembly involving plenty of role-play as the initial launch

- when and where they will offer their service

- how they will be identifiable to other students

- how long they will serve and how they will integrate newly selected peer supporters.

Support

The peer supporters need a lot of support when they are told something in confidence and are upset by it. They may feel very loyal to the person who disclosed this because that person trusted them. Training helps them to know when to report cases to the teacher in charge. That is why debriefing sessions are vital. Never leave a young person worrying over a case he or she has heard that day. Record-keeping and action plans should all be regularly reviewed.

Providing that young people undergo good-quality training and that appropriate safety measures are put in place, the peer support scheme can turn out to be a very valuable contributor to the ethos of the school. It demonstrates that pupils can be responsible, take a lead and help one another. It will not succeed if the team are left to get on with it and teachers step back.

Before a new peer support scheme is set up, staff must understand its purpose and limits. They need to designate someone who will give the time to it that is required and all staff should enthusiastically help 'advertise' it to their classes. Moreover, the leading staff must be given the time and resources to implement and run the system effectively. Peer supporters have told us that when it is led by a headteacher the latter is often too busy to give the scheme the time it requires! It is therefore useful for the leading staff to undergo the same training as the peer supporters. This way, they will understand the rationale and methods of the system and how to ensure that it is effective in practice.

A training course is provided by the Bullying Intervention Group: see *Peer Support Works* by Netta Cartwright (Network Continuum Education 2007).

Top tips for sustainable peer support

- Don't rush it – set it up carefully and work to sustain it.

- Buy in good-quality training.

- Train staff as well as pupils.

- Select a range of personality types as peer supporters and keep the group credible.

- Give the peer supporters status and make sure that they are clearly identifiable.

- Ensure that there are sensible, easy-to-follow safeguarding procedures in place.

- Hold regular, effective meetings with the peer supporters.

- Top up their skills training occasionally via visits from peer supporters in other schools.

- Make sure that pupils know when and where they can receive help.

6

Classroom Activities

Getting the message across

You know the feeling: you announce to a year 8 class that you are going to be doing e-safety and they look bored, irritated even, or rock back on their chairs. They are thinking that they have been learning about e-safety since they were in primary school and probably that they know more than you do about this. In year 9, they are determined that they are not going to share with you their private grief over relationships that have gone wrong and turned into online nightmares or revenge attempts involving personal photos. They may be visualising some images that they absolutely do not want you to see.

The year 7s may look at you politely but 90 per cent of them think they learned about this in primary school and they are so worried about the possibility of being cyberbullied that they may not really be listening when you talk about other types of online risk.

These are generalisations, but 'Oh, not again!' is a phrase I have heard, along with eye-rolling, when e-safety is announced. It is undoubtedly a challenge to engage their interest – to show how relevant e-safety is to their lives here and now. That is why you need a wide menu of activities, a broad, age-appropriate plan and the flexibility to incorporate issues they might raise. The key thing is to make them participants, not recipients. When they do become partners in the exploration of how to manage their online lives, they are transformed. They come alive with bright ideas, think of how they can help younger students and generally take responsibility for e-safety in ways that can surprise you with their creativity. When they are engaged and contributing, you will also be able to note the gaps in their knowledge and plan lessons to address those gaps.

The activities offered in this chapter cover many different aspects of e-safety. Some are short and sharp, while others are lengthier explorations or moral dilemmas. They involve different skill sets. Mix it up with visual tools such as posters and videos, discussions and debates, researching and finding out activities and practical demonstrations of how to set privacy settings or save evidence.

Pick and choose from these ideas, adapt as you see fit and remember to ask the students how they would teach e-safety. You will find that e-safety becomes the most relevant subject, the one that helps with the issues of real life right now for teenagers. Aim to improve the statistics on how many mid-teens adhere to the e-safety advice they have learned. Only 28 per cent say they always follow this advice.

Some of the material in the general text can be used to directly address the students.

THE STEPS CARD

Key stage 3 year 7 30 minutes	Art/computer graphic design
After this activity: Students will have a clear idea of the steps to take in your school if they experience aggression online.	**AIMS** 1. To get students to take ownership of spreading the message on e-safety across the school. 2. Reassurance – the message is that the school will support young people.
Materials: Card, computers and suitable software, printers and scanners, or use only paint and felt tips on cards if you lack the computers. **Preparation:** Guillotine the cards beforehand or have the students cut them.	**OUTPUT** Cards to put in a pocket with clear message on e-safety.

Activity

Design cards with 'help messages' for students to carry around in a pocket using a simple acronym as an aid to remember them.

The Steps card
Introduction

An acronym is a word made up from the first letters of key words. It is a way of helping you remember things. For example, here is an acronym: STEPS. It is a way of making it easy to think about the steps to take if you are cyberbullied or experience any unpleasant upsetting experience online.

> **S**afety
> **T**ell someone
> **E**arly action
> **P**revent it getting worse
> **S**olutions to try

Your task

Design a card to be carried in a pocket.

It should give a clear message to the holder that they can and should get help if they need it over any problem they might have online. You should include where to go for help (such as peer mentors if your school has these, any text line for reporting in school, and the ChildLine contact details).

Before you start, tell me what you would suggest; remember to keep it short and snappy – the card is small.

Your design should be striking and easy to read; think about the font, the colours and the spacing on the small card.

You may think up other acronyms if you prefer.

DESIGN A POSTER ABOUT OUR DIGITAL FOOTPRINTS

This is a good activity to do after you have demonstrated the shaving foam trick in the next activity.

Key stage 3 Homework assignment, research. Plus 34 minutes designing the poster.	Art, photography, graphic design, computer design
After this activity: Students will understand the concept of a digital footprint and be aware that they must manage their online reputation and presence.	**AIMS** Young people learn to be careful about what they upload or say online and respect their own and others' privacy. They understand that material they post, share or upload forms a permanent digital footprint or trail. They learn to protect photos they do decide to upload or post and to show judgement about acceptable use of new technology.
Materials: Card or sheets of paper, computers and suitable software, printers and scanners, or use only paint and felt tips on cards if you lack the computers. **Preparation:** Have the paper and software programs ready.	**OUTPUT** Posters about digital footprints to use around the school or classroom.

Introduction

Did you know that even if you take down something you have posted or remove a photo, it is likely that it has already been seen or copied by other people and spread around the Internet? Every action you take leaves a trail online. We call this your digital footprint. One day when applying to go to college or university a tutor might do a search and find something you are really ashamed of. This is also true if you are starting a new relationship with someone. They might do a search to find out more about you – what would they find? Today we are going to try to design a poster to get this message over to other students.

Activity

Assignment – homework. Find out about digital footprints and what you can do to protect yourself. Suitable sites include:

- ChildNet: www.childnet.com/resources/online-reputation-checklist

- Cybersmart: https://esafety.gov.au/esafety-information/esafety-issues/digital-reputation

- Thinkuknow: www.thinkuknow.co.uk/11_13/need-advice/digital-footprint

Discussion

What might we include in this message? Give me five key things to include. Design a poster that gives a clear message about protecting yourselves online and helping others to be aware of their digital footprints.

The following are some examples that can be photocopied and used as poster displays.

DIGITAL FOOTPRINT

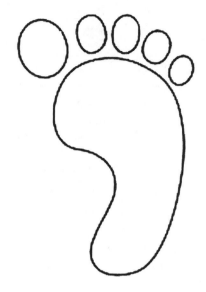

Do you know you are leaving a digital trail or footprint?

Will you be embarrassed by any of it one day?

Would a future employer see things about you that you would rather keep private?

In a new relationship? What can your partner find out about you by a quick search?

Search for yourself online.

Check all privacy settings and photos.

Look at your messages and tweets – what do they say about you?

Write down three steps you have taken to protect your digital footprint.

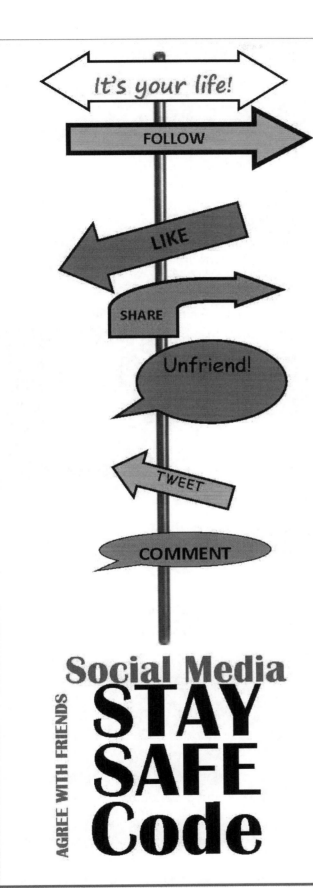

GRANNY TEST Could your granny see it? Have you posted anything inappropriate or illegal, like threats, nudity, alcohol, or drugs?

PEACE TREATY agree with friends not to post or share embarrassing or hurtful comments/images of each other.

AGREE that you'll delete – or report illegal, humiliating or hurtful material, hate speech and racism and block the sender.

REVIEW your privacy settings. They may go back to the original settings when the site is updated. Do you have old photos on it anyone can see? Do you actually know your friends? People on your friends list can see, share, and comment on what you post.

APP HAPPY Keep an eye on 3rd party apps. Do they give companies the chance to gather your personal information? Always read the boring small print before deciding to add one. Are there hidden costs?

LOCATION Don't forget that when you use devices like smartphones and tablets to post something or check in, you could also be sharing your location. Your photos can also give away your location unless you switch off GPS settings on images.

REPORT.

You have the right to be safe online. Don't accept cyberbullying. Save evidence, take a screengrab and report what has happened.

NO TO SEXISM, REVENGE POSTINGS, MISOGYNY, RACISM, HOMOPHOBIA & HATE SPEECH, CRUELTY HUMILIATION, HURT, EXCLUSION AND BETRAYAL

HOW TO USE SHAVING FOAM AS AN E-SAFETY MESSAGE

Key stage 3 10 minutes; follow with discussion or digital footprint activity.	Practical demonstration
After this activity: Students will have understood how content is difficult to retrieve once online.	**AIM** To illustrate that once out there, you cannot take your messages and images back – just like the foam, your content is out there, expanding and becoming unmanageable.
Materials: Can of shaving foam or aerosol cream, one plastic sheet and a plate.	Amusing, quick demonstration may stay in the mind or catch the imagination.

Each week you try to create one symbol that represents one of the safety messages.

In a startling or funny two-minute demonstration which you invite young people to do, the message is reinforced and they can then create posters using this symbol and place them all around the school. This becomes shorthand for the message.

Like shaving foam, anything you post online cannot be put back into the can! Try this with toothpaste or tomato puree.

Activity

1 canister of aerosol cream or shaving cream

One large bowl

Invite a student to come up and squirt the cream into the bowl. Then invite another to try and get any of the cream back into the dispenser. The cream is aerated and foams. It cannot be put back.

Message of the week?

Anything you post online cannot be taken back – it is out there like this foaming cream which cannot be put back into the dispenser.

Ask students to create one image to illustrate the message of the week. Display them on plasma screens, screensavers and on walls, whiteboards and presentations.

Poster making

Create quick posters using a safe image search resource and Publisher or another online graphics program.

TEN TIPS FOR YOUNG PEOPLE ON SOCIAL MEDIA

Key stages 3 and 4 20 minutes	Group activity
After this activity: Students will have explored ten key areas of their lives online and learned some ways to protect themselves.	**AIMS** 1. To explore what the students know about e-safety. 2. To fill gaps in their knowledge. 3. To engage them in taking responsibility for their own online safety.
Materials: Sticky notes and flipchart paper OR Do it online with tablets.	**OUTPUT** Ten top tip lists to use in other re-visit sessions. Materials for display.

Activity

1. All students are asked to write down their ten top tips to share with others on staying safe online. Put each tip onto a sticky note. Stick them onto the flipchart paper.

2. Have a team of three people look through the sticky notes and re-group them under headings.

3. Prioritise and agree the best top ten pieces of advice by allocating each heading to a small group of students to comb through and select their choices.

4. Compare with the top ten tips listed in the handout.

Top ten tips

1 Your reputation

Stop and think before you post anything online! How will this look if someone you respect reads it or sees your photo one day? You might be applying for a job, meeting someone you want to impress… Your post could hang around and come back to haunt you.

2 Nicknames

Use a nickname on sites such as Twitter.

3 Settings

Have you chosen the privacy and security settings so that only friends and family can see your pages? Have you set this for each photo on Facebook – even old ones you posted years ago?

4 Security answers

It is possible to look up your mother's maiden name quite easily, so do not use it as a security or bank password.

5 Private and personal

Give out as little as possible. If you don't have to give your date of birth – don't! It can be used for identity fraud. Check that the site is secure if you have to enter your name and address.

Consider an email address used only for shopping online. This keeps your personal email a little more free from spam.

6 Photos and videos

Think before you upload! Sharing pics of you in school or sports team uniform can allow people to identify where you go to school. Photos with friends and groups of people may be fun, but have you got their permission to upload these? Once your picture is online others can download it and misuse it/share it. If it is yours, do you want to keep it that way?

7 Less is more when filling in forms

Some people simply fill in forms without thinking. Give away as little as possible! If you are registering with a website or signing up for something, use your 'shopping email address' and give as little info as possible – you may not need to fill in every box. Your date of birth can be used to identify you or impersonate you!

8 Why not DM as default?

When chatting with a friend, why not keep it as a direct message? You could so easily forget that your message is being seen by millions of people.

9 Clean out the old

How long is it since you used some of your social media accounts? If you don't use it, close it. This means less of your personal info out there.

10 Fight viruses

Keep your anti-virus software up-to-date. Read the messages from your anti-virus program and stay aware when you are asked to download or install anything on your device.

TRUE OR FALSE: ARE THEY WHO THEY SAY THEY ARE?

Key stage 3 year 7	Online exploration of message senders and requests for information
After this activity: Students will have participated in developing message screening tactics and good responses to requests for personal details.	**AIMS** 1. To explore ways in which people online may not be who they say they are. 2. To practise not giving away personal details online.
Preparation: If required, obtain parental permission to do this exercise. Parents can do their part by reinforcing these messages at home. Set up a Google Hangout or other group messaging tool as a learning tool for a group. Set the privacy setting so that only pupils in this class are able to access this page or messaging group.	**OUTPUTS** 1. Typical scenarios will be shared. 2. Useful responses will be identified.

Divide the pupils into two groups, A and B. Ask each student to create an online name and write it on a piece of paper with their group letter, then fold it in half without anyone else seeing it and hand it to you.

Using their online names, set them all up as members of this messaging group.

Activity

Students in Group A ask those in Group B questions and try to work out whether they are who they say they are from the answers. Group B pupils can answer with true or false answers. Group A have to try and work out whether or not the people they have been talking to are genuine.

Group B have the task of trying to get others in this Hangout to give away personal information. Every pupil has a nickname or online name within the Hangout or messaging group, not their own name.

Discuss

What methods were used to try to get you to give out personal information? How did you resist this? Have you experienced other times when people have tried to get you to give out personal details? What are your options when this happens?

Group the responses into categories

There are tricky situations when you are told:

- You can win something.

- To do something or else…threats.

- You must fill in a form.

- You must log in or register.

- Someone you don't know asks for your personal details.

- Someone wants to connect with you.

Agree on how students could handle these situations.

Add to your wall display or develop a presentation.

'STICKY' E-SAFETY MESSAGES

Key stage 3 Teacher assessment tool	Group activity
After this activity: Students will have demonstrated how much they have understood and remembered of e-safety messages. Messages will be reinforced.	**AIMS** 1. To measure the extent to which e-safety messages are retained after a session or later. 2. To challenge boredom and engage students by making e-safety lessons adventurous and fun.
Materials: Brown paper bags and cards. Existing wall displays developed as explained in this chapter. **Optional:** 'What Do I Do?' grid found later in this chapter.	**OUTPUT** A comparison of your goals for the class with what they have absorbed. This enables you to go back and revisit items on which they appeared weak.

What is stickiness?

In webspeak it usually refers to the extent to which people stay on a webpage or website.

Why are we talking about it here? Because we want to work out how to get e-safety messages to 'stick' and actually be put to use. Too many young people say the e-safety education was good but they don't follow it.

We want to explore...

- Do they become engaged?

- Do they understand?

- Do they retain the message?

- Do they act on it?

- Which of your techniques worked best?

- What helps stickiness?

  o Real-life cases

    o   Potential dilemmas

    o   Problem-solving.

Reinforcing tools

1. 'Catch-up Cards' with short clear messages about the topic for those who are absent or who need a reminder, such as those with difficulty understanding or memory difficulties.

2. 'Take Aways' – students select cards which they think represent what was taught that session and put them into paper bags to take away. If they select different aims/messages, there is a debate.

3. Measure their needs – if some people are very unsure or pick up all the wrong cards, you know they need further support or explanations.

4. Displays – reinforce the learning from the session with attractive displays on walls or screens.

5. Reverse learning using their questions as a basis for a session.

6. 'What Do I Do?' online grid found later in this chapter.

Take Aways

Issue brown paper bags with handles. Ask everyone to write on coloured cards three things they will take away from the session. Then ask them to compare what they have written with the teacher's goals for the session:

Your sample Take Aways   ⟷   Their Take Aways

- Are they the same?

- Could you learn from their TAs?

- Clarify and reinforce your goals, perhaps adding from their lists.

- Display your goals and their cards.

WAVING THE PLASTIC ABOUT?

Before you use your mum's credit card to buy something – have you checked the site is secure? Look for the Verisign logo, or 'https' in the web address of the page that asks for the card details. The letter 's' shows it is a secure page within the website. Use PayPal or a bank secure password.

If a friend sends you a link to a game in a message saying 'Try this!' – don't click on it. Instead, go to the genuine website of that game. Search on Google or another browser and choose the original URL. That link in the message could be a fake site with a 'skin' made to look like the genuine site – these exist to capture your card details.

YOUR PERSONAL DETAILS

Have you thought about having a separate email account for shopping? That way all the adverts and spam don't come into your personal account.

SOCIAL NETWORKERS

Clean your 'friends' list. Don't be fooled into letting just anyone onto your friends list so that you look popular with zillions of mates. Clean out everyone you do not know! Block people who are offensive.

Check all your pics on Facebook – nowadays you have to set the privacy setting on each one separately. It is boring but necessary. They introduce updates all the time, which often causes your settings to go back to their original state, so you have to re-do them.

Did you know that 'Timeline' will bring up all your old pics? Yes, those embarrassing ones from a party that you don't want people to see. Do some housekeeping and set privacy settings for every one or remove them from your Facebook page.

Never circulate private photos from a personal relationship – even if you are mad at someone. For sure you will regret it. They could be used against you.

WEBCAMS

When someone asks you to do a sexy pose in front of a webcam, take a deep breath, make a joke and say no. Even if it is someone you love – things can go wrong and these personal images of you will be floating around on the Internet for all to see.

IN CHAT ROOMS

Be ready to just leave the chat if it is unpleasant, inappropriate or hurtful. You don't have to stay! They are not your friends.

REPORT ABUSE BUTTONS

Learn to recognise these on sites you use in case you need to report an incident or series of attacks. The CEOP button reports to the police and is for serious abuse.

IS IT A FAKE WEBSITE?

Key stage 3 year 8	Students work online
After this activity: Students will understand what safe search entails; they will be aware of fake websites and the steps to take to check the genuine URL.	**LEARNING** Safe search is a basic skill, essential for all actions online. Students will learn how to search safely, use discretion, look for fake sites and spot elements that tell them a site is not safe. Students will learn about some real-life situations in which people have been fooled.
Materials: Fun fake websites set up by Teach ICT: www.teach-ict.com/ks3/year8/information_reliability_bias/information_reliability_spoofs.htm http://zapatopi.net/treeoctopus	**ACTIVITIES** Online working and problem-solving, plus discussion.

Introduction

1. Set the dilemma: *Your friend sends you a message with a link in it saying, 'You've got to see this, it's the best game/app/clip I've ever seen.'*

2. Ask the class: *What do you do? Do you click on the link or look for the URL of this game or app or YouTube clip?*

Could you detect a fake website? Practical work online begins: fun fakes

See www.teach-ict.com/ks3/year8/information_reliability_bias/information_reliability_spoofs.htm

These are fun fake websites created by Teach ICT.com to help you work with your year 8 students to detect spoofs.

For example, this is an amusing example about a weird and wonderful animal called a Tree Octopus:

http://zapatopi.net/treeoctopus

SOME FAMOUS FAKE WEBSITES

Did you know that in 2014 a fake website duped applicants for visas to India?

Also in 2014, people were finally arrested for creating sites made to look like the genuine UK government websites for ordering official documents such as passports, car tax discs, filing tax returns or booking a driving test.

Have you come across any fake sites? You may see emails pretending to be from PayPal or Apple asking you to re-enter your details. These often lead to fake sites.

What to do if you are not sure? Go back to your search engine, search for the original site and think carefully about the options that come up. Is the real site address slightly different? What clues tell you it is the genuine website? Check the 'Contact us' details. Look at the full web address. Check content on the page. Search for the company's address online.

Below is a checklist. Think before you link!

Never click on a link you get inside a text or an email. Even if it came from someone you know, look it up in a search engine or type it into your browser where it can be checked.

Take a look. Is there anything about the website that does not look genuine? Is it asking you for personal information? Does it give contact information (an address in the real world) and say who is behind the website? Is there a phone number and is it in the right country you expected it to be?

The address – also known as the URL. Is the name spelled right or is it just similar to the address you usually use? Fake sites might have an address that is almost the same as the one you want, but the ending or a simple letter change could be different, trying to fool you into thinking it is the real thing.

Don't fall for it! If you are being promised a chance to win something amazing or a chance of a lifetime, then be on your guard!

Did you know you could check the link? Right-click a hyperlink and then choose 'Properties' from the menu. This will show where the link will take you. Is this where you meant to go?

Check that 'https' appears in the address if you are entering credit card or personal details. The 's' tells you that it is using a secure system to keep your information safe. You should also look for the symbol of a little lock. This way your information gets encrypted before it is sent.

LOCATION AND YOUR PHOTOS

Key stages 3 and 4	Practical demonstrations of GPS location settings and creating a webpage of advice
After this activity: Students will be aware of GPS location settings and how to adjust them.	AIMS 1. To make students aware of the risks location settings can bring, especially in cameras. 2. To demonstrate how to turn them off. 3. To engage students in making an advice webpage about location settings.
Materials: Wi-fi access. Students' phones, tablets or other devices. Prepare in advance the 'safe approved photo' described, using the location setting on a phone camera. Upload it to a safe location.	OUTPUT Step-by-step video clips and advice on how to manage location settings on different devices. These and the safe approved photo can be uploaded so that students can use the page to access the advice.

This unit contains advice for you to give students to start off the activity. It is a good example of shared learning. Some students may be able to demonstrate on their phones how to turn location functions off on the phone camera. Others will film the demonstrations to upload short videos of how to do it for the school's page on e-safety advice.

Wherever possible, it is best to combine practical demonstrations with your advice. You can illustrate this by taking and posting one shot, perhaps of the school gate (no students), with the location setting on the phone's camera set to 'on'. Upload it to a safe webpage. A right-click on the photo will reveal where it was taken. Set up an example for the school that is accessible and not blocked by the school's filter. This 'safe approved photo' can be used for demonstration purposes many times by other teachers.

Discussion

- How can a photo give away your location?

- Did you know that when you take a photo with your mobile phone it can store information on where you were when you took that shot?

This can give away your location and be dangerous in some situations. If your phone is lost, the finder can work out where you live or someone viewing your photos can see your location with a simple click. Someone viewing your photo on your social network page can also see where you were when you took it. You may be there still. This is a risk.

You can turn this function off

Ask who knows how to do this and have them demonstrate it on their devices for those with similar models. Have students video one or two of the demonstrations for very short clips.

iOS asks you to opt-in to the location for the Camera app the first time you launch it, but if you change your mind at any time, it's simple to opt-out of and turn off.

If you've already taken photos with your iPhone, iPod touch, or iPad and want to share them from your camera roll, but are worried that they might contain location information, you can quickly and easily wipe them clean before posting.

Have students demonstrate the settings on different types of phone and tablet.

Video the demonstrations and write out a step-by-step guide. Upload to a designated webpage accessible to students and staff.

Don't take risks

Anyone can see your friends' names on your social network page. What if the photo they are using is fake? In fact they are not a young person at all, but an adult.

Abusers look at your interests, what music or sports teams you like. They make sure they can easily talk to you and seem really on your wavelength.

Why is your page public?
Think about setting it to family and friends only.

'It's just between us', or 'If you love me you will send me a photo'
If someone asks you to send photos or videos and says 'It is private, just between us two', you know it is not true. Your images could be shared or misused by mistake or on purpose. Did you know that abusers find it easier these days to get young people to send them photos rather than work hard to persuade someone to meet up and then work to be able to take the photos themselves?

'Now I've got your photo, you have to send me more or I will share it'
Pure blackmail! Report it.

The useful lie
'My webcam's broken but I can still see you. Let's chat.' Don't fall for this one – they do not want you to see that they are not the person they say they are.

'Let's talk somewhere private'
Lots of apps allow private chat. Be careful about this. Don't give away your location either. Did you know that if the GPS setting on your camera is on, anyone can right-click on the image and find out where you were when you took it five minutes ago?

'Let's meet up'
Don't meet up with someone you only know online; and if you do, please follow these rules:

- Let others know where you are going.

- Take someone with you.

- Meet only in a public place.

REITERATE AND RECAP REGULARLY

Key stages 3 and 4	Recap activity, reinforcing the message
After these activities: Students will find e-safety messages reiterated and reinforced with opportunities to ask questions.	**OUTPUTS** 1. Evaluation. 2. An assessment of how much students have (a) understood, (b) retained and (c) intend to put it into action.

It is vital to recap, remind and reinforce before moving on to another level, just as in all good teaching techniques, but so often overlooked in e-safety education. If a guest comes in to your school to deliver an e-safety session, how often do schools revisit what was covered? Do you ensure that everyone accurately understood the messages delivered by the police community support officer (PCSO) or charity? Ask students to tell you what they now plan to do to keep themselves safe. That is how we discover that many students may misunderstand the film or the lesson itself. In the same way in your own lesson cycle, set aside a little time to recap, quiz them or create the colour-themed displays discussed earlier. There are some quiz and wordsearch ideas in this book.

- Later in the chapter is 'Top Five Crimes Online' followed by 'Tell Me Five Ways to Keep Your Secret Stuff Secret!'. Earlier in the chapter is 'Top Ten Tips'.

- Use these in regular short five-minute recaps or quiz questions – 'Name five ways to protect your privacy', 'Give me five common types of cybercrime'.

- Use them as handouts; use them as a guide to poster making; display them; hand them out on cards.

- Test your pupils' retention of the e-safety information you are trying to get across.

INVESTIGATIONS IN CYBERSPACE: WHO ARE THEY?

Key stages 3 and 4	Personal research assignment on key figures in technology
After this activity: Students will have an idea of the possibilities of online entrepreneurship and the history of some of the leading exponents. They will be able to think about how these sites are monetised – understanding that their data is valuable.	**AIMS** 1. To move students from being users of the websites and apps to thinking more actively about what it means to create a start-up. 2. To promote engagement and to encourage girls to think about careers in technology. 3. To encourage e-safety by showing how data is monetised.
Online access required	

A personal research assignment

Find out more about these people. How did they start out? What have they achieved? What message does this send?

- Ken Kutaragi is known as 'The Father of the Playstation'. Born in 1950, he has been Chairman and Group CEO of Sony Computer Entertainment.

- Steve Jobs, who died young, was co-founder and CEO of Apple Inc. and was known for his creative design imagination. Although he dropped out of college, he said he 'dropped in' on a Calligraphy class that turned out to be so important in his later design thinking. Jobs was born in 1955 and many people consider that he transformed the industry. He gave talks to university students about how he followed his curiosity and intuition (see http://news.stanford.edu/news/2005/june15/jobs-061505.html). With his friends Steve Wozniak and briefly Ronald Wayne, he started Apple in his parents' garage.

- Mark Zuckerberg is the well-known T-shirt-wearing founder of Facebook, started when he was at college. By the time Mark was 26 it had 400 million people using what was then called The Facebook.

- Sheryl Sandberg joined Facebook in 2013 as the CEO.

- Marissa Mayer is president and CEO of Yahoo! She previously was an executive and spokesperson at Google.

- Larry Page, born 1973, and Sergey Brin are the co-founders of Google. Page succeeded Eric Schmidt as CEO in 2011. Page invented 'page rank', the foundation of Google's search algorithm.

- YouTube was founded in 2005 by Steve Chen, Chad Hurley and Jawed Karim out of a garage in Menlo Park. It was the most-used site or app mentioned by UK teenagers in the Cybersurvey in 2014.

- Susan Wojcicki is the current CEO of YouTube. She was born in 1968.

- Linus Torvalds is the creator of Linux, and a Fellow at the Linux Foundation. The operating system he created — and the open source method he helped pioneer — changed the software world.

Resources

Here you can read about the 50 most important people in enterprise technology:

www.businessinsider.com/the-50-most-powerful-people-in-enterprise-tech-2012-6?op=1&IR=T

This video talks about learning to code and why it is so important:

www.youtube.com/watch?v=nKIu9yen5nc

Use these resources to take away this idea of fear in our e-safety learning — and instead replace it with competence.

Activity

1. Suggest three key strategies to encourage more women into technology.

2. Find out more about a key leader in the tech industry and prepare a ten-minute presentation about them.

3. Consider how money is made from these sites or apps. Is the data of the users sold or used to push advertising? Does this make you consider what you post?

WHAT SHOULD MAKE YOU SUSPICIOUS?

Key stage 3 year 7	Activity in pairs, exploring suspicious signs or actions online through a game
After this activity: Students will be better able to recognise when behaviour is suspicious and someone is trying to manipulate them.	**AIMS** 1. To improve personal skills in identifying risk. 2. To equip the young people with the signs to watch out for.

Detective game

Here are some possible scenarios:

- If the person tries to insist on having your address or phone number.
- If the person emails you pictures which make you feel uncomfortable and which you would not want to show to anyone else.
- If the person wants you to email them pictures of yourself or use a webcam in a way which makes you feel uncomfortable.
- If the person wants to keep their chats with you secret.
- If the person says you will get into trouble if you tell an adult what has been going on.
- If the person shares information with you and tells you not to tell anyone else about it.
- If the person wants to meet you and tells you not to let anyone know.

If any of these happen to you, it's important to tell your parents or another adult.

Discussion

- What would you do? In pairs talk through each scenario and try to convince your partner that your solution is the right one.
- Partners can disagree.
- Then change roles. Take turns to take a scenario from this list and explain it to your partner.
- Feed back to the group. What consensus was there about how to act on each scenario?
- Collect all the suggestions and put them to the group to vote on.

Did you know that...

- 59% of apps send information about the device and user habits to a third party.
- In 2013, 80 of the top 100 apps were 'free' but made all their money through 'in-app' purchasing.
- You are valuable to the service provider! Everything you do and search for is fed into targeted advertising.

THE POSITIVE FORCE OF NEW TECHNOLOGY — MORE THAN A TOOL FOR GOSSIP

Key stage 3	Personal research and group work
After this activity: Students will have considered how the Internet, social media or mobile phones can be a force for good.	**AIMS** 1. To encourage ideas for useful applications of technology (such as problem-reporting tools within school). 2. To encourage young people to think of creative ways of using new technology to help others. 3. To challenge the use of mobiles as only 'a tool for gossip' and to explore new ways of thinking about them.
You will need: Links to clips about Karen Klein, bus monitor. Copies of Cases 1–4.	**OUTPUT** A code of conduct when using mobiles.

Rationale for this approach

The thinking behind this activity is to challenge the shallow and often damaging way in which many people are using their mobiles to destructively hurt others. By approaching the issue via examples of inspiring uses of mobile technology, it is hoped that young people's interest will be sparked and they will be more receptive to the idea of negotiating an agreed code of conduct when using mobiles. Some may think of ways that mobiles can be used to report concerns at school or to support one another. I have found mid-teens saying they are bored with e-safety rules and advice and this has led to low adherence to e-safety guidelines. This and many of the other activities given here are an attempt to engage them in different ways. Who knows, we might trigger an idea that one of them will develop into a life-saving app.

Activity

Divide the class into groups:

1. Ask them why they think their mobile phone is essential to them.

2. Ask for examples in which they might have used their mobile to help someone else.

3. Remind them that for victims of cyberbullying a mobile can be an instrument of torture and, prior to mobile phones, bullying was something you could escape from in your bedroom or by leaving the scene. Explain the case of the bus monitor Karen Klein (Case 1 below).

4. Ask the groups to come up with or research ways in which mobile phone technology changes the world in a positive way.

5. Compare the ideas they have come up with to their original reasons why their own mobile is essential to them. Emphasise the enormous potential of mobile phone technology and agree a code of conduct when using a mobile.

Here are a few examples.

Case examples

1   *The bus monitor Karen Klein*

After a video of bus monitor Karen Klein receiving heart-breaking jeers from students was posted to YouTube, people became outraged. A fund was set up and sympathetic online 'bystanders' raised more than $700,000 for Karen who had given years of her life to helping students. Klein received emails, letters and Facebook messages from supporters that amazed her.

In this situation the 'good' people outweighed the people who tormented Karen and the person who filmed the taunts on their mobile and uploaded it to YouTube.

For the full story about the public reaction to what happened to Karen Klein see www.today.com/id/48764355/ns/today-good_news/#.UuKzpxAo5pg.

2   *Mobile phones used in medicine in the developing world*

In the developed world, with ageing populations and rising rates of chronic disease, what is called 'm-health' meets a desire from patients to take a more active role in managing their health. And also enables medical professionals to monitor them from a distance.

On the other hand, in the developing world with its shortage of health services, mobile phone technology is making diagnostic services more accessible. Mobile technology is portable and could help link patient and doctor in new ways.

3   *Mobile phones used in banking in the developing world*

Mobile phones are used in Indonesia, for example, to provide banking services to a population in rural areas without this access. Working with women who are typically stall-holders in markets, they provide banking services to their customers on a basic mobile phone that does not need Wi-Fi. This enables women to save for an emergency, unlike the old way of saving money under the mattress from where it was often raided by other family members who needed money.

4   *Floods or disaster management*

Some recent disasters have seen imaginative uses of new technology. One was the Haiti disaster when an Australian doctor called Paul Gardner-Stephen developed a way to allow mobile phones to communicate directly with each other even when no network coverage was available. In a crisis this can allow medics and rescue workers to operate successfully. In an earthquake or a tsunami it is likely that mobile masts are damaged or downed. The system is called 'mesh networking', and is a web of users who can text, call or send data to other users nearby.

Haiti triggered a wave of developments in which phones are used in disaster zones. One of these allows rescuers to view mobile phone activity on a computer screen which shows where people are clustering and gets messages to them. The Red Cross is now using this system in 40 countries across the world.

The importance of mobiles in crisis situations has been recognised. The UK government has dropped solar-powered battery chargers with humanitarian aid for the Yazidi community in Iraq, and Facebook used satellite technology to help those working to combat Ebola in the recent outbreak in Africa to be able to communicate. Doctors can diagnose a distant patient in some cases via a mobile phone, and mobiles are used to send information about crops and to make payments.

MOBILES – A REVOLUTION IN A FEW SHORT YEARS

Key stages 3 and 4	Comprehension exercise followed by activities
	This could take place over more than one lesson and some sections could be set as homework.
Learning objectives: To tailor e-safety advice more specifically to the young people's behaviour and needs by engaging them in the history and rapid development of mobiles.	**AIMS** 1. To explore how the changing mobile phone has altered our behaviour. 2. To explore the actual lives students are leading online and to engage them in identifying risks and protective measures they can take.
Preparation: Project the eight points given below in the classroom and make copies of the text or upload it to an accessible page.	**OUTPUT** Tailored e-safety advice to fit the lives the students are leading.

Clunky 'brick' to 'wearable tech?

Figure 6.1 How many of these phones or devices can you identify? What is coming next?

Comprehension exercise

Give the students the text below and ask them to answer the questions. Then move to the activity below the text. It might be a good use of time to set the comprehension exercise as homework and then to do the activity in class as a follow-up.

THE ERA OF THE MOBILE PHONE

The first mobile phone was a weighty Motorola used by a senior engineer and he called a rival company on it. The phone actually weighed over one kilogram and gave 30 minutes of talk time after a whole 10 hours of charging up! That is like carrying around a whole bag of sugar compared with the lightness of today's phones.

In 1973 Martin Cooper made the first handheld cellular phone call in public (although this was not the first cellular call since car phones have been around before then). Walking down the streets of New York, Cooper talked on the phone. The phone was also known as the 'Brick' cell phone.

By 1982 mobile phone systems were allocated a frequency for a network and this kick-started their rapid development. Motorola released a commercial mobile phone with 30 minutes of talk time. It cost as much as a second-hand car!

By the late 1990s mobile phones were much cheaper and increasingly available to all. Along with Motorola, Nokia, Sony Ericsson, Panasonic, LG and HTC would soon enter the market followed by Samsung, Apple and, of course, Blackberry.

At first phones were bulky and had long aerials. Displays were grey. They offered basic functions such as text messaging, a calculator, games and a phone book. Nokia phones also came with a very popular game, the Snake game. A flip-phone was born in 1997 which, although small and neat, did not last long.

It was only in 2001 that phones had a multi-coloured display, but now things began to change rapidly. Wi-fi appeared alongside faster broadband and in 2002 the first camera-phone was on offer; by 2004 the idea of the phone in your pocket was becoming widespread with lighter models on sale. The design and development of mobile phones really took off. The arrival of cameras in phones led to a spate of bullying incidents in which people used the camera to be nasty or to humiliate another person. Some people even provoked fights in order to take a photo of them or video them and the media coined a phrase 'happy slapping', which has almost died out now. But there were positive aspects to having a phone in relation to bullying too – people could photograph evidence.

It was not until 2005 that the first Walkman phone delivered music. Then followed a golden age of design and change. Mobiles were to become stylish and could reflect the owner's taste. Cases came in colours and styles. Phones became a life essential. Then in 2007, Apple unveiled the world's first iPhone – a touchscreen smartphone. This phone was the first of its kind and it enabled users to run apps (applications) designed for specific purposes. Apps offer the software to enable a wide range of functions including viewing movies, books, games, navigation and security.

After 2006 manufacturers changed from focusing on mobiles for business people to thinking about mobiles as a personal entertainment device. In 2011 touchscreens were the new standard in a competitive market in which many companies were fighting for market share with new models. In a short span of time, mobile phones became the mini-computer that is still able to fit in our pockets, complete with location GPS. Service providers began offering more generous packages with unlimited data downloads or large amounts of talk time and batteries charged faster and lasted longer.

Phones developed to become an essential accessory and life manager with Internet access, maps and GPS features, calendars, photos, videos and an app for everything from train timetables to finding which of your friends is in the area.

Adapted by Adrienne Katz from an original article by Kanika Saini, first published in the August/September 2013 issue of Engineers' Forum at Virginia Tech: www.ef.org.vt.edu/wp-content/uploads/2013/10/EF2013aSeptember.pdf.

Rapid and recent changes in mobile phones that affect our lives

1. When do you think the first mobile was used to make a call?

2. What change kick-started the rapid development of commercially available mobiles?

3. When did mobile phones first become cheaper and within reach of many people?

4. When did mobile phones first offer a coloured display instead of grey?

5. When was the first camera-phone offered for sale and how did this change behaviour?

6. What was 'happy slapping'? Does anyone talk about this any more?

7. It is only ten years since phones changed to be light, colourful and with multiple features: has our society caught up fast enough? Describe how our socialising behaviour has changed.

8. Describe some of the risks mobile phones brought alongside their wonderful convenience.

Group activity

Discuss in pairs. Feed back to the group.

1. Write on sticky notes the different features of your phone.

2. Set aside features you do not use much.

3. Which are the most used features of the phones you and your friends use?

4. How have these features altered your social life and relationships with other people?

5. How have these features increased the risks you might meet?

6. What steps do you take to protect yourself from these risks?

7. Imagine the next developments in mobile phones – what would you rate as the most important design features and the most important technical features?

8. Create a stay-safe guide for a child who is getting their first smartphone ever.

Consider the 'most used features' your class identifies. Use this as the basis of advice you can directly link to these features they are using and their behaviour online.

Later in the chapter I suggest using the grid from the 'What Do I Do?' activity as a guide to exploring the actual life young people are leading online and tailoring the advice to their needs. Young people complain that the e-safety advice they receive is often not relevant to them personally. By this age they have had the generic universal e-safety advice delivered to them a few times and are 'switching off', in their own words. They tune out as they think it is old hat and they know it already. On the other hand, there is much evidence that too many of them are not following e-safety advice.

The idea of exploring 'What do I do online?' or 'What are the most used features on my phone?' is to help them come to understand specific risks relating to their personal patterns of use and how they might protect themselves from harm. Focus on chunking the material and giving advice in digestible portions. Use opportunities for students to teach one another.

Extension

Below are some questions students can research.

When were the first mobile phone services launched in the UK?	1985
Two operators launched these initial services, who were they?	Cellnet and Vodafone
When was the world's first text message sent?	1992. 'Happy Christmas' was the message sent on Orbitel's phone to Vodafone director Richard Jarvis by Neil Papworth of Orbitel
When were mobile phones first offered to UK consumers?	1992
What year was the first phone with the Nokia tune launched?	1994. The phone was designed by Frank Nuovo. It was the smallest, lightest GSM phone and had a new type of user-friendly menu system
When was the first camera-phone launched?	2002. The Nokia 7650 was the first camera-phone
When was the Blackberry launched at consumers? (Formerly it was aimed at business people.)	2006
When was the first iPhone launched?	2007
Did you know? The UK's first mobile phone users were motorists in Manchester. A car radio phone system began in Manchester in 1959. The General Post Office, or GPO, ran the network. Subscribers in South Lancashire could connect for £195 (more than £3000 in today's money). There were only six channels, which meant only six calls could take place at the same time, and all calls were placed through the operator. There were 86 subscribers by 1963, but the GPO made a loss on the service.	Read more here: www.mobilephonehistory.co.uk/history/mobile_phone_history.php

THE WEB WE WANT

Key stage 3 year 7	Group work, research, negotiating rules, creating a campaign. More than one session.
Learning objectives: 1. To teach pupils about acceptable behaviour online. 2. To reinforce the school's AUP in ICT. 3. To explore the ethics of behaviour in a democratic way with pupils to enhance a sense of ownership.	**AIMS** 1. To be a good digital citizen. 2. To explore the principles decided on when the web was born. To develop a new set of rules to achieve the web we want. 3. To include participation by all in creating new rules and promoting them.
Link to article Software to create artwork and presentations.	**OUTPUTS** • The web we want. • Our web rules. • Campaign for the web we want and rules. • Making the AUP in ICT known to all. • Graphic posters, online news flashes, advertisements, assembly presentations, flashmobs in the playground, songs or short dramas.

Preparatory reading

Tim Berners-Lee, *An Online Magna Carta*: www.theguardian.com/technology/2014/mar/12/online-magna-carta-berners-lee-web.

Introduction

Begin with these questions:

- Today we are going to think about the future of the Internet. If you see an address of a shop or a company, how do you know whether that address is online or down the road?

- Who knows what www stands for in website addresses? (World Wide Web.)

- Today we cannot imagine our lives without the Internet, but how old do you think it actually is? (The first website was built and tested in 1991.)

- Often called the inventor of the World Wide Web, Tim Berners-Lee thinks it is time for a debate about the direction of the web in the next 25 years. He suggested we think about 'The Web We Want'. Can you think of any decisions that were made about the web (Internet) when it was first developed? (It is free; it is open to anyone; it is neutral.)

- What principles do you think should be discussed? Possibly:
  - Free speech is acceptable only when it does not harm others.

- ○ Plagiarism/copyright and intellectual property: what if a singer posts a song she has written, performed and recorded — how does she get paid for it if people download it and share it without payment?

- ○ Is my work my own or is it acceptable for people to copy it and pretend it is theirs?

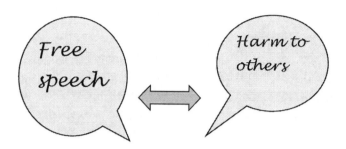

Discussion

While governments have to think about issues like privacy and free speech, we could choose to discuss how we behave online and what kind of online world you are creating for the next 25 years.

Divide the class into two groups. Make two handouts, one for each group:

Group 1	Group 2
Your task is to work on the big picture of The Web We Want	**Your task is to work on Our Web Rules**

Each group discusses their views, agrees on their key messages and prepares a presentation to the class. Their goal is to 'sell' their ideas to the other group.

Plenary

1. How closely do the two groups' key messages work together? For example, do Our Web Rules help to create The Web We Want? Is there anything to add?

2. Does our school Acceptable Use Policy in ICT cover the rules Group 2 has developed?

3. How many people know what is in the AUP?

A week later

Create a campaign to make the AUP and Our Web Rules known to all pupils in the school. This can be graphic posters, online news flashes, advertisements, assembly presentations, flashmobs in the playground, songs and short dramas.

THEY WERE WRONG!

A video and song activity to provide help and support.

(From an idea by Okehampton Academy Anti-Bullying Committee and Mr Philippe Messer.)

Year 7 Key stage 7	Create classroom mobile on resilient responses. Video, design, flash song. Four activity options. Multiple sessions.
Curriculum areas: PSHE/SMSC development, shared humanity Behaviour and safeguarding	**AIMS** 1. To reinforce self-esteem. 2. To reduce bullying/cyberbullying. 3. To improve relationships and inclusion. 4. To show that almost anyone could be victimised or turn the experience around.
Preparation: Strips of paper 76cm x 10cm Video equipment	**Enhancement:** To create messages to use across the school in displays, video, graphic art or drama scenarios. **Extension:** Literature: Consider figures in novels or movies who have triumphed over the odds. (See Maya Angelou in the next activity.)

Activity 1: Responses

Provide each pupil with a strip of paper at least 76cm wide and no less than 10cm high.

Ask them to write, on one side of the page, words completing one of these sentences:

- They said I was...

- They called me a...

(These can be true real-life examples or they can dream up suitable roles to play.)

Then turn the paper over and write a positive outcome or how they challenged this. Sentences on the other side of the page start:

- BUT...

Examples

- They called me shortie/But I have more leg room!

- They said I was ugly/But now I have a modelling contract.

- They said I couldn't sing/But I recorded my first track with a band last week.

- They said I couldn't play football/But I play for my county now.

- They said I was small/But I crawled into a small space and rescued a dog.

Humour is encouraged; no names are to be used.

Everyone lines up with their strips and one by one they show their first side, then turn the paper around to show their second side. Hang the strips from cotton thread from the ceiling, so that they turn in the wind like a mobile, always changing to the positive message.

Activity 2: Video

Young people can make a video with their cards using a music track that gives the message (see the list of music tracks later in the chapter).

Activity 3: Graphic design

Young people can design graphics to convey these messages on school walls, plasma screens or a PowerPoint presentation for assembly.

Activity 4: Flashmob

Young people can organise a flashmob when at a signal on their phones they all produce their cards and hold them up high in the air.

The Okehampton video can be viewed on www.bullyinginterventiongroup.co.uk/bigideas. php.

MAYA ANGELOU: RESILIENCE IN THE FACE OF IMPOSSIBLE HARDSHIP

Upper Key stage 3 and Key stage 4	Poetry appreciation
After this activity: Students will be better able to use resilience in the face of difficulties.	**AIM** To use this inspiring poem about resilience to help young people explore their own resilience and find practical responses to difficulties in their lives.
This poem is in many anthologies and can be found online in a quick search. Poem Hunter is a useful resource. Biographies of Angelou are widely available, including one on mayaangelou.com.	Search on YouTube for a video of Maya Angelou reading this poem herself. This is very rewarding.

Maya Angelou said she had thousands of daughters. I wonder if she ever knew really how many...

Maya Angelou said often that although she gave birth to one son, she had thousands of daughters. 'I have daughters who are black and white, Asian and Spanish-speaking, and native American,' she said. 'I have daughters who are fat and thin, pretty and plain, gay and straight. I have all sorts of daughters who I just claim. And they claim me.'

I wonder if Angelou ever knew really how many – girls who were told about her, named after her, or like me, growing up in a suburban corner of England, clinging fiercely to her books and even when not reading them, inhaling the spirit of her struggle from the titles alone: *A Song Flung Up to Heaven*, *I Know Why the Caged Bird Sings* and *Gather Together in My Name*.

Afua Hirsch, The Guardian, 31 May 2014

www.theguardian.com/books/2014/jun/01/maya-angelou-appreciation-afua-hirsch

For more information on Maya Angelou, see www.wdchumanities.org/video-remembering-dr-maya-angelou-great-american-humanist.

Rationale

Why look at this example of resilience when thinking about cyberbullying and e-safety? Maya Angelou has served as an inspiration for many, and young people need examples of resilience as much as ever. To be crushed, to overcome and still rise...that is the message of this extraordinary woman and writer, whom you might be studying in literature class. This is an example of cross-pollination in which the work in one subject can be so usefully used to develop ideas in another. An icon for all women and girls and an icon for anyone concerned with the history of people of colour, Maya Angelou is a one-woman anti-racism and anti-misogynist crusader. These are issues that urgently need addressing in the online world where images of women are constantly misused and racism is rife. Anti-bullying work has long used inspirational figures to help targeted young people realise that they are not alone and that they can cope. Inspirational figures make an impression.

BOARD GAME ON E-SAFETY SKILLS

Upper Key stage 2 and Key stage 3	Exploring online situations and dilemmas
Materials: Board, dice and two types of cards: safe and unsafe.	**Board game**
AIMS 1. To give a greater understanding of how to conduct oneself online to selected students who need targeted support. 2. To use in peer support sessions when supporting a young person, or in a whole class as an end-of-term activity before the holidays when they will be online for longer.	**OUTCOME** Improving knowledge of age-appropriate online situations and problem-solving solutions.

Preparation

- Print out copies of the board on A3 paper (laminate to use again).

- Have pairs of dice available.

- Make cards in two colours, one colour for Safe and another colour for Unsafe, and print each sentence below onto a card (further examples are given below).

Instructions

Players begin at START and, when it is their turn, they throw the dice and advance by the number on the dice. If they land on an Unsafe stop they must pick up a card from the Unsafe pile. It may tell them to go back a number of spaces. If they land on a Safe stop, they pick up a Safe card, which might advance them a few spaces. The first player to reach END wins. (The board can also be downloaded in A3 format at www.esafetforschools.com/resources.)

Variation

Another layer of this game is to discuss the following each time a card is picked up:

- Why is this action unsafe – what is the risk or possible harm?

- Why is this action safe – what have you avoided?

- Are there other options you might have chosen?

Cards

Each card contains one of the following scenarios. To illustrate the cards, a few have been laid out in a card design with answers.

Safe

- You did not open the email with the subject 'You have won a prize'. (Go forward two spaces.)

- You did not open an attachment in a message from someone you've never heard of. (Go forward two spaces.)

- When you shopped with your mum's credit card online you helped her check that the site was safe before using the card. (Go forward six spaces.)

- You have a strong password (letters and numbers). (Go forward five spaces.)

- You use different passwords for different clubs and services. (Go forward five spaces.)

- You remembered to turn off the locator service on your phone's camera. (Go forward three spaces.)

- A friend sent you a message saying 'You must try this game'. But before you clicked on the link he sent, you checked the URL of this game so that you did not land on a fake site. (Go forward three spaces.)

Ideas for more cards for this activity

- You did not share a photo sent to you of someone in your class because you can see it was meant to be private/between them only. (Go forward six spaces.)

- You reported abuse to a website or service after saving the evidence. (Go forward five spaces.)

- You told your friend not to post a private photo in revenge because he had broken up with his girlfriend and was feeling really hurt and angry. (Go forward six spaces.)

Unsafe

- You have hundreds of friends on your SNS account. (Go back four spaces.)

- You post photos online without making sure only your friends and family can see them. (Go back four spaces.)

- You post webcam shots of yourself online. (Go back five spaces.)

- You carelessly gave away the name of your school when you posted photos of yourself and friends in school uniform online. (Go back three spaces.)

- You keep logged in to your favourite apps on your phone all the time. (Go back two spaces.)

- You use the same password on lots of different sites or services. (Go back three spaces.)

- You agreed to meet up with someone you only knew online. (Go back six spaces.)

- You pressured a girlfriend to send you revealing photos. (Go back five spaces.)

- You shared revealing photos of your girlfriend with others. (Go back to Start – this is against the law.)

- You tried to pressure someone into giving you money. (Go back six spaces.)

Student Handout

Digi-Dilemmas Board Game Cards

You did not open the email with the subject 'You have won a prize'. (Go forward two spaces)	What is the risk if you open this type of message? Hoax messages like this are usually phishing to get your email address.
You did not open an attachment in a message from someone you've never heard of. (Go forward two spaces.)	What is the risk if you open attachments from people you have never heard of? Clicking on the attachment can let a virus or malware into your computer.
When you shopped with your mum's credit card online you helped her check that the site was safe before using the card. (Go forward six spaces)	What is the risk if you do not check the website is secure? Having her credit card details stolen or hacked.
You have a strong password (letters and numbers). (Go forward five spaces.)	What is the point of a strong password? It is harder for people or software to guess it and get into your account.
You use different passwords for different clubs and services. (Go forward five spaces.)	What is the reason you should have different passwords when it is easier to remember just one? If one of your passwords is hacked at least your other accounts will be safe.
You remembered to turn off the location service on your phone's camera. (Go forward three spaces.)	Why should I turn off the location service on my phone's camera? Because when you post the photo online or send it, people can click on it and find out exactly where you are. This is not a safe situation.

Copyright © Adrienne Katz 2016

A friend sent you a message saying 'You must try this game'. But before you clicked on the link he sent, you checked the URL of this game so that you did not land on a fake site. (Go forward three spaces.)	Why can't I just click on the link? I know him. If this is a virus email using his address, it might be taking you to a fake site made to look like the game, but in fact it is a 'skin' only there to capture your details when it asks you to sign in. Always check the URL first.
You did not share a photo sent to you of someone in your class because you can see it was meant to be private/between them only. (Go forward six spaces.)	Why shouldn't I share it with friends? Everyone else is doing it. It's a joke. Sharing photos of nude under 18s is against the law. Your friends are entitled to some privacy, so don't make a bad situation worse if this is a revenge action after a break-up.
You reported abuse to a website or service after saving the evidence. (Go forward five spaces.)	Why should I bother to report abuse? Nobody ever does anything about it. Actually, that is not true. If the behaviour is against the rules of the site the person can be stopped and the offensive material taken down. If it involves sexually exploiting children the police can be alerted to stop it.
You have hundreds of friends on your SNS account. (Go back four spaces.)	I like to look popular, so why shouldn't I accept friend requests? But you do not know more than 20 of these 'friends' and you are revealing your personal life and photos to all these people who might misuse the material. Nothing is private.
You post photos online without making sure only your friends and family can see them. (Go back four spaces.)	Why does it matter who sees my photos? Not everyone means well and people could misuse your photos in many ways. They could also share them with even more people. You might give away a lot about yourself in your photos without realising it. One day someone you care about might see a photo you are desperately ashamed about when they do a search about you.

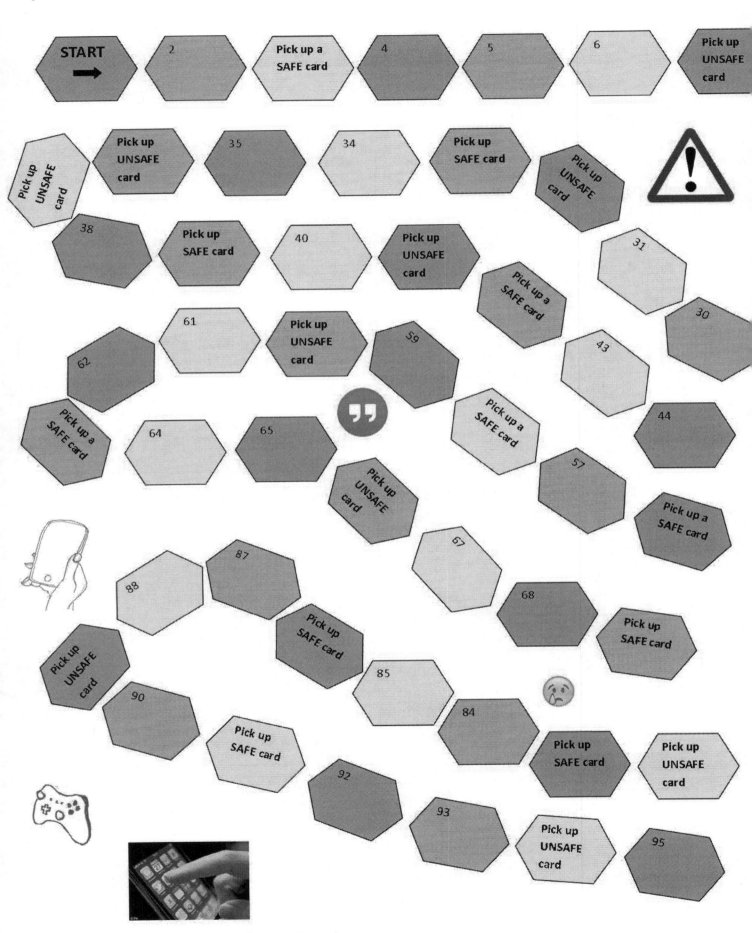

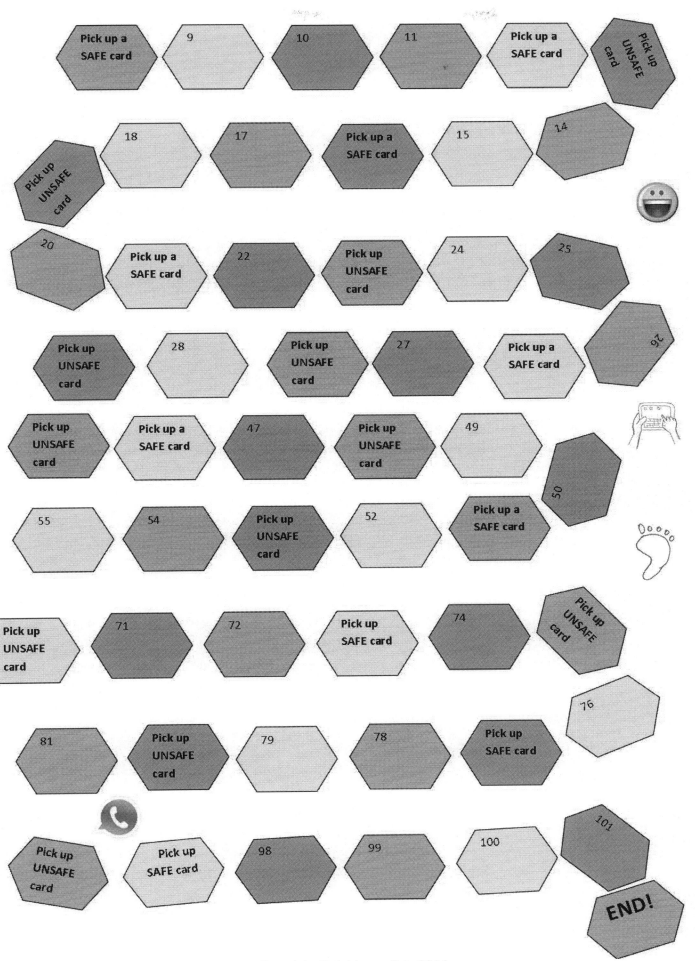

Pick up a SAFE card — 9 — 10 — 11 — Pick up a SAFE card — Pick up UNSAFE card

Pick up UNSAFE card — 18 — 17 — Pick up a SAFE card — 15 — 14

20 — Pick up a SAFE card — 22 — Pick up UNSAFE card — 24 — 25

Pick up UNSAFE card — 28 — Pick up UNSAFE card — 27 — Pick up a SAFE card — 26

Pick up UNSAFE card — Pick up a SAFE card — 47 — Pick up UNSAFE card — 49 — 50

55 — 54 — Pick up UNSAFE card — 52 — Pick up a SAFE card

Pick up UNSAFE card — 71 — 72 — Pick up SAFE card — 74 — Pick up UNSAFE card

76

81 — Pick up UNSAFE card — 79 — 78 — Pick up SAFE card

Pick up UNSAFE card — Pick up SAFE card — 98 — 99 — 100 — 101

END!

NEW APPS AND GPS — OVERSHARING

Key stage 3 years 7 and 8	Group work Practical demonstration Creative writing
After this activity: Students will understand the importance of protecting their location and how to do so.	**AIM** To explore the use of GPS and how to switch it off.
	OUTPUT Creative writing: guide for younger students.

Young people love secrets and love meeting other young people. They flock to new messaging apps where there are spaces to communicate anonymously online using their smartphones. Whisper and Yik Yak are just two of these. They use GPS (Global Positioning System) in the same way your SatNav in the car works out where you are, and they can share anonymous posts from people nearby. This clearly poses many risks for a young person who might agree to meet someone they are talking to, or if they reveal their location.

On any of these sites or apps that allow anonymous posts there is a high risk of cyberbullying or harmful material. They are meant to have some age restrictions, but teens do not always heed this if their friends are using an app.

Giving out information about where you are to people you do not know is not a good idea! But often a young person is so excited to meet or talk with others and, as one put it, 'safety goes right out of my head'.

Ask the class:

- Can they explain GPS?

- How many use applications that rely on GPS?

GPS is useful if using a map for directions – it can show you where you are. But the age limits on dating sites and SNS are there for a reason and should be respected.

Demonstrate: It is a good idea to show them how to turn off the GPS feature on their phone to avoid giving away their location. Check in app and phone location settings as well as camera settings. Photos taken with the GPS feature enabled can give away to the viewer where you are or were when it was taken.

Explore what the risks might be: Teens should always let someone at home or a friend know where they are and when they are coming home.

Activity: Creative writing

To explain this to younger children, we told them how the wolf in the story of Red Riding Hood managed to locate her because she posted a photo of herself walking along the path in the wood to her grandma's house and the wolf was able to work out where she was and lie in wait for her under the covers of grandma's bed.

If you were explaining the issues around location to someone younger than you, how would you explain how GPS works and what they should do to conceal their location? Can you think of inventive ways to introduce this idea? How would you help them to stay safe?

SLAY YOUR DRAGON!

Key stage 3	Comprehension and creative writing 40 minutes
After this activity: Students will have used 'healthy scepticism' to assess a message. They will have considered re-tweets and sharing. They will have a better understanding of the coercive tactics used to get you to re-tweet the message.	**AIMS** 1. To explore pupils' behaviour in social networking sites. 2. To encourage pupils to use their own judgement when urged to forward and share messages. 3. To examine online communication.
Preparation: Upload a slide with the message.	**OUTPUT** The teacher will have examples of coercive or risky messages currently seen by students and teach suitable responses.

Reading

One day this arrived in my Facebook messages:

> Please put this on your status if you know someone or are related to someone who has been eaten by a dragon. Dragons are nearly unstoppable and they can breathe fire. 93% of people won't copy and paste this because they've already been eaten by dragons. 6% are sitting in the shower armed with fire extinguishers, whilst the remaining 1% are awesome and will re-post this.

This message has been discussed on the following website where people have added pictures and ideas: http://verysrs.com/phpbb3/viewtopic.php?f=21&t=27020.

There is also a Facebook community: www.facebook.com/pages/Being-eaten-by-dragons/157308210974610.

Comprehension

1. What does it tell you about the stupid things people post online?
2. What is healthy scepticism?
3. Why do you think most people do not re-tweet or re-post messages?
4. What tactic is the writer of this message using in order to get you to re-post the message?

Creative writing

Try and write your own crazy or funny message that reflects the sort of messages people send and the way we behave online. Your aim is to do this in a way that helps people understand how silly some of this is. You want to help them view these messages with some healthy scepticism.

Use your creative writing and humour. Then read out a few to the class.

Plenary

Share some of the ideas. Discuss students' options to respond/ignore/re-tweet.

WHAT DO I DO?

Key stages 3 and 4	Exploration of online activities and risks
After this activity: Students will have identified their own risks and considered how to protect against these.	**AIMS** 1. To make e-safety education more personal and relevant by exploring each student's individual online life. 2. To encourage them to weigh up risks and to work out possible ways to protect against these.
Preparation: Ask each student to draw up a blank table of three columns. Add in the headings in column 1 (left-hand side).	**OUTPUT** The teacher can identify the most actively used features, apps and sites and tailor the e-safety advice to meet the needs of students.

Give each student a copy of the 'What do I do?' table.

Risks and precautions

What do I do?	What might the risks be?	What steps can I take?
Search for information	If I accept the first choice listed by my search engine I may be getting incorrect information. Google will give me more of what I already like, reinforcing one view.	Look to verify information in more than one location. Do not believe everything you read. Retain a healthy scepticism. Learn to cross-check information and select with discernment. What seems to be a free service may be possible because information on users is sold to advertisers. Be careful on any free service or search engine.
Contact people/ friends via SNS (Facebook)	Someone wants to befriend you but they are not who they say they are. Your profile is public and information about you falls into the wrong hands. Someone you met online wants to meet up. You are bullied by a former friend on Facebook. Someone gets your password and changes your profile or sends messages as if from you.	Contact with friends is enjoyed by everyone. But take simple precautions – admit as friends only people you know. If you are not sure about a new request, check someone is genuine by doing a search. Keep your profile and your address and phone number private. Having huge friends' lists to look popular is a sure way to get into difficulties. Remove from the list people you are no longer friends with. Avoid meeting up with people you only know online; but if you insist on meeting, take a friend with you or meet in a public space and tell someone where you are going and when. Keep the evidence. Do not reply. Remove the sender from your friend list. If the behaviour breaches the terms of service of the website, report it to the SNS site. Talk to a person you trust. Keep your password safe, always opt for two-stage verification when offered and change your passwords from time to time. Always log out and shut down your browser if you walk away from the screen.
Arrange social plans	It is possible to find out where you are going to be and when. This could get into the wrong hands.	When you reply to a group message, check who is in that group.

What do I do?	What might the risks be?	What steps can I take?
Visit chat rooms	Sometimes people who are not feeling good about their social life or their relationships at home may seek that friendship and intimacy in chat rooms. It can lead them into dangerous situations or into being bullied.	Students who use chat rooms heavily have told us that they are cyberbullied more than other people. This suggests you should take great care about the groups you join and the chats you have. You may also get drawn in to a group looking to involve young people and you should be very alert to deliberate grooming. Operate with all your antennae on full alert! Get out of an unpleasant situation by logging out. Use a nickname or change names. Stay in charge in chat – your personal profile should not have your address or phone number, or even your real photo. Tell a parent or carer if something makes you worried. Learn how to keep a conversation in chat in case you need this evidence to report something. Check out how to report on the site or through the CEOP button.
Gaming	When gaming, why is it dangerous to play on a third party site rather than the originator site?	Many amateur sites also host a game. These can be risky or malicious. Play only at the game site. Some games require Active X or JavaScript controls to let your computer interact to a greater extent. These can be useful to hackers, so turn these controls off in the configuration menu when you are finished. Symantec recommends you have a separate user account for online gaming with only a web browser installed on it. When finished gaming, you switch back to the full user account.
Shopping	How would you protect your personal details when shopping online? Your credit card details? What could you do to guard against phishing?	Consider opening an email address only for shopping. Use Hotmail or Gmail for a spare address. Use your bank's verifying service or PayPal to verify the card – this is an extra layer of security. Check the site is genuine. Never follow a link a friend has sent you but search for the store's Internet address yourself to check it is authentic. Check what they will do with your data and do not agree to it being used for promotions or sold to other parties. Watch out for phishing – online fraud where someone tries to trick you into giving them personal details. Never enter your password after following a link in an email from someone – go onto the website via your own search first.
Sharing music and files	You could be illegally downloading music or other material.	Join a legal music downloading site and make sure your music is downloaded from this site.
Share jokes	By passing on a 'joke' am I joining in the bullying of someone?	Think twice before pinging on a joke if it is about someone or some people.
Share photos	Would I be embarrassed if one day this photo came up when I was in a job interview or my Nan saw it?	If you upload photos to Facebook you can now choose a privacy setting for each one. Keep some personal. Be careful what you share with friends or make public.

Taken from *Cyberbullying and E-safety: What Educators and Other Professionals Need to Know* (Adrienne Katz, 2012, Jessica Kingsley Publishers).

What do I do?	What might the risks be?	What steps can I take?

FLASHMOB: SONG

All Key stages	To plan and stage a flashmob
A lead group and mobile phones, a large open space or hall to meet.	**AIM** To get pupils engaged in spreading the 'stay safe' message.
Output: Song about e-safety that can be used in many ways within school and with future years.	**Activity:** Competition to create song or rap about e-safety.

You need

A school or group where young people have their mobiles with them or have tablets for school use. Alternatively you will need another way of giving the signal that the event is starting.

Activity

1. Invite pupils to enter a competition for a song or rap that gets across the stay safe online message. The song could be about Cyberbullying, Staying Strong and Our Rights, or 'Use your voice to speak out'.

2. Select a winner.

3. Use your peer supporters to teach the song to a large number of people.

4. Agree that at a given signal everyone will stop what they are doing and stand up and sing the song.

5. On the day and time, give the signal via texts to mobiles or a signal on school plasma screens, or agree a time and place beforehand.

6. At the signal, as many people as possible stand up and sing the song.

It could be in the lunch queue, on the field, in the hall, at a school sports event, at a parents' evening, or as part of an assembly.

Tip: Enforce secrecy as far as possible – the element of surprise draws people's attention!

Alternatives

If you do not run the competition to create a new song, your flashmob event could use a well-known song that has an inspiring message. There are many songs that work well. Some are commonly used against bullying. Some express resilience or defiance, rather than sadness – these work best. Your pupils will provide an up-to-date list that will put mine to shame! Lyrics are online on www.AZlyrics.com.

Should you wish to use an existing song that is often seen as an anthem to resilience or to fight bullying, you could choose from this list:

Title	Artist	Comments
Not Afraid	Eminem	
Born This Way	Lada Gaga	The song gave its name to the foundation she set up to support 'the wellness of young people and empower them to create a kinder, braver world'
Security	Joss Stone	From the *Mind, Body and Soul* album
Eye of the Tiger	Survivor	A survivor song
Walking on Sunshine	Katrina and the Waves	Cheers everyone up
We Are the Champions	Queen	
I Will Survive	Gloria Gaynor	
Ain't No Mountain High Enough	Diana Ross and The Supremes	
Alice	Avril Lavigne	About getting up when you've been pushed down and not letting anyone stop you. It is used in Tim Burton's *Alice in Wonderland*
Can't Hold Us Down	Christina Aguilera	About not taking sexism and standing up for yourself
Hero	Superchick	Inspires to take a stand against bullying
Firework	Katy Perry	
Heal the World	Michael Jackson	Inspires to help people
Imagine	John Lennon	
Keep Holding On	Avril Lavigne	
A New Day Has Come	Celine Dion	
One Tribe	The Black Eyed Peas	
Respect	Aretha Franklin	
Shine	Vanessa Amorosi	
Soar	Christina Aguilera	Supportive and inspiring
Survivor	Destiny's Child	
You Are Not Alone	Michael Jackson	
You're the Voice	John Farnham	
Beautiful	Bethany Dillion	'Who I am is quite enough'
Strong Enough	Stacie Orrico	
We All Need Saving	Jon Mclaughlin	We all need saving sometimes
U.N.I.T.Y.	Queen Latifah	
Who's Laughing Now?	Jesse J.	
Mean	Taylor Swift	
Titanium	David Guetta ft Sia	
Fly	Nicky Minaj ft Rihanna	
Who Says	Selina Gomez & The Scene	
Make it Stop (September's Children)	Rise Against	
Skyscraper	Demi Lovato	
Stronger	Kelly Clarkson	
You Had to Pick On Me	Matt Kennon	
Hey Bully	Morgan Frazier	
Stupid Boy	Keith Urban	About a boy who treats a girl poorly – she gets a better life
Don't Laugh At Me	Mark Wills	
Fix You	Coldplay	

ARE OUR MESSAGES REALLY SAFE?

Key stages 3 and 4	Explore a real-life high-profile scenario involving Angelina Jolie
After this activity: Students will have a clear sense of the harm that can be caused by thoughtless messages and emails.	**AIMS** 1. To use contemporary true scenarios to engage teenagers and explore how thoughtless messages can come to light with devastating consequences. 2. To explore how so-called banter can be racist or otherwise offensive.
Preparation research: Photo Action Press/ Rex Jolie Pascal meeting for the first time since the hack: www.theguardian.com/commentisfree/2014/ dec/12/movie-moguls-might-be-monsters- but-their-emails-are-still-private Reuters report by Lisa Richwine: www. reuters.com/article/2014/12/12/ us-sony-cybersecurity-obama- idUSKBN0JP29N20141212	

Rationale

Using real-life high-profile stories that link to an industry in which pupils of this age have an interest is a route to engage their interest and consider the consequences of careless messages and emails.

Students can search for photos of this meeting at the above link. The story is widely reported online.

Introduction

When we are chatting with friends online or sharing messages or emails, we usually feel that our messages won't be seen by other people, let alone hacked and leaked. But for Sony films this is exactly what happened. Their system was hacked.

Emails were leaked which showed a senior executive saying some rather embarrassing things about Angelina Jolie. When this senior person met publicly with Angelina the photo also went round the world in a flash. This must have been pretty awkward. Among the damaging leaks, including unreleased films, were personal emails that nobody expected would ever be made public. But these emails allegedly described Jolie in very unflattering terms and criticised her talent. Imagine the moment when this executive and Jolie came together in public with the world's press watching. This kind of embarrassment could happen to any one of us if we are not careful about what we say online.

In these emails, the world also learned that there were jokes about the President's taste in films. Some people thought this showed racist overtones.

But the executive concerned denied this, telling the Hollywood website 'Deadline' on 5 February 2015 that she did not want to be defined by these emails after a 30-year career. She argued that there are stupid things we say in rash moments – but it is wrong to hack/share them.

This row rumbled on in the media and in a live interview on stage, and in a media statement the executive admitted, 'The content of my emails…were insensitive and inappropriate but are not an accurate reflection of who I am.' She later met with civil rights campaigner Al Sharpton, and promised to work on a taskforce to ensure diversity in the film industry.

Discussion

In pairs, discuss the following:

1. The Sony executive says she does not want to be defined by these emails. Do you think her name will always be associated with what she put in these emails or do you think this incident will be soon forgotten?

2. Are our messages and emails reflections of who we are, even if we do not want to see ourselves that way?

Put your views on these questions on sticky notes and post them onto flipchart sheets.

Leader

- Group or sort the answers into like-minded viewpoints and describe the messages given in these notes.

- Agree with the class an overall message from this exercise. For example: 'This class believes that…(we are or are not defined by casual emails or messages…).'

Further questions to ask might be:

1. Does banter often border on racism? Can you think of examples?

2. If you were thinking of employing someone and you came across messages they had posted or sent that were either racist or homophobic, how would you see this person fitting in to your team and working with everyone in an organisation?

Nowadays employers and university or college admissions officers search the Internet before interviewing someone for a job or a place. What might they find out about you? Think of photos you posted after a party or some jokey comments on other people's pages you made to look witty. Perhaps they could be interpreted as saying something about you as a person?

Students

Explain what you plan to do after this lesson. Examples might be:

- Take a look at my messages as if I were a stranger and clean up.

- Be more careful what I text or share in future.

CHALLENGING 'UNWRITTEN RULES' OR SOCIAL NORMS

Key stages 3 and 4	Group activity and analysis of social norms and pressures
After this activity: Students will be better able to recognise pressure to conform.	**AIM** To challenge the pressures teenagers face to conform to the group behaviour and 'unwritten rules'.
Extension: Read or view Malcom Gladwell's TED talks.	**OUTPUT** Optionally, students can create an illustrated humorous guide to surviving unwritten rules.
I will be able to recognise peer pressure. I will be better able to understand that I do not need to conform to unwritten rules all the time if I profoundly disagree with them.	

Introduction

Social norms are powerful, and we are extremely reluctant to challenge them. People will simply crash and burn before they break these unwritten rules.

In a gang, for example, the members may be ruled by a culture of fear: they may need protection, they might fear other gangs, or fear being alone. There is a hierarchy and they must be loyal and they must obey the leader. This is an extreme example, but some social groups echo this. Other social groups are a loose bonding of equals.

So if it is agreed in a group that an unspoken rule is that nobody tells – then this can be a powerful pull in the opposite direction of your anti-bullying policy.

Equally, if it is tacitly agreed that everyone has to be witty and cruel online or on mobiles, then this plays a part in people vying for power or acceptance.

- How do we recognise these unwritten rules?

- How do we challenge them?

- What is a 'norm'?

- Can we replace the unwritten rules with other norms?

- What would prompt people to change?

When asked what message he wanted people to take away after reading his book *Outliers*, journalist, thinker and best-selling author Malcolm Gladwell responded, 'What we do as a community, as a society, for each other, matters as much as what we do for ourselves. It sounds a little trite, but there's a powerful amount of truth in that, I think.'[42]

Activity

Thinking about your 'society', the young people you know and your friends:

1. Write on sticky notes some of the unspoken rules you think are in place (don't put your name on them). You can use as many notes as you need – one rule or agreed behaviour on each note.

2. Stick these up on the wall.

3. Now group the notes with similar 'unwritten rules' together.

4. Would the group agree that these are powerful messages that your class/group/year are aware of?

5. Which of these 'rules' do you think are positive?

6. Which could be challenged?

7. What could we do for each other that matters as much as what we do for ourselves to make our friendships really matter?

Extension

Malcolm Gladwell is the author of *The Tipping Point*, *Blink* and *Outliers*. His TED talks can be viewed online and he is a writer for *The New Yorker*.

FILM TO EXPLORE NEGATIVE ATTITUDES TO PEOPLE WITH LEARNING DIFFICULTIES

Key stage 3 years 7 and 8	View film and follow-up activities
After this activity: Students will have a greater understanding of victimisation of people with learning difficulties.	**AIMS** 1. To explore respect in relation to someone with learning difficulties and a slight disability. 2. To agree how everyone wants to be treated. 3. To have the students work out what needs to be done with the characters in the bullying story and to consider what might have happened if this had occurred today with the advent of smartphones added to the mix.
Locate film online: This is a free DVD created for the DCSF and comes with a resource booklet that you may need to search for – it is not always displayed with it. www.youtube.com/ watch?v=Cw0VrC5ODKA	**Film run time:** 5 mins 12 secs plus other chapters that illustrate the views of the characters as well as separate useful interviews with other people who have disabilities.
Time needed: 45 minutes plus homework and a follow-up session of 30 minutes to hear suggestions.	

Questions

Ask the group this question:

• How do you want to be treated?

List their responses under headings such as 'With respect', 'Fairly', 'Kindly', 'Equally'… Establish agreement: we all want to be treated this way.

Then ask:

• Do you think this is any different for people with disabilities?

Film

Prepare them for the story in the film (some may find it sad and it may remind some of their own experiences. People often cry during this film). Example:

'This is a story about a group of young people who bully someone. Afterwards we will be able to hear what the different characters say and have our own discussions about what

we think. Then we can plan together what work we think should take place with each character to stop them bullying so they learn to respect people with disabilities.'

Show the film *Make Them Go Away* (www.youtube.com/watch?v=Cw0VrC5ODKA; 5 mins 12 secs).

Show also the several additional two-minute chapters in which characters from the story talk about their points of view. There are also interviews with many different people with disabilities who explain their own real stories.

- This film was made before cyberbullying was so central an issue. Add this to the story by suggesting that when the bullies grab Ben's wallet outside the school they get a friend to film it; and in the shopping centre, the bullying group film Ben as he goes to get the old lady's handbag. This is because they have been uploading their videos of cruelty to Ben. The police find that there is a whole series.

Follow-up

Divide the students into groups:

- One group will consider what work is needed with Aaron.

- One group will consider how to support Ben.

- One group will consider the role of Vicki and the other bystanders in the group.

Ask them to briefly discuss what they think should happen next with the person they have been asked to focus upon.

For homework they can write a short couple of paragraphs of their suggestions on what they would do if they were the school involved.

Discuss these in a **plenary group**.

HOW DO YOU LOOK TO OTHERS ONLINE?

Upper Key stage 2 and Key stage 3	Pair work followed by report back
AIM To give students an opportunity to explore their own online presence and make adjustments.	**OUTCOME** After this activity students should have an understanding of their digital footprint, how their online image is viewed by others and where they have weaknesses in their privacy settings. They should be able to report that they have made some change to their online settings or learned from the exercise about what to avoid.
Online access required	
I will know what my digital footprint is and how to protect my online privacy and reputation.	

Introduce the topic

The Internet knows a lot about us. Every time we share a photo, change our status or sign up for what seems to be a free online service, click 'Like, follow, get tagged in a photo' or chat on social media, we leave behind a digital trail that gives an impression of us. This is not always the impression we want. We are going to think about our digital identity today and check our privacy settings.

1. Google yourself.

2. Search for images of yourself.

3. Deactivate any old social network accounts.

4. Check privacy settings on the ones you do use.

5. Think about what you have actively disclosed about yourself.

6. Think about what you have passively disclosed about yourself.

7. Check that images of you do not give away where you were when they were taken (right-click on the image to see the location).

8. Think about what your friends may have disclosed about you. Are you tagged in their photos?

9. Make a note of changes you make and share good tips with the class.

10. Know the basics, clean up often, use the tools that are there and decide on any extra steps that increase your privacy.

Then ask students, working in pairs, to complete the handout.

HOW DO YOU LOOK TO OTHERS ONLINE?

Imagine you were a little green man from Mars who saw what you had posted for the first time. What sort of messages do you think he would get about you?

- Have you chosen a sexy nickname?

- Are your photos a bit too revealing?

- Is your banter a little OTT?

- Google yourself and check what anyone is able to see about you.

Make a list with your partner of what you could do to improve your digital footprint. Below are some tips to help you. Report back when asked.

Did you know?

Abusers tend to look for young people who use a sexy name or post sexy images online. They especially like people who talk about sex online. We don't know what little green men like! This could put you at risk.

Do you have hundreds of 'friends'?

Abusers know that you do not know most of them personally, so it is easier for them to become a friend and flatter you because it is obvious you are too keen to look popular.

Do you give out your personal stuff too easily?

Don't say too much about your personal details to someone you've only met online. Why are they asking you for this information anyway? Girls love to share in confidence. Don't do it – think twice.

I'm a friend of your friend

If they say they are a friend of someone you know – why not check this out? Is it really true? Anyone can see your friends' names on your social network page. What if the photo they are using is fake? Abusers look at your interests, what music or sports teams you like. They make sure they can easily talk to you and seem really on your wavelength.

Why is your page public?

Think about setting it to family and friends only.

'It's just between us', or 'If you love me you will send me a photo'

If someone asks you to send photos or videos and says 'It is private, just between us two', you know it is not true. Your images could be shared or misused by mistake or on purpose. Did you know that abusers find it easier these days to get young people to send them photos rather than work hard to persuade someone to meet up and then work to be able to take the photos themselves?

'Now I've got your photo, you have to send me more or I will share it'

Pure blackmail! Report it.

The useful lie

'My webcam's broken but I can still see you. Let's chat.' Don't fall for this one – they do not want you to see that they are not the person they say they are.

'Let's talk somewhere private'

Lots of apps allow private chat. Be careful about this. Don't give away your location either. Did you know that if the GPS setting on your camera is on, anyone can right-click on the image and find out where you were when you took it five minutes ago?

'Let's meet up'

Don't meet up with someone you only know online; and if you do, please follow these rules:

- Let others know where you are going.

- Take someone with you.

- Meet only in a public place.

A RESPONSIBLE DIGITAL CITIZEN

Year 8 Can be adopted for Key stage 4	Citizenship. Discussion and pair work, research
After this activity: Students will know about UK law and understand the implications of unacceptable behaviour.	**AIMS** To explore aspects of the law that young people should know and understand in relation to discrimination and harassment. To build a concept of a responsible digital citizen.
Curriculum link: National Curriculum in England: Citizenship Programmes of Study for Key Stages 3 and 4, Sept 2013. **Useful resource:** Citizenship: www.amnesty.org.uk/sites/default/files/book_-_right_here_right_now_0.pdf.	This is a series of activities and discussions. Some can be assigned for independent study, while others are suitable for facilitated classroom work.

Purpose of study

A high-quality citizenship education helps to provide pupils with knowledge, skills and understanding to prepare them to play a full and active part in society. In particular, citizenship education should foster pupils' keen awareness and understanding of democracy, government and how laws are made and upheld. Teaching should equip pupils with the skills and knowledge to explore political and social issues critically, to weigh evidence, debate and make reasoned arguments. It should also prepare pupils to take their place in society as responsible citizens, manage their money well and make sound financial decisions.[43]

Aims

The National Curriculum for Citizenship aims to ensure that all pupils:

- acquire a sound knowledge and understanding of how the United Kingdom is governed, its political system and how citizens participate actively in its democratic systems of government

- develop a sound knowledge and understanding of the role of law and the justice system in our society and how laws are shaped and enforced

- develop an interest in, and commitment to, participation in volunteering as well as other forms of responsible activity, that they will take with them into adulthood

- are equipped with the skills to think critically and debate political questions, to enable them to manage their money on a day-to-day basis, and plan for future financial needs.

Key stage 3: Pupils should be taught about:

- the nature of rules and laws and the justice system, including the role of the police and the operation of courts and tribunals.

Key stage 4: Pupils should be taught about:

- human rights and international law

- the legal system in the UK, different sources of law and how the law helps society deal with complex problems.

Activity

The handout gives a series of questions and discussion activities about the law. This is to explore how much young people know and to offer an opportunity to discuss what laws there are that cover cyberbullying and to explore ethics and principles of behaviour.

In these discussions you will want to cover the preserving of evidence, situations when it is appropriate to report a case to the police and the rights and responsibilities that are set out in your Acceptable Use of ICT Policy.

Working in pairs, pupils look through these questions and make their notes. Then in feedback a discussion is held to explore whether the answers indicate any gaps in their knowledge or understanding.

WHAT DO YOU KNOW ABOUT THE LAW?

Is there a law against cyberbullying?

At the moment there is no single law against cyberbullying, although politicians are discussing whether to create one or to add a clause to an existing law. But there are several other laws we need to know about and understand, because they are used in some situations where online behaviour is involved.

1. Can you name any of the laws that apply?

It's the law!

2. Can you think of situations where our UK law would not apply?

If you were being trolled by people who were anonymous on a website that was not based in the UK or Europe, it might be difficult for the police to act unless we had agreements with that country.

If a website or app is based in the USA, it might be a case where the right to free speech cancels out your right to have it removed because you find it offensive.

If you have no evidence or saved screengrabs, it would be very difficult to investigate and you may need these if you are reporting to the police or asking the service to take down or close an account because it goes against the terms and conditions of the site or app.

HOW OLD ARE YOU AND DOES IT MATTER? YOU LOOK OLDER THAN YOU ARE ANYWAY!

At what age can you be held criminally responsible?

That means you could be charged with a crime, because you are thought to be old enough to know right from wrong. A person who gets a criminal record can be affected by this for life as it can be checked by employers, for example. You cannot go to the USA if you have a criminal record. There are some professions you would be blocked from.

Circle the age you think is correct:

10   12   16   18   21

The age of criminal responsibility in England and Wales is ten years old.

This means that children under the age of ten can't be arrested or charged with a crime. There are other punishments that can be given to children under ten years old.

On the whole, policy is not to criminalise children and young people where possible, but warnings may be given and in some cases further action might be taken. These may be serious.

Did you know that a young person might be committing an illegal offence if they share sexual videos and pictures involving indecent images of under-18s?

Under the Protection of Children Act 1978 and Section 160' Criminal Justice Act 1988
It is a crime to take an indecent photograph or allow one to be taken of a person under 18 years of age:

1. Make an indecent photograph – includes downloading or opening an image that has been sent via email or messaging or shared via SNS.

2. Distribute or show such an image.

3. Possess with the intention of distributing images.

4. Or simply possess the images.

HUMAN RIGHTS

Human rights belong to everyone; knowing what these rights are and how they relate to our own lives is a first step towards a culture where everyone's human rights are routinely respected.

This quote is adapted from *Right Here, Right Now* (see below).

We have our own Human Rights Act and we are also part of a bigger picture in which young people's rights are protected by the United Nations Convention on the Rights of the Child (UNCRC).

What are your rights?

The UNCRC is the most signed convention in the world. It sets out many rights for children. Two of these could apply in cyberbullying situations (italics added):

> - **Article 16** (Right to privacy): Children have a right to privacy. The law should protect them from attacks against their way of life, *their good name*, their families and their homes.
> - **Article 2** (Non-discrimination): The Convention applies to all children, whatever their race, religion or abilities; whatever they think or say, whatever type of family they come from. It doesn't matter where children live, what language they speak, what their parents do, whether they are boys or girls, what their culture is, whether they have a disability or whether they are rich or poor. No child should be treated unfairly on any basis.

Resources
UNCRC

- *Child-friendly version:* www.unicef.org/rightsite/files/uncrcchilldfriendlylanguage.pdf.

- *Brief overview for teens:* www.unicef.org/crc/files/Rights_overview.pdf.

Human Rights Act, Citizenship

Right Here, Right Now: Teaching Human Rights through Citizenship, Amnesty International with Ministry of Justice, British Institute of Human Rights, and Department for Children, Schools and Families: www.amnesty.org.uk/sites/default/files/book_-_right_here_right_now_0.pdf.

CHALLENGING DISCRIMINATION

Key stages 3 and 4	Activity to challenge discrimination
AIMS 1. To understand what is meant by the terms stereotype, prejudice and discrimination. 2. To be able to recognise stereotypical and prejudicial attitudes in oneself and others. 3. To be aware of the negative consequences of prejudice and stereotypes.	This discussion explores stereotypes and prejudice. After it, young people will be able to recognise stereotypes. They will be aware of the rights of the child in the UNCRC, which include the right to be protected from discrimination.
Materials: A copy of the UNCRC.	A creative writing element is included.

Questions

- What does the UNCRC tell us about abusive or discriminatory behaviour online?

- Do you think people go against these rights everyday online? Can you give an example?

- What is a stereotype? In what way do we judge other people before we know them?

A stereotype is an oversimplified or exaggerated idea about a group of people pre-judged because of just one aspect of who they are. It suggests that all the people in this category are the same and is usually a lazy way of criticising them:

- Why do you think this could be a dangerous thing to do?

- How could people who think like this lose out?

- Have you ever felt judged by one aspect alone?

Activities
Short story

Write a short story starting: 'It was because of his hair...'

Poster

Make a poster against 'labelling' people or stereotyping them.

In the work to explore how we stereotype others, there are many ways of illustrating what we mean. But commonly people choose to talk about 'labelling' anyone who is different from them. Humour can be a great communicator and this silly poster idea has been enjoyed in several schools. It can be used together with the activity – displayed on walls, projected on screen or handed out as a postcard. It reinforces the idea that labelling someone is unacceptable. Do not label people! Labels are for cans!

EQUALITY AND RIGHTS

Key stage 2	Logo design
AIM To recognise and promote symbols of equality.	**OUTPUT** Artwork on equality for a display in school that can be used for an assembly theme on equality.
Materials: Art materials or computer design programs.	

Design an anti-discrimination logo

- Think about symbols people can easily understand.

- Rainbow colours are universally accepted as a symbol of equality.

- Posters should be easy to read from a distance, striking and bold.

The Universal Declaration of Human Rights

Download a student booklet on the Universal Declaration of Human Rights (1948): http://f.edgesuite.net/data/www.youthforhumanrights.org/files/YHRI_what-are-human-rights-booklet.pdf.

Introduction

In 1948 the world was exhausted and war weary. Nations declared a set of universal rights that they hoped would make the world a better place. Here are the words of Eleanor Roosevelt:

> Where, after all, do universal human rights begin? In small places, close to home – so close and so small that they cannot be seen on any maps of the world. Yet they are the world of the individual person; the neighborhood he lives in; the school or college he attends; the factory, farm, or office where he works. Such are the places where every man, woman, and child seeks equal justice, equal opportunity, equal dignity without discrimination. Unless these rights have meaning there, they have little meaning anywhere. Without concerted citizen action to uphold them close to home, we shall look in vain for progress in the larger world.
>
> *UN Human Rights for All, Eleanor Roosevelt*[44]

This activity will think about this question:

- How can we give rights 'meaning' in our dealings with one another?

We will think about the law and how our behaviour might need to change.

THE UNIVERSAL DECLARATION OF HUMAN RIGHTS

The Universal Declaration of Human Rights has 30 rights, but the few listed here could apply to cyberbullying, discrimination and online abuse:

1. We are all born free and equal.

2. Don't discriminate.

3. The right to life. (This includes the right to live in freedom and safety.)

4. We're all equal before the law.

5. Your human rights are protected by law.

6. The right to privacy. (Nobody should try to harm our good name. Nobody has the right to come into our home, open our letters, or bother us or our family without good reason.)

7. The right to our own things.

8. Freedom of thought.

9. Freedom of expression.

10. The right to play and relax.

11. The right to education. (We should learn about the UN and how to get on with others.)

12. Copyright.

13. A fair and free world.

14. Responsibility. (We have a duty to other people; we should respect their rights and freedoms.)

Write down your answers to these questions:

1. Does cyber-abuse, bullying and trolling interfere with these rights or prevent people from enjoying their rights?

2. Do you think the Internet is misogynist (anti-women)? Give an example to support your answer.

3. The Universal Declaration of Human Rights was created in 1948 after years of war. Is there a right you would add now in the age of cyberspace and new technology if you were drawing up the Universal Declaration of Human Rights today?

4. What was the first Human Rights document in this country? (*The Magna Carta of 1215, making the King subject to the law.*)

A few years after the Universal Declaration of Human Rights, the European Convention on Human Rights (ECHR) was drawn up. It is an international treaty to protect human rights and fundamental freedoms in Europe. The Convention established the European Court of Human Rights (ECtHR).

SEXTING AND THE LAW

Key stages 3 and 4	Quick survey, case analysis
After this activity: Students will have a good understanding of the law on sharing explicit images. At KS3 it is important for pupils to more actively manage online risks through well-informed choices, consideration and respect for others and by taking responsibility for both their own conduct and keeping others safe online. (ICT) At KS3 pupils must also consider the consequences of sharing the personal information of others such as friends or family and recognise the appropriate behaviour around this concept. (ICT)	**AIMS** 1. To enhance understanding of the risks of sexting. 2. To assess and manage risks associated with personal lifestyle choices and situation, try new ideas and face challenges safely. (PSHE) 3. To demonstrate effective ways of resisting negative pressure, including peer pressure. (PSHE) 4. To discuss ways that relationships might change over time and demonstrate how to negotiate within relationships. (PSHE)

Ask your class to answer the three questions in the worksheet and then discuss the answers. There is information on the law for the teacher below.

SEXTING AND THE LAW

1. What does the law say about sexually explicit photos of children and young people?

2. What is the age limit when referring to children and young people here?

    10   12   16   18   21

About sexually explicit images of children and young people...

Circle the answer you think is right:

You can possess them	Yes	No	In some circumstances
You can share them	Yes	No	In some circumstances
You can view them	Yes	No	In some circumstances

Discuss with the rest of the class:

- Ask those who selected 'in some circumstances' to explain what they meant.

- What does it mean if you are put on the sex offenders register?

- Explain who, if anyone, is breaking the law in the scenario here...

Darren has got his girlfriend Selena to send him explicit photos of herself. She wants to please him and keep him, so she agreed because they are an item and she trusts him. He can't help showing them to his best mate Steve. Steve has always fancied Selena himself. He thinks that if he shares her photo then she will think it was Darren and they might split up and then he is in with a chance. So Steve shares them with half the class.

- Discuss both the legal and moral issues of this situation.

Guide to the law for the teacher/facilitator

The legal age for children and young people to consent to sex is 16 regardless of sexual orientation. However, young people are unlikely to be prosecuted for mutually agreed sexual activity where there is no evidence of exploitation.

The law does not affect young people's right to confidential advice on contraception, condoms, pregnancy and abortion, or their ability to consent to treatment, even if they are under 16.

Sexual offences legislation in all parts of the United Kingdom assumes that children and young people under 13 do not have the capacity to consent to sexual activity.

It is illegal for an adult who is in a position of trust to a child or young person under the age of 18, such as a teacher or carer, to have sex with them.

The law covers all intercourse with, or sexual touching of, a child. It includes sexual touching of any part of their body, clothed or unclothed, in any form.

It is also against the law to persuade a child to take part in sexual activity, to engage in sexual activity in their presence, to cause them to watch a sexual act (including videos, photographs or on websites) or to arrange to meet them following sexual grooming.

Discussion

- What does the law say about encouraging violence or trying to get people to act together to injure someone else or a group of people?
- What does the law say about spreading hatred or trying to encourage others to hate someone or some group of people?
- What does the law say about racism?
- What does the law say about discrimination because someone has a disability?
- What does the law say about discrimination because of someone's sexual orientation?
- What does the law say about discrimination because of being either male or female?

FROM 'A BIT OF FUN' TO AN OFFENCE – HOW WELL DO YOU UNDERSTAND THE LAW?

Key stages 3 and 4	Group discussions and cases to explore
Citizenship and Digital Literacy	Exploring what is against the law
After this exercise:	

After this exercise:

1. Students will know how to recognise five of the most common online scenarios of relational aggression.

2. Students will understand what is legal or illegal.

Case examples

Take a look at the cases below. Are any of these actions against the law? Could they be against the law in some circumstances? Are these incidents discrimination? Is this considered bullying or harassment?

The teacher can divide the class into five groups and hand each group one of the cases. In the group the students discuss the case. Then all five groups report back on their case and their discussion in a plenary. Alternatively the cases can be handed out and students can work in pairs discussing every case.

1. Dean, 12, and his friends enjoy a bit of banter – they call each other nicknames and have a laugh most of the time. They all seem to enjoy it. Stevie is in the group – he notices that some of the banter is aimed at Raj and it seems more cruel than usual. It goes on and on, becoming threatening and violent. Raj is called a Paki and there are references to his 'tan' and other messages Stevie feels uncomfortable about. He says something to Dean, but Dean laughs and says, 'Look mate, if he can't take it, he shouldn't hang around with us.' Then Stevie begins to see 'banter' in the group messages that say he is 'so gay', suggesting he is keen on Raj. He knows this phrase is often used in his school to mean anything rubbish, but he feels uneasy. He begins to worry about how he must seem to others. He is not sure about his sexuality. He knows his parents often use homophobic language, so he feels he cannot talk to them about what is happening. The insults grow and there is a daily barrage of racist and homophobic language among the group. He is becoming very worried and feels increasingly an outsider in this group.

   o   What does the law say about racism and homophobia?

   o   If this were happening in the workplace, what do you think would happen?

   While bullying at school is not usually seen as a crime, if it escalates to hate crime it could have very serious consequences.

2. Maeve is the most popular girl in the group and she has an adoring group of girls around her who hang on her every word. The girls gossip a lot and rate each other's looks and dress sense all the time. Most of the time it is fun and amusing but Maeve

turns on different girls in the group at various times and she seems to get everyone else to do the same. Her judgement counts, she is the queen bee, and once someone is named by her as looking awful/fat/unfashionable – that is it. Nobody knows when they will be the target. Some are scared to do anything that will make Maeve pick on them so that they will be targeted in endless online insults, photos taken when they were not aware of it and endless secret nicknames describing them. One day she chooses DeeDee. The group does not know it but DeeDee has just learned that her mother is seriously ill, so when she is around her friends she is not very lively or cheerful. Her thoughts are not on how she looks; in fact that is the least of her worries. Maeve quickly finds that her cruelty hits home with DeeDee, who seems to get really upset each time Maeve attacks or humiliates her. Maeve feels powerful and keeps on at it. At one point she threatens her. DeeDee becomes more and more depressed as one by one Maeve takes away her few friends and one day she does not come to school. Later the students hear that DeeDee has a serious mental health illness.

o   Could Maeve have contributed to this situation?

o   Could other students have stopped it?

While it cannot be proved that Maeve's actions alone caused DeeDee's problem and nobody would like to lay this type of guilt or responsibility on a young person, nevertheless there is another dimension. Should students who knew what was going on have intervened? Should Maeve have been more mature and changed her behaviour? Should the school have protected DeeDee?

o   What do you think should happen now?

3.   Two boys have been friends for ages. They have a real argument one day about something one of them has said about the other. They exchange angry messages online and face to face. It looks as though they may never be friends again unless there is an apology. They avoid each other for a few days. The mother of one of them rushes in to school saying her son is being victimised.

o   How would you describe this incident?

o   Is this bullying or discrimination, or just a friendship-fallout?

4.   Suze sent some messages to her former friend Rosie criticising how she looked and saying nasty things about her sense of fashion. She included lots of awful old photos. Rosie told her to get lost and go and sort out her own look.

o   This is also a friendship-fallout. It is not bullying or discrimination...yet. But what if Rosie had not been so resilient and had begun to starve herself in an effort to please Suze or to stop her making fun of her? Sometimes the consequences are not what the perpetrator imagined. What do you think?

5.   Joe hangs around with a group of young people from his school. He has learning difficulties. They manipulate him a lot because he does not always realise what is happening when they laugh at him. He thinks they are his friends because they let

him go around with them. They always send him 'commands' on his phone and he feels he must carry out what they tell him to do. One day they persuade him to steal some alcohol for them but he gets caught.

- o Pick apart what has happened here. What age do you have to be to buy alcohol? Is Joe the only one responsible? Theft is against the law. Joe is 14 years old.

How far do you agree?

- My friends and I do joke around with each other, but we know when to stop and not cross the line. (Where is this 'line'? How do you know when you cross it? How do you become sensitive to possible problems?)

- You have to be able to take some jokes and show you have a sense of humour.

- It is normal to play pranks and make jokes around your friends, but if a prank has the potential to be harmful then it could be bullying.

The next set of questions could be a student handout or alternatively be projected onto a whiteboard for discussion. (The answers will need to be removed!)

Against the law?

Which of these actions could get you into trouble with the law?

1. Taking a shot of another boy in the changing room and sharing it around amongst your mates. (It is against the law to 'distribute indecent images of young people under 18'.)

2. Jermaine hacked his friend Danny's account on iTunes and bought some downloads that were charged to Danny's mum's credit card. (This could be fraud and theft – especially if it escalates.)

3. Seb was devastated when his girlfriend broke up with him. He sent her texts, and messages using IM, Facebook, WhatsApp, Twitter and Instagram. When she did not reply, he began slagging her off on all of his accounts. He even threatened her. He began trying to control her and find out where she was and who she was with all the time. (This could be stalking and harassment.)

4. Pete, 15, was very proud of his lovely girlfriend, Sam, who was the same age. She had even sent him some very personal photos – she trusted him. At first he showed nobody, it was between them. He could not stop looking at these photos. But one day he and a mate were playing games on his phone and he couldn't resist showing his best mate a photo of Sam. Pete's mate was impressed. He fancied Sam. He became jealous that she was not interested in him but only in Pete. One day he grabbed Pete's phone when his friend had left it on a table, and he sent a photo of Sam to all his mates. This went viral around the school.

5. When Lucas and his girlfriend split up he was really hurt and angry. To get back at her for leaving him and humiliating him in front of their classmates he posted a photo of her in a sexy pose on a website advertising sex. He put her contact details with the photo.

Online trolling

Here are some examples of recent cases where action was taken about online trolling – causing harm, harassment and inciting hatred.

Caroline Criado-Perez

This case involved the appalling harassment or trolling of Caroline Criado-Perez, who merely campaigned to have a woman represented on our bank notes. Along with her, supporters such as Stella Creasy MP were also trolled.

A British journalist and feminist activist, Caroline had been involved in high-profile campaigns for women to gain better representation in the British media via a site she co-founded, called the 'Women's Room', as well as for women to be depicted on banknotes. The banknote campaign was successful, but in turn led to sustained harassment on Twitter of Criado-Perez and other women who were targeted with threats of murder and rape – at times up to 50 per hour. Twitter at first denied the need for change, but finally announced plans to improve its complaint procedures with a one-click report as a result.

The court case revealed that one of the trolls was a woman.

Two people were arrested from Tyne and Wear and charged with the improper use of a communications network. John Nimmo (25) and Isabella Sorley (23) pleaded guilty to the charges brought against them. Sorley was sentenced to 12 weeks and Nimmo 8 weeks.

Peter Nunn, 33, was jailed for 18 weeks almost a year later for sending similar messages to the MP Stella Creasy.

The CPS has since put out a series of guidance documents, one of which is on hate crime: www.cps.gov.uk/legal/p_to_r/racist_and_religious_crime.

Another guidance document from the CPS is specifically on social media: www.cps.gov.uk/legal/a_to_c/communications_sent_via_social_media.

Tom Daley

Until the Twitter outrage when Olympic diver Tom Daley was targeted with hate messages, the general public knew very little about the Malicious Communications Act. But when Daley failed to win a medal in one of his specialist events at the London 2012 Olympic Games, he was subjected to a torrent of abuse from a young person who posted a series of tweets, on Twitter, in which there was a threat to 'drown' him.

The young man was arrested under the Malicious Communications Act and later released with a formal harassment warning. Section 127 of the Communications Act 2003 makes it an offence to make improper use of a public electronic communications network such as grossly offensive, indecent, obscene, menacing or annoying phone calls and emails.

Fabrice Muamba

But sports stars in the public eye continue to be targeted. Student Liam Stacey was charged with a racially aggravated offence under the Public Order Act 1986. He had posted racially abusive tweets after the shocking on-pitch collapse of ex-Bolton footballer Fabrice Muamba during a match with Tottenham Hotspur. Muamba suffered a near-fatal cardiac arrest.

Ex-partners

The Criminal Justice and Courts Bill has now passed and this new law makes it a crime to share intimate private photos or videos as an act of revenge against a former partner after a relationship has broken down.

Discussion

- How much do you know about the law?

- Do you agree with the new law?

- Do you think if enough people disapprove of trolls and cruelty online they can change the online society by massing together?

In the cases above we can see how fast we have to respond as a society. What next steps would you suggest? Figure 6.2 shows some serious incidents that are or might be against the law. Also, you can read about the Equality Act in Chapter 12.

Serious incidents that are or might be against the law
What do we mean?

Downloading pornographic images of under 18s

Sharing/distributing child pornography images including 'sexting' where the young person in the image is under 18

'Sexting' where an adult is involved with a child

Hacking or otherwise attacking a system

Inciting hatred of a particular group of people

There is talk of making 'revenge porn' illegal, but if images of under 18s are shared this action is already illegal

Inappropriate communications between staff and a student

Promoting discrimination against the protected groups in the Equality Act 2010

Stalking or harassing someone

Malicious communication

Promoting illegal acts

Persistently downloading and sharing pirated content

Some things are offensive but not actually illegal. Remember the law will distinguish between these two.

CEOP works to prevent child sexual exploitation; do not use it for bullying cases!

In certain situations the police may give a young person a warning but, if repeated, this behaviour could land them with a criminal record. A caution was recently given in a case of teenagers 'sexting' and sharing the image.

Internet Watch Foundation

Laws relating to the IWF's remit

The Internet Watch Foundation's remit covers three types of Internet content:

- Child sexual abuse content hosted anywhere in the world
- Criminally obscene adult content, including extreme pornography, hosted in the UK
- Non-photographic child sexual abuse images hosted in the UK

Figure 6.2 Serious incidents that we are or might be against the law

QUICK ACTIVITIES

How weak are your online passwords?
The worst ten you should never use

Every year a report is issued highlighting the least secure online passwords.

In January 2015, online security company SplashData announced its annual list of the 25 most common passwords found on the Internet. It is this predictability which makes these the 'worst passwords' because they could expose anyone who uses them to being easily hacked or having their identities stolen. In its fourth annual report, compiled from more than 3.3 million leaked passwords during the year, '123456' and 'password' are still in the top two spots that they have held each year since the first list was issued in 2011. This shows how reluctant users are to change their ways or to believe 'it could happen to me'!

There were a series of major security breaches in 2014 involving iCloud, Snapchat and Sony Pictures. Despite these high-profile hacks and the media coverage of hacking generally, it seems people still don't know how to protect themselves with strong enough online passwords.

Read this list to check you are not using any of these, or anything close to them. Then write out what could make a password strong.

The top ten worst passwords

1. 123456
2. password
3. 12345
4. 12345678
5. qwerty
6. 1234567890
7. 1234
8. baseball
9. dragon
10. football

Web experts say many people continue to put themselves at risk by using weak passwords.

What makes a weak password

- A password that is formed from a sequence of letters on your keyboard may appeal to you as easy to remember, but it is extremely weak.

- Passwords that use only numbers are also easy to crack, especially those in sequences.

- Longer passwords made up of numbers and letters are being asked for in websites; and even then, if you choose something very obvious like football66 because it reminds you of when England won the FIFA World Cup, you could be creating a weak or guessable password.

- Avoid using your favourite sport – football and baseball both make the list of the weakest ten passwords.

- Don't use your birthday or one of your family members' birthdays – it is too easy to find these in Facebook pages.

- Trying to be too clever and choosing 'trustno1' or 'keepoff23' is not so clever after all!

- Weak passwords that are very common seem to hang around year after year, making it even easier for hackers. Avoid the famously weak and popular ones by doing a websearch and checking them out.

QUIZ A–Z

A useful filler for those who finish work early, or an assignment for homework.

From apps to zips, find out what it all means in this A–Z of online terms. How many more can you add?

- A is for... Apps and Android

- B is for... BlackBerry, BBM, Browser, BinWeevils and Blog

- C is for... CEOP, Computing, Cyber, Call of Duty, Club Penguin, Cloud and Chrome

- D is for... Dongle, Download and Desktop

- E is for... E-learning and Emoticon

- F is for... Facebook, Firewall, Firefox and Flash

- G is for... Google, Gigabyte and Grooming

- H is for... Habbo, Hacker, Halo and HTML

- I is for... iPod, iPad, iPhone, Instagram, Internet and Icon

- J is for... Java and JPEG

- K is for... Kilobyte, Keyword and Kindle

- L is for... Leetspeak, Like and LinkedIn

- M is for... MovieStarPlanet, Moshi Monsters, Malware and Megabyte

- N is for... Navigation Bar, Netiquette, Network and Nomophobia

- O is for... Online, Offline and OoVoo

- P is for... Pinterest, Palm Top, Parental Control, PayPal and Phishing

- Q is for... Quantum Computers, QuickTime and Quora

- R is for... Raspberry Pi, Ratting, Rollover, Redirect and RAM

- S is for... Snapchat, Storage, Safari, Search Engine, SEO, Server, Sexting and Skype

- T is for... Tags, Texting, Toolbar, Trolls, Twitter and Tweets

- U is for... URL, Ubuntu, Upload, Undo and Undelete

- V is for... Vine, Virus, VLE and VoIP

- W is for... Whatsapp, Windows, Webinar and Wizard

- X is for... Xbox

- Y is for... YouTube and Yik Yak

- Z is for... Zip files and Zipit, an app to help teens

If students do not know what some of these mean, they can search and find out, then explain to the class.

TOP FIVE CRIMES ONLINE

There are lots of ways that people try to steal personal information and cause trouble online. Here are the top five. The student handout lists these and asks students to explain what the names mean.

1. **Hacking**

   Hackers try to break into other people's computers to steal files and personal information, or cause trouble.

2. **Phishing**

   Criminals set up fake websites which look like real websites, such as Facebook or a bank. They send emails pretending to be from that site saying you need to update your details. If you click on the link in the email, it takes you to the fake site. If you enter your details, hey presto, they've got your password and can take over your account.

3. **Viruses and malware**

   Viruses are 'malware' – nasty pieces of software that can mess up your computer, delete files or make your screen freeze. Once your computer is infected, viruses then try to spread to other computers, often by email. Criminals also use malware like 'Trojans' to get access to computers and make trouble.

4. **Ratting**

   RATs are 'Remote Access Trojans'. A Trojan is software which is put on your computer without you knowing it. Remote Access means criminals can take control of your computer, spy on your private files, delete stuff and even turn on your webcam!

5. **Clickjacking**

   Criminals try to get people to click on links which download viruses, RATs or other malware by making the links look interesting. The link might advertise a funny video with a caption like 'OMG! You won't believe what this girl did' or say 'Click for a free iPod'. Don't click on links from people you don't recognise or seem too good to be true!

TOP FIVE CRIMES ONLINE

There are lots of ways that people try to steal personal information and cause trouble online. Here are the top five. Can you explain what these names mean?

1. **Hacking**

2. **Phishing**

3. **Viruses and malware**

4. **Ratting**

5. **Clickjacking**

TELL ME FIVE WAYS TO KEEP YOUR SECRET STUFF SECRET!

Though there are criminals who might try to steal your personal details or photos, it's easy to protect your computer. Tell me five things you should always do:

1. **Set strong passwords!**

   Your password is like the keys to your house. You should use a different one for each site you use and make sure it's a mix of letters, numbers and symbols. Don't use ones which are easy to guess, like QWERTY, 123456 or Password! Avoid your pets' names or your football club. These can usually be discovered by looking at your social network page.

2. **Check URLs.**

   The URL is the address of the website. You can find it in the address bar at the top of the page. The URL for Thinkuknow is www.thinkuknow.co.uk – can you see it when you go there? When you click a link you should always check that the URL is the one you would expect for the site before you enter any details.

3. **Don't click on links from people you don't know.**

   These could take you to phishing sites or download viruses or malware onto your computer. Never enter your details into a site you're not sure about – even if the link has come from a friend.

4. **Always use antivirus software.**

   If you've got your own computer, make sure you get anti-virus software. If your parent or carer bought it for you, ask them to make sure you've got one installed. Find out more at www.getsafeonline.org.

5. **Treat your password like your toothbrush and lock your phone!**

   Don't share your password, even with your best friend! If you share your password or leave a phone or computer unlocked, then someone else could access any accounts you haven't logged out of. They could spread rumours about you, say nasty things about other people and get you in trouble. They could pretend to be you!

WORDSEARCH

Below is a simple wordsearch. Doing a wordsearch as a short Rewind exercise, or as a filler for those who have finished first, can inspire your students to create new ones using their knowledge.

There are 25 words in this wordsearch; 3 are about risky problems online and 22 are sites, services or apps.

Answers:

Scam

Bot

Hack

Snapchat

WhatsApp

Vine

Tumblr

Facebook

Instagram

iTunes

Spotify

Twitter

YouTube

Netflix

Ebay

Google

Tumblr

Whisper

Kik

Ask.fm

Skype

Snapchat

Social network

ISP

WORDSEARCH

There are 25 words in this wordsearch; 3 are about risky problems online and 22 are sites, services or apps.

How many can you find?

S	K	I	K	I	N	S	T	A	G	R	A	M	R
N	O	H	A	C	K	W	H	A	T	S	A	P	P
A	I	C	H	A	T	R	O	O	M	X	J	B	N
E	C	C	I	S	P	Z	Y	A	H	O	O	Y	E
B	W	R	K	A	S	K	F	M	S	R	S	W	T
A	G	O	O	G	L	E	P	A	O	L	R	H	F
Y	S	C	A	M	Z	N	S	L	K	E	P	I	L
O	B	O	T	V	I	N	E	P	T	A	J	S	I
U	S	N	A	P	C	H	A	T	O	X	Z	P	X
T	U	M	B	L	R	S	I	B	W	T	V	E	L
U	S	K	Y	P	E	W	T	N	K	O	I	R	C
B	A	V	N	I	T	U	N	E	S	B	R	F	U
E	E	P	M	F	F	A	C	E	B	O	O	K	Y

1. Can you describe what these are?

2. Are there risks using some of them?

3. How would you protect yourself from these risks and still enjoy the site, service or app?

Work with a partner and explain to each other what these all are.

Student Handout

SECURITY WORDSEARCH

Can you spot 12 words to do with security online?

Can you explain what they mean?

P	V	E	R	I	F	Y	M	Y
Z	A	U	P	D	A	T	E	D
X	U	S	E	R	N	A	M	E
S	E	L	S	G	V	U	R	L
U	P	O	M	W	B	U	G	R
R	C	G	B	L	O	C	K	T
I	F	I	L	T	E	R	F	E
V	W	N	S	C	A	N	D	O

WHAT DID WE LEARN TODAY? REWIND AND WRAP UP

This is a quick activity to be used at the end of a lesson or the end of the week to revisit what was learned.

1. What is e-safety all about? Tell your partner three things.

2. What kind of things can you do now to stay safe? Start with the words: 'I learned how to...'

3. Let's rewind and think about what we did in this lesson.

4. Name three messages you will take away from it.

5. What kind of things will you now do to stay safe?

6. Quiz time with some games... (See the quick activities above.)

7. Text to this school number if you have any questions you'd like answered next time. (*Set up school phone to receive texts, not your own.*)

8. Contact peer supporters or report anything you are worried about to the worry box or text number or email address. (*School email address for reporting incidents.*)

About debates

A debate is a structured contest about an issue or a resolution we call the 'motion'. A formal debate involves two sides: one supports a resolution and one opposes it. The rules are agreed beforehand.

Debates are judged in order to declare a winning side. Those in the room will vote at the end. In some cases you might like to take a vote at the start and at the end, in order to measure how many people have had their views changed by the persuasive debaters.

Why are debates so useful to young people?

We use debates in democratic societies to explore and resolve issues and problems. There are many different kinds of debates, and this skill will be useful to every citizen in various situations where decisions are taken or influenced, such as at a board meeting, a public hearing, local council or national government level.

I have found them an inspirational way to explore issues related to the Internet with young people, whether we are debating who is responsible for children's safety online, whether gaming is bad for children, or issues related to violence in relationships. Teachers listening to the debate can find out how much their pupils know about an issue and prepare lessons to fill in any gaps they note during the discussions.

Structure for debates

In a formal debate there are two teams: one, consisting of three people, supporting a resolution (affirmative team); another, also consisting of three people, opposing the resolution (opposing team). And those who are judging the quality of the evidence and arguments and the performance in the debate – the audience. A chairperson is required.

Preparing for the debate

- Develop the motion to be debated. (There are several suggestions for debates in this book.)

- Organise the teams.

- Establish the rules of the debate – how long will each speaker in each team get to speak? (No more than 3–5 minutes each is suggested.) Who will speak first, second and third? The first speaker introduces the team's argument, the second speaker backs this up with further evidence and the third speaker can strongly sum up the argument for the whole team.

- Research and prepare the arguments on both sides.

- Try to imagine what the other side will argue and prepare your counter-arguments or rebuttals.

- Prepare the room for debate. The most successful debates I have enjoyed with young people have taken place in the council chamber of some local authorities. There was electronic voting with the results instantly visible on screens (try voting via Twitter and relay to a screen where the Twitter feed is displayed). Another feature of the council chamber venues is that they have microphones at each seat and a button for an audience member to press to show they wish to speak. One person controls it all, and when it is your turn to speak the light flashes green at your seat and your microphone is live. Each speaker is shown on screen and everyone can see and hear them.

DEBATE ON GAMING

Key stages 3 and 4	Debate
AIMS 1. To explore e-safety issues via debates. 2. To encourage inquiry, articulacy and fluency. 3. To explore different perspectives on key e-safety matters. 4. To encourage critical thinking.	**OUTCOMES** After holding these debates students will have learned: • formal debating techniques • how to disagree assertively and politely • about e-safety • details for their team's motion.
Materials needed: Useful web addresses and books to look up information.	**OUTPUTS** Photos and transcripts of the debate can be shared around the school.

Introduction

By looking at the evidence for and against the proposition for the debate, students learn:

- the inquiry process (conducting research)

- to write and speak persuasively

- to articulate perspectives on issues

- to deal with controversial issues and to disagree with others in a controlled formal, courteous way

- critical thinking.

Students will also learn several skills related to online searches for evidence:

- Not to believe everything they read online.

- To analyse different pieces of evidence and form a nuanced viewpoint.

- How to use various pieces of evidence in their arguments.

- To decide whether or not to break down the different kinds of games to consider their impact – that is, not a blanket 'all games are good or bad' approach.

Evidence generally falls into three categories:

1. There is research that claims all gaming is bad for children – it causes obesity, violence and antisocial behaviour, while encouraging children to be isolated and even become addicted. Some claim it wires their brains differently.

2. Others claim that kids learn to be quick, dexterous and smart through gaming as well as computer literate. They also argue that co-operative games teach them teamwork and skills.

3. Yet other research found the impact of the games was less strong than whether a child was from a functioning family, had good social relationships and other social or economic factors.

Adding this third category demonstrates that arguments are not always clear-cut and evidence cannot always be simplistic.

Activity

- **Action 1:** Divide people into teams for the motion and against the motion.

- **Action 2:** Decide whether or not to look at all games or some types of games; for example:

  o co-operative model games

  o prosocial games

  o antisocial games

  o violent aggressive games.

Do you think their impact varies?

- **Action 3:** Determine the parameters of the debate. Remind everyone of the motion – 'Computer games are harmful for children's development' – and that debates have a formal structure before the discussion is opened to the floor.

Below is some evidence that can be used in the arguments. Students can also be encouraged to search for their own evidence.

Evidence for the motion: Video games are bad for you

In a carefully constructed study of the impact of games on aggression, researcher Craig Anderson and colleagues concluded that high exposure to violent video games is a significant risk factor for later aggressive behaviour. They tested this in Japan and in the USA, two different cultures. They found that regular violent video game play early in the school year predicted later aggression.[45] The Palo Alto Medical Foundation[46] argues that video games with violent content are linked to more aggressive behaviour in teens. They believe that players engage on a deeper level when they play these games than they do watching TV. Players identify with the characters on an emotional and physical level.

Part of the increase in aggressive behaviour is thought to be linked to the amount of time children are allowed to play video games. The Cybersurvey in the UK found that, of young people who were gamers, 35 per cent spent more than five hours a day online and another 36 per cent spent 3–4 hours a day online. A few said they spent between 7 and 12 hours a day online. Twenty-eight per cent said their parents limit the amount of time they spend online. The rest said their parents did not. More than half said they were at a friend's house most of the time they were online, but 98 per cent were online at home.

According to the UK's Internet Advertising Bureau, the average gamer uses three or more different devices. When gaming time is analysed, consoles account for 30 per cent, followed by computers (24%), smartphones (21%) and tablets (18%). Some games are more time-consuming than others. Titles such as *World of Warcraft* and *Call of Duty* tend to swallow large chunks of time, whereas games on smartphones and discs appear to take less time.[47]

This contributes to the argument that young people are becoming obese and physically unfit. National figures show one third of children in England aged 10 and 11 were overweight or very overweight in 2012/13. Overweight children have a higher chance of getting serious health problems such as type 2 diabetes in later life.[48]

For more evidence on the impact of video games, see www.pamf.org/parenting-teens/general/media-web/videogames.html.

Evidence against the motion: Positive impacts of video games on adolescents

It seems that the true impact of a game can depend on what is in it. If the game is rewarding players for being kind, or helping others to create something, it seems the young people tend to show more empathy and help other people more.[49]

According to the Internet Advertising Bureau,[50] 99 per cent of 8–17-year-olds in the UK play video games. Gaming has developed into a huge industry that brings millions to our economy. Thirty-three million Britons are playing these games, so if they were so harmful, surely we would have seen a rising crime rate if their impact were to raise aggression? Because many people now use their smartphones to play video games, it seems that more females are becoming players. That could change the kinds of games on offer.

The University of Auckland in New Zealand[51] found that playing games such as SPARX could help young people diagnosed with depression.

Gaming is thought to help develop physical skills and motor skills, such as those needed to catch or grab a ball. Some surgeons are said to use games to help keep their fingers fast and dexterous.

A German team found that you could train certain areas of the adult brain through gaming and are considering how this could be adapted for therapy. This study at the Max Planck Institute found that certain types of video gaming causes increases in the brain regions responsible for spatial orientation, memory formation and strategic planning, as well as fine motor skills.[52] Other research says it could be a way to retrain the brain after a stroke.

The *Huffington Post* summarises nine ways that video games could be good for us.[53]

Evidence for moderation: A little game playing can be good for you

Research at Oxford University has found that children who play video games for a relatively short time each day are showing more positive outcomes than children who do not play at all. These outcomes show that the children are happier, more sociable and less hyperactive. The conclusion was that playing up to an hour a day could be good for you.

The study tested a large number of children and compared those who do not play at all with those who spend different amounts of time playing console games or computer-based games.

Compared with those who played for very long periods of three hours or more, and those who never played, the children who played for about an hour were happier and better adjusted. But playing for very long times was linked to harmful effects. This type of entertainment is more interactive than passively sitting and watching TV. This means it can have both positive and negative impacts, depending on the content and time it is played.

The study argued that it was factors such as a child's family life, their relationships at school and whether they experience poverty that make the most difference to their lives rather than the fact that they play video games.[54]

The American Psychological Association devoted a special issue to looking at the impact of violent video games: 'Video Games: Old Fears and New Directions'.[55] In his paper in this edition, 'Blazing angels or resident evil? Can violent video games be a force for good?', Christopher J. Ferguson argues that the negative impacts of violent games may have been exaggerated by some in the scientific community, while he thinks research should be broadened out to include some positive effects such as 'visio-spatial cognition, social networking and use as educational tools'.

Also in this special edition, Patrick Markey and Charlotte Markey found that only some individuals are adversely affected by violent video games and that those who are affected have pre-existing dispositions, which make them susceptible to such violent media.

A different study by Brock University, Canada, explored the behaviour of pupils by trying to unravel the relationship between the kinds of video games young people played, the time they spent playing them and how this might affect their thinking.

They found that very violent games that involved killing, maiming or decapitating human characters were popular and widespread. So it would be difficult for parents to stop their children from playing or seeing them. They found that while many teenagers could play these sorts of games without any change in their attitudes, for teenagers who played for more than three hours a day without much other human interaction there were problems. This isolation and the long time spent on these games seemed to delay the development of social skills and empathy, trust or concern for other people. They lacked positive social experiences. So screen-obsessed teens who are not having a healthy social life might fail to see other people's points of view or care about anyone else.[56]

Discuss

So could children who are unhappy or lonely be turning to gaming more than their happier friends? Which comes first: gaming or poor adjustment?

DEBATE ON PRIVACY

Key stage 3 years 8 and 9	Debate: Exploring the meaning of privacy

Who do you think is thought to have said these things?

1. 'Privacy is dead.'

2. 'I have as much privacy as a goldfish in a bowl.'[57]

3. 'Most of my songs have names of people I've met or are dear to me. There are people who have privacy issues about people knowing about their private life. But for me, I like to include a few special names and a few details about them to make the song very special to me.'

4. 'I don't want to write an autobiography because I would become public property with no privacy left.'

Answers

1. This is Mark Zuckerberg, talking at the Crunchie Awards in San Francisco in January 2010 when he explained that people no longer expect to have privacy. 'People have really gotten comfortable not only sharing more information and different kinds, but more openly and with more people.'

   He went on to say that privacy was no longer a 'social norm'. The social norms are evolving with time. He said if he was creating Facebook now he would have a lot more public by default than he did then. He was then widely quoted as saying privacy was dead.

   Read more at http://readwrite.com/2010/01/09facebooks-zuckerberg-says_ the_age_of_privacy_is_ov.

2. This is thought to be Princess Margaret speaking as she refers to the media interest in her life, lived in the glare of being a royal.

3. This is Taylor Swift on her Facebook page.

4. This is Stephen Hawking in an interview.[58]

Debate: What do you think about privacy?
Motion

Privacy is dead, get over it. There is no longer any need to protect your individual privacy online.

Discuss

- Can you still protect your privacy in this day and age?

- Are you entitled to protect your privacy?

- What should be public and what should be private?

  o Would you make your medical records public?

  o Do your likes and dislikes matter? Do they put you at risk?

- Instead of 'getting over it', should citizens demand clear rules on privacy, security and confidentiality?

A recent real case for discussion

A mass leak of images stored in cloud services which revealed nude photos of many well-known stars in August 2014 is thought to be linked to hackers who, a few months later, posted hundreds of images retrieved from Snapchat that the senders thought would self-destruct in seconds. The hack involved a third party website called Snapsaved.com and users were lured there by an offer to let them use the app on a website instead of the usual way only available on a mobile.

But the site was set up to save the users' log-in details unbeknown to them. It also stored all the images that were uploaded. This is a different site from the very similar sounding app called Snapsave – as many scams and fake sites often are. The difference is often very tiny and the similarity great – this seems to fool many people. Once the fake site had the user's details, the hackers could use them on Snapchat itself without the knowledge of the user.

Read more at www.theguardian.com/technology/2014/oct/12/teenagers-snapchat-images-leaked-internet.

7

Staff Training

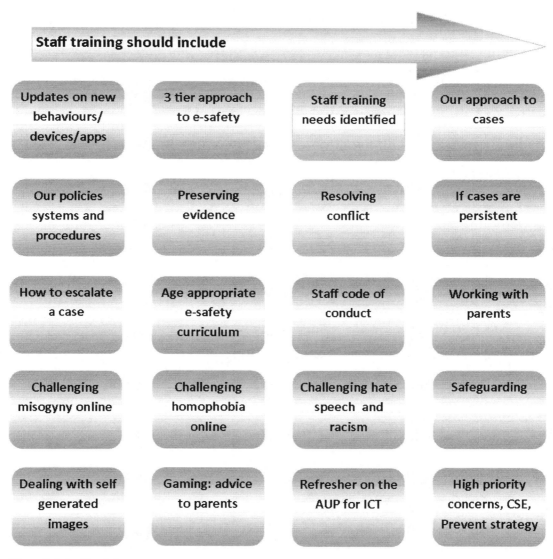

Staff training should include

Updates on new behaviours/ devices/apps	3 tier approach to e-safety	Staff training needs identified	Our approach to cases
Our policies systems and procedures	Preserving evidence	Resolving conflict	If cases are persistent
How to escalate a case	Age appropriate e-safety curriculum	Staff code of conduct	Working with parents
Challenging misogyny online	Challenging homophobia online	Challenging hate speech and racism	Safeguarding
Dealing with self generated images	Gaming: advice to parents	Refresher on the AUP for ICT	High priority concerns, CSE, Prevent strategy

Figure 7.1 Staff training

The sweep of staff training should cover all the matters shown in Figure 7.1 and be flexible enough to add new issues at any time. Right now some young person is sitting in a backroom inventing the next online craze. You will have to be ready to adapt.

It is a given that your policies and procedures need to be known and understood by everyone and regularly reinforced, but the 'three-tier approach' – a new way of thinking about e-safety education – is the fundamental building block that anchors delivery of e-safety advice and support to students. It is explained in this chapter.

Explore your staff training needs using the staff training needs survey given here as an example. Also here are discussions on determining your school's approach and setting it out simply in the 4S diagram (Figure 7.2). There is a focus on how to think about vulnerable groups of students and help those who report problems to get a good outcome. A number of typical case scenarios are given here to ensure that your training covers discussions on how to respond in these situations.

You will find:

- policy and procedure discussed in Chapter 5

- serious cases discussed in Chapter 8

- working with parents discussed in Chapter 11

- the Equality Act explained in Chapter 12

- the law as it relates to online issues discussed in Chapter 12

- what is needed for inspection discussed more fully in Chapter 9.

Tools in this chapter:

- staff training needs survey

- the 4S diagram

- icebreaker quiz

- discussion on change student handout

- creating a safe space for discussions with students

- identifying a web of support for a student

- responding to disclosures

- safeguarding simple check.

The challenge

Staff training has consistently been singled out as an area for development. There is a marked diverging pattern as some teachers are highly skilled and regularly updated by their schools to be at the cutting edge, while other teachers and non-teaching staff still laugh nervously and say 'I'm not a digital native' to excuse their lack of understanding of the online world. The latter are rather stubborn! In a secondary school they may also tend to feel that there is an expert in school, the IT manager, so they do not have to get their heads around this difficult issue on top of everything else they are doing!

In 2012 and again in 2015,[59] Ofsted found staff training in online safety to be weak or inconsistent. They also reported that 28 per cent of secondary students did not have confidence in their teachers' understanding of online safety – a fact reinforced by teachers who in turn said that they didn't believe that they had received sufficient training focusing on online safety. This message was further illustrated in research by Professor Andy Phippen who found that staff training is consistently the weakest area of schools provision.[60]

What is needed?

- Induction and at least annual training (in-service or online) for all staff, teaching or non-teaching.

- Awareness of the school's Acceptable Use Policy; professional conduct as it relates to electronic media and online matters; plus links to safeguarding practices within school.

- Developments and changes in training content each session to reflect advances in technology and changes in youth culture as well as staff needs. Avoid simply delivering the same messages repeatedly.

- An e-safety group or committee or designated individual with e-safety responsibility.

- Age-appropriate progressive e-safety curriculum with staff guidance and support to deliver it.

- Excellent staff support in the form of incident flowcharts that illustrate how to escalate or report a case; quick routes to advice and support; and debriefing after a serious or distressing incident.

Better support for students who experience e-safety incidents is a priority

This is one of the most pressing needs for staff training and yet it is often overlooked. A young person may choose any member of staff to talk to about their problem. They are likely to make their choice based on trust and the friendliness of that adult, rather than the staff member's digital prowess.

The issue is usually excruciatingly embarrassing or humiliating and they may have kept it hidden for a long time. But things do not always go well when young people do report. Unless we can improve the response they get when they report an online safety incident, it is unlikely that many more teenagers will come forward. This could allow deeply dangerous situations to escalate and desperate young people to go unsupported.

SWGfL concluded that 74 per cent would prefer to report issues to their friends rather than a 'trusted adult'.[61] Young people in my own work in the Cybersurvey revealed that telling someone was not a very successful strategy for them: a worrying half of all young people did not tell anyone about their problem, and of those who did report it, not all were successfully helped.

Of those who had told someone or reported their problem online:

- 50% said 'the problem stopped'

- 23% said 'things improved a bit'

- 11% said 'things stayed the same'

- 17% said 'things got worse'.

This means that more than a quarter of those who came forward did not see any appreciable positive change in their situation, while for a considerable number things actually worsened. Once young people in your school realise this, much of the work to try to get them to come forward is undone. Trust is weakened. This alone is an argument for improved staff training to include better responses to incidents for all staff, whether teaching or non-teaching. The situation is dire, as we learned that around a half of those who experienced cyberbullying did not tell anyone.

Good practice in tackling bullying includes multiple reporting routes, consistent whole-school approaches, good auditing processes and regular self-evaluation.[62] This could equally apply to e-safety incidents and problems. It is difficult to know which route or method a young person might select to report a problem. It could be an anonymous text to a helpline set up by the school. Or they may present with a lesser issue at first, before they go on to reveal the real problem. They are unlikely to label their personal situation as 'cyberbullying' – rather, it might be 'I'm having a drama with friends' or 'I've got this situation'. Coming forward to report cyberbullying may in fact mask a far more serious problem such as sexting, blackmail or extortion. Among young people who were personally sharing explicit images of themselves, we found that more than two thirds had been cyberbullied and this may be what they choose to tell you in the first instance, if they finally decide to talk to someone.

This is why it may be useful to have some key questions to ask in the form of a screening tool to identify when to escalate a case. For example, it is easier to ask if the student has ever had their SNS page hacked than to ask if they are engaged in high-risk but embarrassing behaviour involving posting explicit images. It was found that people involved in sexting were also more likely to have experienced the hacking of their SNS page and a range of other incidents described in Chapter 8. Knowing this can help you frame the questions and checks you might give your staff to use to explore a young person's needs and provide support and e-safety advice.

While it is distressing that far too many young people feel they did not get the help they were seeking, the other side of the coin is to clarify what help cannot be given. For example, it may never be possible to retrieve and remove all images that have been shared online. Nor is it possible to promise confidentiality or that the police or parents will not be informed. And no, sadly, there is no sheriff in the sky somewhere who keeps order on the Internet – something that many young people feel there must be, if only they could contact this authority figure.

Chapter 9 discusses how to prepare for inspection, but Table 7.1 sets out a very summarised view of what should be in place regarding good practice in e-safety.[63]

Table 7.1 Good/bad practice in e-safety

Outstanding	Inadequate
Whole-school consistent approach	Inconsistent approach
Robust and integrated reporting routines	Children are not aware of how to report a problem
Effective staff development	No evidence of staff training
Clearly communicated and respected policy	Policies are generic and not updated
Progressive online safety curriculum	No progressive, planned e-safety education
Secure and effective infrastructure	No Internet filtering or monitoring Personal data is unsecured Security of passwords is ineffective
Effective monitoring and evaluation	No effective monitoring or evaluation

Ten quick points for e-safety educators

Your training should not be so structural that it overlooks these messages. Educators should:

1. model positive and exciting use of technology
2. involve students as co-researchers
3. involve students as peer-teachers
4. chunk the information into digestible bites
5. consider the age and gender of their audience
6. ask for feedback on what they have learned
7. poll students to keep up with trends and their view of risk
8. monitor the effectiveness of what they do
9. engage with parents and ensure they are up-to-date
10. update themselves regularly on safety advice from hand-held devices, SNS sites and all other available safety advice, which often changes.

Getting started: What are your staff training needs?

Staff training sessions are precious and time can be short. That is why finding out the most pressing needs of your staff can guide you when planning the content. The following is a sample staff training needs survey which you can adapt to your school's requirements.

I find it tells a great deal and helps to focus the training session where it is needed most. You can keep it anonymous, which encourages people to be frank without fear of being thought to be a weak link.

Questionnaire for school staff to identify training needs
(Please adapt to suit your own school and any current concerns)

Dear colleague,

Thank you for your help with these questions. This is to help us understand your training needs and to aid us in reviewing policy and strategy relating to e-safety and the use of our ICT systems.

The school's Acceptable Use Policy relating to all ICT use
Please circle the number of the statement that most closely reflects your view

1. I have seen it but not used it
2. I have seen it and used it
3. I have seen it but not fully understood it
4. I saw it a long time ago
5. I don't think it applies to me
6. I have not seen it
7. I refer to it frequently in my role
8. I teach it to pupils
9. I teach it to staff
10. Other

If you have seen it or used it, please answer the following: (1 = least, 5 = most)	1	2	3	4	5
How well does it suit our purpose?					
Is it still up-to-date?					
Is it comprehensive and thorough?					
Is it easy to understand and act upon?					
Please tell us aspects of the AUP that require reviewing or updating					

	Yes	Maybe	Not
Would you be willing to be involved with a policy review?			
Would you be willing to lead pupils in a policy review?			
Would you be able to lead staff in a learning session?			

NOT AT ALL   VERY

How confident are you in the following actions?	1	2	3	4	5
Reporting abuse					
Putting Serious Incident Protocols into action					
Demonstrating privacy settings to pupils					
Dealing with online incidents					
Responding when pupils report cyberbullying					

How aware are you of the following?	NOT AT ALL				VERY
	1	2	3	4	5
Advice to staff on contacts with pupils via SNS or email					
Protecting your own privacy from students or parents					
Professional conduct on electronic devices					
Protecting data/encryption/removing data from school premises					
Taking photographs of school events within the guidelines					
Keeping evidence if a pupil reports incidents of bullying or harassment					
The risks of location software					
The issues surrounding plagiarism and copyright					
The Equality Act 2010					
Safeguarding procedures if an incident occurs involving online behaviour					
The risks of radicalisation online					
How to recognise CSE and act appropriately					
The law relating to possessing or sharing explicit images of young people					
The law covering malicious communications					
The law relating to so-called 'revenge porn'					
The law relating to incitement of hatred					

My training needs

Please identify your priorities for training on a scale of 1–5 (1 = of interest, 5 = priority need) You may add your suggestions in the blank rows.

	1	2	3	4	5
Updates in e-safety advice (such as: hand-held devices and games consoles with Internet access)					
Trends we have noticed and how we might respond					
How to respond to cyberbullying incidents					
E-safety and professional conduct for staff					
Embedding our AUP					
Training in our Anti-Bullying Policy and strategies					
How to help students with special needs or disabilities to use the Internet safely					
Appropriate responses to cyber-homophobia and other prejudice-related bullying					
Appropriate responses when pupils access sites encouraging anorexia or suicidal activities					
Discussions following pupil surveys or incident-monitoring results, e.g. 'How effective is our strategy and how do we know?'					
How to work with parents: our proactive approach and how to respond when incidents occur – real-life cases					
My own digital skills need a brush-up					
Training in the Serious Incident Protocol					
I am new in the school and need a full induction					

Big decisions: What is the over-arching approach of your school?

When thinking about staff training, consider the overall approach of the school – is it 'Lock down and ban' or 'Educate'?

The debate about locked-down systems has largely been overtaken by technology. Today children and young people can access the Internet in so many ways that a locked-down system and banning phones will certainly trigger work-arounds or fail to prevent students accessing blocked sites on their own or their friends' devices.

A key finding of the Ofsted report *The Safe Use of New Technologies*[63] was the following:

Pupils in the schools that had 'managed' systems had better knowledge and understanding of how to stay safe than those in schools with 'locked down' systems. Pupils were more vulnerable overall when schools used locked down systems because they were not given enough opportunities to learn how to assess and manage risk for themselves.

The Byron review, *Safer Children in a Digital World* (2008),[64] identified the need for building 'the resilience of children to online issues through progressive and appropriate education.'

The words 'progressive and appropriate' here are critical. It is often notable that e-safety sessions are not age-appropriate, that pupils are bored, or they have heard it all before. On the other hand, truly progressive education is not only age-appropriate but it moves with the times, new developments in technology and changing youth culture. It should be exciting and challenging, engaging and supportive rather than filled with threats of what might happen if you do not comply. It should be responsive. E-safety education should also be appropriate for those with learning difficulties, language barriers and emotional or mental health problems:

- Involve pupils.

- Train peer mentors.

- Cater for those with special needs.

- Embed age-appropriate e-safety across the curriculum.

- Draw up and agree a diagram such as the 4S guide for staff, 'Severity, Sanctions, Strategy and Support' (Figure 7.2). This type of plan helps to clarify your school's approach and gives staff a quick reference point on what you expect them to do. Discretion is of course important when dealing with individual cases, but a guide can help establish some consistency and give confidence to staff members.

The 4S guide for staff. © Adrienne Katz   Please do not be rigid! This is a guide only. Use your judgement on strategy or support depending on the case.

Severity	Sanctions	Strategy	Support
1. Friendship issues Unintended hurt caused Name calling/insults	Missing break Work in isolation Making amends Apologies	Record incident and check whether there are other incidents by this person Work on good relationships	Support target, offer alternative break-time activities. Introduce peer mentors. Teach skills, i.e. responses and technology options/solutions. Activate Anti-Bullying focus group.
2. Repeated Name calling and nasty comments continue online or offline despite warnings Physical injury Damage to belongings Deliberate rumour spreading Alienating friends Relational aggression	Isolation Fixed period exclusion Miss school outing or trip Supervised during breaks Confiscate mobile phone if necessary. Deny use of school IT. Note in pupil file or allocate any negative behaviour points	Record incident and evidence. Make action plan. Inform SLT. Intervene to challenge prejudice, if present. Request meeting with parents. If appropriate, consider mediation. Report and get offensive material deleted if online Work with bullying child to explore motivation and underlying issues. Police visit.	Support the target, engage peer mentors or buddy groups. Empower target and encourage decision making in next steps. Put a signal in place. Check wellbeing regularly. Pair up target with others, or suggest clubs. Build self-esteem and online skills. Work with whole class or year group/henchmen if needed. Reinforce behaviour agreements, AUP in ICT and AB messages. Work with perpetrator to change

3.

Persistent:

Physical, emotional, verbal, sexual or cyberbullying

Prejudice based:

Homophobic, racist, disablist, appearance

A 'campaign' against someone

Misuse of images

Fixed period exclusion. Follow the school Behaviour Policy steps.

If 'hate crime', involve police. To miss school outing/event. If necessary confiscate device, preserve evidence.

Counselling

Assign work on difference

Record incident, preserve evidence. Get images taken down. Report abuse to site or service.

Meeting with parents and SLT, plus outside agencies as required Action plan to be agreed by all parties and monitored for change. Set dates for checks. Try to turn around perpetrator's behaviour/mindset.

Develop support package for target: Engage parents and arrange for regular contact to monitor progress. Increased e-safety education and possible professional support or counselling for target.

Alert all staff. Plan classroom dynamics or change class option.

Ensure safe travel. Work with entire class. Teach relationships. Conflict resolution. Restorative approaches.

4.

High risk.

Target known or thought to be vulnerable

Depression/anorexic/self-harm or suicide attempts/online risks evident/mental ill health or sexting or CSE

Radicalisation or involvement with incitement to hatred

Involve police as necessary

Permanent exclusion may be considered

Perpetrator/s may not be known or in school

Adults may be involved

Mental health professionals may need to be consulted

Explore target's online life, look for signs of high-risk behaviour. Check their privacy settings, help with social media. Report abuse to websites or service providers. Request offensive material be taken down but preserve evidence.

Consider whether perpetrator is acting this way because of their own troubles

Engage target and their parents in a web of support including outside agencies

Counselling and specialist advice are likely to be required. Intensive e-safety education and support are needed.

Debrief and support any staff dealing with case.

Review school systems. Policies and strategies in light of this case.

Figure 7.2 The 4S guide for staff: Severity, Sanctions, Strategy and Support

How do we keep up?

Keeping up with new trends, text slang and changing apps and devices is always going to be a challenge. Remember that for some of your staff members the digital world might seem daunting, whereas for others it is their home turf. Rather than have some people feeling intimidated, your goal in staff training is to show everyone that they do have the skills to address e-safety and to bring them all up to a level that enables them to cope well and know where to get the help they need with more serious issues. You will need to bridge the gap between those who are digitally skilled but have little experience of counselling, supporting and empathising, and those who have good empathy and listening skills, but little digital skill.

One light-hearted way of adding to the knowledge base of your staff is to start a staff training session with an icebreaker. This could be a quiz such as the one below or a discussion on the changes they have seen – such as 'Keeping an Eye on Changes' which follows.

Jargon or geekspeak

The jargon, though fun to learn about, is not the most important aspect unless you are investigating a case – then it might be critical to understand or look up what is being said.

A specialised language has developed and it changes so fast that adults using out-of-date jargon can seem laughable, especially in the Twitterverse. Used as effective shorthand and secret language, it is popular and sometimes funny. What you do need to know is where to look it up if you need to – for example, on www.netlingo.com. Another point to think about is that some of the language used can seem very shocking to those on the outside – and yet some young people claim to be unperturbed by it. Some language does indeed indicate a life-or-death situation.

Don't worry if you or your staff cannot remember all the terms – it is more important to know where you can conveniently look it up. In some cases you will need to look up the netlingo or cyberslang to know what is being said. Some terms for this are: geekspeak, textspeak or netspeak.

But there are some phrases you should always be on the lookout for: 'See you on the other side' or abbreviations of it can suggest someone is thinking of suicide. Be alert to all references to depression, self-harm or anorexia.

ICEBREAKER QUIZ – HOW MANY DO YOU KNOW?

Media stacking	
Media meshing	
Android	
Cloud	
Nomophobia	
Selfie	
Ana and Mia sites	
YOLO	
Munch	
See u on the other side	
Sock puppet	
Mopper	
Tweeps	
Alphanumeric password	

Answers

Media stacking	Using multimedia to multitask – for example, shopping online while watching TV and ringing a friend
Media meshing	Using multimedia in connection with the programme you are watching on TV
Android	Android is an operating system (OS) currently developed by Google, based on Linux, and designed primarliy for touchscreen mobile devices such as smartphones and tablets
Cloud	Online storage of data
Nomophobia	Fear of losing your mobile
Selfie	Self-taken photo of yourself
Ana and Mia sites	Anorexia and bulimia sites
YOLO	You only live once
Munch	Screengrab
See u on the other side	Reference to suicide
Sock puppet	False identity used for deception
Mopper	Mobile shopper
Tweeps	Twitter peeps – followers
Alphanumeric password	One that uses letters and numbers mixed together

What are they using?

Recent polls of young people's online experiences show that while YouTube is the most used site, they are increasingly also turning to apps to circumvent their phone account. This trend allows them to talk to friends and groups without paying for the call via their account or using up their minutes. Some popular apps are discussed in this section. It is not necessary for every staff member to know and understand what every app offers – indeed, they change so often that would be impossible – but it is important for them to understand the trends. These new apps can make tracing a culprit much harder than if you were to ask a conventional service provider for assistance. This feature, and the promise of anonymity, can create a permitting environment for bullying and aggression or secret behaviour.

Some apps are relatively safer than others for teenagers, if used correctly. Among them are the giants who have moved to improve safety, reporting and privacy features, such as Facebook, Instagram, LinkedIn (for older students 14+) and Twitter. These offer options to share privately or to report problems. But of course no technology is safe if the human using it misuses it. All these, other than LinkedIn, are for those aged 13+.

YouTube offers a kids' YouTube which is useful for very young children, but teens want the real thing. While there are many inspiring and educational videos on it, and the temptation to make your own is exciting, there are of course tragic and upsetting or unsuitable videos too. It is necessary to talk this through with young people.

OoVoo is one of the popular messaging apps teens love. But it can allow adults to contact young people in the video chats where a group is chatting. Posing as a young person, predatory adults can attempt to join in.

Snapchat allows users to send messages that disappear. This can mean no evidence trail, but of course someone has created an app to capture the message or image on Snapchat and a message intended to self-destruct can be saved without the knowledge of the sender and easily misused.

Anonymity can mean that hurtful messages are shared, people are threatened, and not knowing who is talking about you to others can be deeply distressing.

Tumblr has grown to be one of the most popular blog platforms on which users hide their real names. All accounts are visible to the public and the content is unmonitored.

Vine, the video sharing app, is intended for age 17+ but is in fact used by younger users.

WhatsApp (16+) allows users to bypass their phone account and share location, contacts and messaging with other users freely via the app. This can make bullying hard to trace.

On several other apps such as Ask.fm or Kik messenger there are higher risks due to anonymity or the way that people can contact a young person directly. Kik also allows users to circumvent using their phone account and connect with anyone on the system, who might be an adult posing as a young person.

It is not necessary for all staff to know about each app – the bigger picture is important, and the knowledge that some allow anyone to see what is posted, or allow direct contact from other users, or lack privacy, is really important.

There are online guides to the latest apps that can provide updates in this constantly changing environment. Wired and Gismodo collaborate to produce a guide to 400 apps, but as these change all the time it is best to keep checking the web reviews.

Below is a discussion exercise usually done in small groups of five, in which staff can discuss influences and new behaviours they are seeing. It is useful to get everyone working together and allows participants to air concerns. Feed back to the wider group on each item.

KEEPING AN EYE ON CHANGES

What are the changes you see that affect cyberbullying and risky online/mobile phone behaviour?

What are the changes in **technology** you see that affect cyberbullying and risky online behaviour?	What **stories in the news** have an impact on bullying, hate crime and risky behaviour?
What are the changes in **provider packages** that have had an impact on young people's behaviour?	What are the changes in **youth culture/ icons/music** you see that show up in online cases?
What are the **family issues** you see that affect young people's behaviour?	What are **local neighbourhood issues** you see turning up in youth conflict or abusive cases?

Any other changes – such as focused grooming, new tactics of abusers, new sites…

Some answers

> What are the changes in **technology** you see that affect cyberbullying and risky online behaviour?
>
> *From Brick to iPhones*
>
> *Cameras and videos built in*
>
> *GPS*
>
> *Google Glass*
>
> *Powerful Wi-Fi everywhere – high speed*
>
> *Webcams*

> What **stories in the news** have an impact on bullying, hate crime and risky behaviour?
>
> *Stories about Muslims*
>
> *Stories about Travellers*
>
> *Denigrating certain groups or crime among certain groups*
>
> *High-profile cases, parents in prison*

> What are the changes in **provider packages** that have had an impact on young people's behaviour?
>
> *'All you can eat' versus dial up and pay per minute or per GB*

> What are the changes in **youth culture/ icons/music** you see that show up in online cases?
>
> *High-profile suicides*
>
> *Magazines push images of sex and thinness*
>
> *Gossip sells – moves to new sites*
>
> *Pornified music videos*

> What are the **family issues** you see that affect young people's behaviour?
>
> *Young carers*
>
> *Domestic violence*
>
> *Overstressed parents*
>
> *Parenting by text*
>
> *Lack of filters, support and knowledge*

> What are **local neighbourhood issues** you see turning up in youth conflict or abusive cases?
>
> *Inter-estate feuds*
>
> *Local gangs*

> Any other changes – such as focused grooming, new tactics of abusers, new sites...
>
> *Self-deleting messages*
>
> *Ask.fm or other anonymous sites*

A three-tier approach for e-safety education

There can be no 'one size fits all' in e-safety education. Whatever made anyone imagine that e-safety education could be delivered in some uniform universal way? That if we delivered a standard box, gift wrapped with a clear set of rules, it would be enough?

If you give it a moment's thought, it is plain that some pupils are more vulnerable than others, while their resilience and judgement varies hugely. Some have a lot of support from parents, while others have none. Young carers turn out to be in need of some targeted support, while those in care require an almost bespoke package.

Age and gender studies show different forms of cyberbullying and online behaviours. Pupils with multiple problems can be risk-takers online. Pupils who are homophobically bullied were more likely than their peers to claim that the e-safety education they received was 'not good enough' or 'useless'. I describe these findings in depth in my book *Cyberbullying and E-safety: What Educators and Other Professionals Need to Know*. Let's take a moment to think about who might need more than the universal delivery. There is a sizable minority, amongst whom are serious and worrying cases, and very needy young people. They tell us that they either do not follow the e-safety advice they were taught, or that it is irrelevant to their online lives, was given too late or too early, or in other ways is not understood or 'sticking'. Most often it did not address the life they actually lead online.

Children with special needs may not understand or remember the e-safety rules, while for children in care there may be other risks they take in their efforts to locate family members or to be in touch with people from their old neighbourhood. The Cybersurvey has shown that young carers are particularly vulnerable to being cyberbullied and they tend to say that the e-safety education they have received was in their opinion 'not good enough' or 'useless'. If they miss out on socialising with friends due to responsibilities at home, are some young carers turning to the Internet for a social life to a greater extent even than their peers?

Responses from young people to the Cybersurvey, now in its seventh year, show us that delivering one universal format of e-safety education is simply not enough. While this universal level is suitable for the majority, there is a sizable group for whom this is not enough. I propose a three-tier strategy, as illustrated in Figure 7.3.

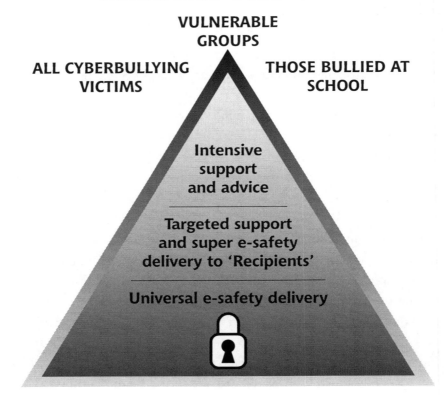

e-SAFETY EDUCATION
UNIVERSAL AND TARGETED SUPPORT

VULNERABLE GROUPS

ALL CYBERBULLYING VICTIMS   **THOSE BULLIED AT SCHOOL**

Intensive support and advice

Targeted support and super e-safety delivery to 'Recipients'

Universal e-safety delivery

Figure 7.3 Three-tier approach to e-safety education

Tier 1: Universal delivery

This involves engaging students in new and participative ways in order to deliver age-appropriate, progressive and relevant e-safety advice that teaches skills, problem-solving, risk recognition and an understanding of how to stay safe online. This is not a top-down approach in which you simply teach them a few rules and hope they stick to them. (They have told us they don't.) It is an enquiring approach that takes the students on a journey of discovery from which they can develop the ability to manage their online lives. They are seen as partners in a dialogue rather than the recipients of a set of rigid instructions. The classroom activities in this book, along with the quick activities to revisit and recap what was learned, plus the dilemmas to solve, are all examples of this style and approach.

Tier 2: Targeted support

In the second tier for targeted students, I have placed a group called Recipients. They are people who are receiving abuse or aggression online, including cyberbullying. They are possibly bullied in school and there is a risk that this might migrate to cyberbullying or retaliation might occur. People who are bullied offline often go online to find other friends and validation, leaving them vulnerable to groomers and other malign users. This second tier also includes people with special needs and anyone who, for whatever reason, may require a top-up on the universal delivery. Students can be vulnerable for a period due to problems in their lives or they may be vulnerable because of a fairly permanent situation such as being in care or being a young carer. They may struggle with English or have a learning disability. We know from our research that they require more than the universal delivery on e-safety.

Your staff training should pay special attention to students with special educational needs.

More than one in five respondents with special needs said, 'I was taught about e-safety too late.' They are more than twice as likely as their peers to say, 'I have not been taught how to stay safe online.' Of those who had been taught, more than a quarter said they never follow the e-safety guidelines (Cybersurvey, Notts 2013).

Training your staff to be sensitive to the needs of those students for whom the universal delivery of e-safety is simply not sufficient is a key element in safeguarding these young people. It is also making 'reasonable adjustments' in the interests of equality.

Messages from young people with special educational needs

There is evidence that bullying of pupils with disabilities and special educational needs is disproportionate. This can leave them isolated and looking for friendship. They often try to do anything to please those from whom they crave acceptance, putting themselves into an even more vulnerable situation.

- 62% of disabled pupils have been bullied, 19% daily or weekly, and 38% at least once per month.[66]

- 40% of children on the autistic spectrum have been bullied at school.[67]

- 90% of people with a learning disability have been bullied at school, two thirds on a regular basis.[68]

- 37% of learners with special needs experienced cyberbullying compared with 20% of their peers.[69]

Being on the autistic spectrum should not mean that a child is more likely to be bullied, but it is in fact the case unless good prevention work is undertaken. The National Autistic Society (NAS) consulted parents and reported that: 'Eighty-three per cent of parents tell us that their child's self-esteem was damaged, and three quarters reported that being bullied affected their child's development of social skills and relationships.'[70]

Mencap carried out similar research involving children with a learning disability (*Bullying Wrecks Lives*).[71] It found that eight out of ten of them had been bullied and six out of ten had been physically hurt. One respondent, aged 17, recalled:

'When I went to school I got bullied really badly. I got bullied at break times by other children at school. They would call me names, spit on me and throw stones and bottles. I told my teachers at school and they said that I had special needs so I should get used to

it as I would be bullied all of my life. They also told me to stop playing out at break times then I would not get bullied.'

Since these pieces of research, which both took place before the arrival of smartphones, we have seen the cruel way that humiliating images are now used and uploaded, how people are goaded online and then jeered at – and more. The Cybersurvey showed that respondents with special needs required a dedicated version of e-safety education and support as they were being failed by a universal delivery intended for most young people.

Highly vulnerable online

In addition to the offline bullying targeted at them, children with disabilities and special educational needs can be highly vulnerable online and are often left to their own devices, especially if they love gaming. In autumn 2014 the Cybersurvey found that young people with special needs were very active in posting photos of themselves online (40% did so) and more than a third said they spent more than five hours a day online. Alarmingly, more than a quarter said they 'often' visit websites urging self-harm or suicide and a quarter visit websites 'urging you to be very thin'. Sixteen per cent of young people with special needs had their personal details stolen and 13 per cent were visiting gambling sites. One in five often visited websites meant for adults. They raised the issue of advice that might be dangerous – more than a quarter said they had visited sites giving advice they thought might be dangerous. Very often they struggle to tell if this is the case. One quarter said they had encountered very violent images or videos 'I did not want to see' and 14 per cent had been involved in sexting.[72] Here are some support activities you can use:

- Devise a range of ways to deliver the e-safety message making adjustments for their difficulties. Use images, film, drama, art and instruction and social stories.

- Create wall displays with clear visual images.

- Deliver e-safety advice in short sessions with intensive recaps. Use a variety of techniques and kinetic activities to reinforce the message. Then revisit it frequently.

- Work closely with families and other services such as care settings if required in order to be consistent.

- Demonstrate with practical hands-on sessions.

- Ask families to check their child's online history and set filters at home and on mobile devices.

It is not only the experience of being bullied personally that is damaging, but also the impact of having their social development delayed even further if a child is socially excluded or shunned by other young people, as we can hear in the views of parents in the NAS research above. The depressing realisation of isolation and the dread that you might be bullied blights the education and wellbeing of so many children and young people. Research has described the impact of bullying on children with SEN as 'double jeopardy'[73] because, on top of all the usual impacts bullying delivers, children with SEN or disability can be doubly impacted if their development does not benefit from the boost of interaction with other children.

While the usual types of bullying behaviour are seen, there are others. Alongside types of bullying such as verbal, physical, indirect, emotional and cyber, and appalling prejudice-based bullying or 'disablism', children and young people with special needs have told us of other types of bullying they experience:[74]

- **Exploitative** – exploiting their disability or difficulty by goading them to trigger certain behaviours or bombarding them with sensory sensations when they need to be calm and quiet.

- **Manipulative** – manipulating the target child into doing something the bully or group wants to make them do. This can mean humiliating them for the entertainment of the group.

- **Conditional friendship** – when a group and their leader 'allow' the target child to think they are in a friendship group with them, but in fact this is only conditional on the target child doing something for the group, such as steal from the newsagent or allow them to slap him about a bit for their entertainment and power.

- **Relational aggression** – describes situations in which someone finds their friends deliberately alienated by one manipulative or controlling person, or situations are contrived especially in order to make the victim feel humiliated or embarrassed, isolated or 'stupid'.

Now that so much of bullying behaviour takes place online or on mobile phones, it is more vital than ever that pupils with special needs are catered for with e-safety advice that they can understand, easily remember and put into practice with real help and demonstrations.

Breaking the information into short chunks and ensuring regular recaps, with 'idea of the week' or a quiz, form the foundation steps that help to keep the e-safety message to the fore.

No longer can these different aspects of life skills be taught separately in silos. Anti-bullying work, e-safety education and SRE need to be delivered in an interlocking way that really strikes home, along with personal privacy and safeguarding messages. Only those who need help with English and young carers are cyberbullied more than pupils with special needs, but all three groups require the more targeted level of e-safety integrated into life skills.

Tier 3: Intensive support

The intensive support and advice in Tier 3 is for those few people who are cause for serious concern. Their online behaviour is high-risk, they may self-harm or be an anorexic, they may be depressed or anxious, and they might of course have any other major life worry due to their home life.

They are often known to be vulnerable and the school may be providing some form of support to them already. But does this include advice and help to stay safe online? These may be the very people who are seeking intimacy or friendship online; they may also be easily persuaded or coerced into doing things they do not want to do.

If a student has once shared a nude selfie and you are aware of this, they are candidates for the intensive support group. At any time they could be blackmailed. Their multiple difficulties could lead them to send increasingly inappropriate images, seeking 'love' and intimacy and what they feel is affirmation. They are more likely to be persuaded to agree to meet someone who is grooming them.

Students in care

Of those in care:

- 28% say they were taught about e-safety 'too late'.

- 26% relied on a website to learn about e-safety.

- 24% 'don't really' or 'never' follow the advice.

- They are three times more likely than their peers to try to get round blocks and filters.

- One in five said that what they had been taught was 'not good enough' or 'useless'.

Your staff training should explore how to support students who may be at risk or vulnerable in some way, whether temporarily or over a long period of time:

- What new ways of delivering e-safety messages can be used to help those with special needs? Devise resources. Plan a curriculum to suit.

- How can we address the e-safety needs of those with emotional difficulties?

- What are the sanctions, strategies and support available to us?

Special areas of concern
Sites promoting anorexia

Staff must be trained and prepared to tackle the obsession with appearance that is dominant in the teen years. It is advisable to include a session to familiarise them with the issues and how easily search engines keep providing browsing teens with prompts to keep visiting sites like this if they have once done so.

In a study supported by Nominet, Emma Bond looked at pro-eating disorder websites and online communities and found that these:

> …promote a disordered view of perfection in relation to body image which normalises an ultrathin/emaciated body. There is often extreme or dangerous dieting advice given which promote harmful behaviours. The sites reinforce an eating disordered self-identity and bullying is frequent. There is an increasing availability of pro-eating disorder forums and blogs but the nature of the sites varies according to the type of online space. The risks vary according to the type of content and the frequency of visits and young people who have low levels of self-esteem or are lacking in self-confidence are especially vulnerable. For people

with an eating disorder there is a problematic relationship between feeling isolated from family and friends and finding support in online environments which makes treatment and recovery complex. The research concludes that health professionals, educators and parents need to be aware of Pro-Anorexia sites and the risks they may pose but it is important not to unnecessarily advertise their existence to children and young people. Educational strategies aimed at children and young people should emphasise the importance of critical thinking around visual images in relation to the wider context of harmful content online.[75]

This obsession with appearance is seen right across the spectrum, from mild to severe. Among teenagers being bullied, 'how I look' is the overwhelming reason given by respondents to the BIG Award survey.[76] Among secondary school students who have been bullied, 22 per cent think the reason they were bullied is to do with race, religion or culture, while 17 per cent link it to homophobia – 'insults because I am gay or they think I might be'. Eleven per cent think it was simply sexist and 14 per cent say it was linked to their special educational needs or disability. Seven per cent think it is to do with the fact that they have some form of long-term or chronic illness, but 81 per cent said they thought it was because of 'how I look'.

This denigration of other people's appearance shows up in the high number talking about being called a 'slag' or a 'slut', which is extremely common, especially when sexual jealousy lies behind the bullying. Being bullied for being 'ginger' is surprisingly still a common reason cited, despite high-profile actors, musicians and radio DJs with red hair being immensely popular. It is also possible to be bullied for your appearance when it is not even your own body that is ridiculed:

> 'I was bullied where someone put a picture of my head on a picture of a naked person and said it was me and the Photoshop looked pretty convincing that it was me.'

Who is most likely to visit sites promoting anorexia?

Compared with their peers with no difficulties, the following groups of young people were more likely to have visited pro-ana sites (Cybersurvey, Autumn 2014):

1. Young carers and young people with a long-term illness are twice as likely to visit 'sites that urge you to be very thin'.

2. Young people in care and young people involved in sexting are *more* than twice as likely to visit pro-ana sites.

3. Those with mental health difficulties are more than two and a half times as likely to do so.

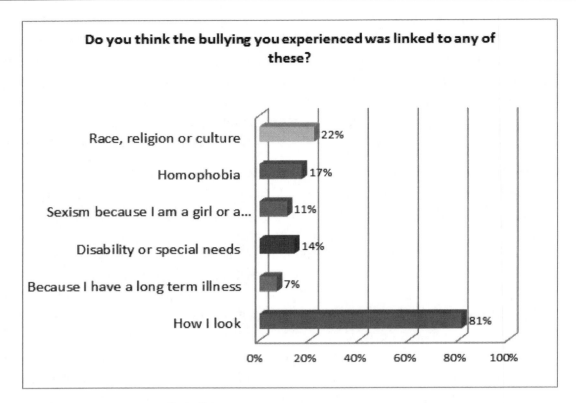

Figure 7.4 Reasons given for bullying

Cyberhomophobia

Most standard e-safety education does not address the homophobic cyberbullying that is common from the age of ten and increases in the mid-teens. Often finding it extremely awkward to report, victims suffer alone as they feel unable to tell their parents in many situations. When they do report it, they tell us of totally inappropriate responses, often without asking them if this would cause them tremendous problems.

Faith communities' attitudes are not always considered, and for some victims merely reporting it can give them a 'label' they may not welcome or even be able to cope with if their families are informed. They tell us that the e-safety education often failed them as it was not relevant to their lives. If isolated and lonely in class, they may take risks seeking replacement friends online. This is worrying, as they are less likely than peers to follow the e-safety advice they have been taught. They are almost twice as likely to look te-safety education they received was 'not good enough' or 'useless'. They are also more likely to say they got this e-safety education at the wrong age. They could be searching the net for advice and information if your SRE teaching has not helped them.

The homophobic insults appear to be loaded with racist words or comments and insults linked to disability in a multiple victimisation. They are twice as likely to report that the online homophobic bullying is carried on from what is happening in their lives in school.

Worryingly, too, they are more likely to tell us they have received messages from strangers asking them to meet up. Meeting a 'like-minded' stranger online can lead to a high-risk meeting in real life.

Indirect bullying is a powerful tool, and we see that other people deliberately send humiliating or altered photos of the targeted person around the group; this happens twice as often as malicious photo sharing in the peer group generally.

Homophobic bullying is rife whether the victim is gay or not, and is often linked to the lifestyle of a relative. Desperate students are driven to desperate measures, and the culture of silence they adopt is only breached if the school has an inclusive ethos and makes it known that it does not pass judgement on someone trying to get help. It is essential to make it known that this form of cyberbullying is equally as unacceptable as any other.

- Ensure staff are well prepared to handle these cases.

- Confidentiality cannot be promised but discretion can.

- Ensure the young person is safe before planning next steps.

- Consider whether there are any signs this person is contemplating attempting to take his or her life and prioritise this aspect of their care.

- If grooming is suspected, preserve all evidence.

- Promote equality in the school community.

Children using dating websites heavily used by adults

A great deal of experimental behaviour is to be found online as teenagers seek relationships and adrenaline highs among the flirting and sexting common today. This can be without serious consequences in some situations, as we see in the Cybersurvey, but where sites allow children and adults to mix, host forums with dangerous content, reveal users' location and actively urge users to self-harm, this is quite a different level of risk.

This problem has been brought to light by organisations such as the National Society for the Prevention of Cruelty to Children (NSPCC) who are deeply concerned about what they see. They are campaigning for sites to separate their audiences by age and to prevent the location of children being revealed. All too often, troubling topics turn out to be unmoderated. This creates a perfect hunting ground for predators or – as the NSPCC puts it – 'a playground for paedophiles'. Some adults with an insider's knowledge of music, for example a DJ in a recent case, are able to persuade teenagers that they are teens too. This knowledge of music, computer games or sport helps them build rapport and pass as a teen. Predator adults may seek out sites where they can freely mix with young people in unmoderated forums in which age is not verified.

Young people can be at further risk if the site uses technology to reveal their whereabouts. In addition, many of them do not realise that the photo they upload can give away the location where it was taken, if this GPS feature on their camera is on. Then again, young people might also be checking Twitter, Facebook or other SNS, or using Bluetooth to find people nearby. Young people can give away their location unwittingly. Tiny details such as school uniform or local football clubs can give away information that can be exploited. When reporting problems to these sites, moderators are often not humans! Thirty-three per cent of children have been asked to meet offline when using these sites.[77]

Risks involved in using teen dating apps and sites

- 75% of young people think dating apps could be risky and things could go wrong.

- 33% who have used a dating app or site have been asked by someone they have met on a dating site/app to meet offline.

- 29% who have used a dating app or site have been contacted by someone they suspected or knew was over the age of 18.

- In 72% of these cases the adult knew they were talking to a child.[78]

When telling an adult who had contacted them from a dating app that they were under 16 years old, more than two thirds of the adults still continued the conversation. Almost a third actually went on to ask for the child's number or email or some other way they could be contacted. Forty-four per cent asked for or sent an image, and almost a third asked to meet up with them. A respondent in the Cybersurvey wrote simply: 'An old man tried to talk to me.'

Activities with staff

- Ensure that staff all know about this high-risk behaviour and are alerted to watch out for any cases and refer them at once to the appropriate person in the school.

- Devise sessions to tackle pressures and discrimination around appearance. Enlist art and drama departments to actively develop art and scenarios or short plays.

- Challenge what these websites say with vulnerable students.

- Alert all staff to notify heads of year if they note sudden extreme weight loss.

- Challenge all forms of bullying around appearance.

- Include sessions on healthy eating.

- Develop sensitive screening questions to ask about online history and habits where necessary.

- Encourage parents to block these sites where possible.

- Use case scenarios to train staff, plan for eventualities and give them the confidence that they are prepared. (See the typical serious case shown below and scenarios at the end of this chapter.)

- Draw up and agree a diagram such as the 4S diagram (Figure 7.2).

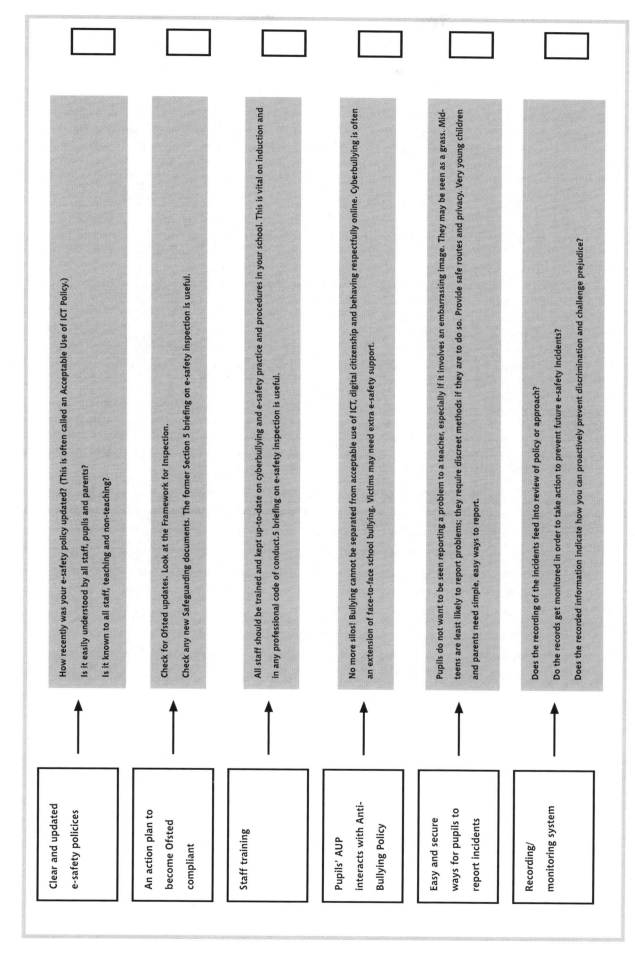

Clear and updated e-safety policies	How recently was your e-safety policy updated? (This is often called an Acceptable Use of ICT Policy.) Is it easily understood by all staff, pupils and parents? Is it known to all staff, teaching and non-teaching?	☐
An action plan to become Ofsted compliant	Check for Ofsted updates. Look at the Framework for Inspection. Check any new Safeguarding documents. The former Section 5 briefing on e-safety inspection is useful.	☐
Staff training	All staff should be trained and kept up-to-date on cyberbullying and e-safety practice and procedures in your school. This is vital on induction and in any professional code of conduct.5 briefing on e-safety inspection is useful.	☐
Pupils' AUP interacts with Anti-Bullying Policy	No more silos! Bullying cannot be separated from acceptable use of ICT, digital citizenship and behaving respectfully online. Cyberbullying is often an extension of face-to-face school bullying. Victims may need extra e-safety support.	☐
Easy and secure ways for pupils to report incidents	Pupils do not want to be seen reporting a problem to a teacher, especially if it involves an embarrassing image. They may be seen as a grass. Mid-teens are least likely to report problems; they require discreet methods if they are to do so. Provide safe routes and privacy. Very young children and parents need simple, easy ways to report.	☐
Recording/ monitoring system	Does the recording of the incidents feed into review of policy or approach? Do the records get monitored in order to take action to prevent future e-safety incidents? Does the recorded information indicate how you can proactively prevent discrimination and challenge prejudice?	☐

Figure 7.5 Steps to compliance

A typical serious case

The case below is an amalgamation of many similar cases. It does not describe or reflect any single person.

'I am really desperate. I have had so many worries with my daughter replying to sexy messages from boys on social media, despite the fact that we have been there before and the end result even involved the police, a huge drama, and me taking her out of school. She is due to start a new school in a short while. I saw this as a clean start! I've allowed her back on Facebook again, only to find a boy from the new school is asking her to post pics!! She is falling for it AGAIN. And she seems to be loving it or thinking he actually does care about her. I have talked till I'm blue in the face about the dangers, and told her this is her chance for a fresh start away from what happened before. I feel so frustrated and upset.

Her confidence is rock bottom and she experienced a lot of bullying at her old school, both before and after the sexting thing. She self-harmed and said she wanted to die, but has really been better for a couple of months. My heart sinks as I can see it all starting again. We are moving to get away for a fresh start, in around a month, but what's the point if it will all start again? What could actually make a difference? HOW do I let her know she doesn't need to do this to get people to like her? Help please!'

How would staff respond?

Set up a group discussion. Here are some pointers to cover.

This student needs a lot of work with mental health professionals to explore why she needs to validate herself in this way. Her past is obviously important, as are her coping and relationship skills. Moving from school to school will make her always the newbie and most likely to be bullied. Moving house is not really likely to actually change her online life all that much. It is highly likely that she will soon be visiting the same sites and services again. She may feel she does not exist socially unless she is interacting online, particularly if she is being bullied in real life in school.

Pupils at her new school can find her online images or learn of her reputation quite easily, so the move is not likely to provide the clean slate her mother hopes for. It would be interesting to know why the boy at her new school thought she was a good mark for his request for her to sext, and to explore what work on e-safety and relationships has been done in the new school prior to this girl's arrival. Why did he think this was acceptable? Had he been contacted by anyone at her former school? It would help to know whether their planned education programme for teaching SRE and issues of consent and appropriate relationships is strong before this girl even goes to the school. Does the school have anything in place to safeguard this new girl?

Her online life will need monitoring, but if this monitoring is too overt or stifling she may conceal it. Two girls in Ireland (where a spate of suicides among young girls were allegedly linked to cyberbullying) explained to me how they did this. They had two Facebook pages, one in their Irish name and one in an English name. Other girls have shown me how they have a tame Facebook page that their mum can see and they do all their social interaction via apps and in chat rooms or other social networking sites such as Ask.fm where posters can remain anonymous.

The case is an example of a Tier 3 situation. For this girl, universal e-safety is not going to be sufficient. Her mother too requires support, both therapeutic and technological. Using software that allows her to monitor all activity on her daughter's phone and computer/tablet from a distance must be balanced with the question of trust. This girl may be visiting pro-ana or self-harm websites, or websites urging suicide. Windows 10 offers a wide array of parental controls.

Within school there is a great deal of work to be done, starting with SRE and building into it e-safety for the modern era. Boys must know that if they ask for photos of this sort they could be found in breach of the law. If they are found with explicit photos of an under-18-year-old on their device or found to have shared these images, the consequences will be serious. Invite a police officer to school to discuss with the whole year group the law and the consequences of cases of sexting. The law is explained in Chapter 6 and in an activity which can be used with young people to explore how much they know about the law. A school's Safeguarding and Child Protection procedures need to work in close tandem with all e-safety policy.

This case has similarities to the story of Amanda Todd in Canada. She too had shared self-taken images when very young, and when this became known among her school mates she was bullied mercilessly. She was also bullied online by people she did not know. After moving house and school, it continued and she suffered extortion and trolling. Amanda told her heartbreaking story in a video that went viral. She self-harmed and had multiple problems. She eventually took her life. I have been saddened to be asked by children as young as ten in London whether I have seen this video of a Canadian teen. It is a very distressing video you would not want a ten-year-old to view, yet so many have done so on YouTube. We would do well to be aware of what children are viewing and talking about.

The danger of Amanda's story being so widely known is that it could suggest to someone feeling vulnerable that suicide might be an answer. The massive publicity given to cases like these and the series of tragic girls' deaths that took place on this side of the Atlantic in 2013 is alarming. In the cases in Ireland the dead girls were revered, dressed like princesses and very publicly mourned. There was a sense that they were in a better place. People (implying the bullies) would be feeling sorry now for what they had done. How must this play in the mind of a girl feeling distraught, disturbed and isolated? The Samaritans have warned against glamorising suicide because of the 'copycat' tendency, while Dr Jitender Sareen, a psychiatrist and professor at the University of Manitoba, argued that much of the coverage of Amanda's case gave the facile notion that cyberbullying causes suicide, overlooking possible mental health issues.

'Being cyberbullied can be the straw that broke the camel's back, but the media and politicians at times simplify the issue to bullying equals suicide,' Dr Sareen said. He gave the example of someone with a lung disorder who then dies from a common cold to explain that many young people who take their own lives after being bullied had mental health issues that affected their coping skills. In the same article Wayne MacKaye, the author of a major report for the Canadian Government, said: 'It's really important to not in any way popularize or glamorize [suicide], which then can lead to a kind of bizarre copycat effect.' He argued for better links between mental health professionals and schools.[79]

But are professionals trained to handle this type of case?

A shortage of trained professionals has been identified, with research for the Marie Collins Foundation revealing: 'More than half of health, education and children's services workers did not feel confident in helping online abuse victims.' Eight in ten said they had no training in rehabilitating these victims – but nearly all said it would be of value. In the study, carried out by Dr Emma Bond and Stuart Agnew at University Campus, Suffolk, and supported by Professor Andy Phippen, of Plymouth University:[80]

- 70% of the 692 respondents stated that they had not received training in online risk assessment and 96.5% said they would value such training

- 81.1% of the respondents said they had never had any training in helping children in their recovery from online abuse; 94% said they would value such training

- more than half said they did not feel confident about helping children who had experienced harm or abuse online.

The professionals who took part in the survey included school nurses, health visitors and paediatricians, social workers, child protection advisors, family and education welfare officers, teachers and learning support assistants.

It is vital that educators and other professionals receive e-safety training as part of their initial training and their continuous professional development. They need regular updates and advice, as this case demonstrates. Perhaps consider co-training events with other agencies? I have found that training days can be enriched when teachers are working with other agencies and community services in the training day discussions.

A sad truth is that in cases like this one the images are unlikely to have disappeared from the Internet. In 2012 IWF analysed public reports of self-generated child abuse images. They found that 88 per cent of them had been taken from their original location and uploaded or misused elsewhere, showing the extent to which young people lose control of their own images without their knowledge. As the 'Shaving Foam' activity in Chapter 6 shows, once your image is out there, it is nigh on impossible to retrieve it. Nevertheless, in the immediate group of young people in your school, you can take swift action to prevent any further sharing of the image and put in place support for this student. It is vital to stop any 'shaming' continuing among students, and then comes the difficult work of a professional working with the girl to unpick her need to do this.

Gaming

Another issue for staff to be aware of is that of gaming. There is evidence that young people with behavioural difficulties are often gaming for very long periods of time. It allows their carers a break and the young person can be feeling 'addicted' to playing. It brings skills. But it can also bring them into contact with other gamers, games that are unsuitable for their emotional age, and extreme violence or porn. Sadly in the Cybersurvey this proved also to be true for those in care and may be a concern for many young people left to their own devices for lengthy periods. Table 7.2 shows the experiences they describe while gaming online.

Table 7.2 Experiences while gaming online of young people aged 10–16 (Cybersurvey, 2013)

Experienced when using online games consoles	Looked after children	Special educational needs	Peers with no difficulties
Messages with threats	47%	43%	24%
Being bullied carried on from life in school	35%	32%	10%
Name-calling	45%	43%	24%
Being asked by a stranger to meet up	42%	30%	11%
A message from a stranger asking you to share your location	40%	31%	16%
A message that tried to make you do something you did not want to do	38%	33%	15%
Unwanted sexual suggestions, jokes or threats online when gaming	40%	32%	15%
A message with racist comments or names	33%	31%	15%
A message calling you gay whether true or not	43%	41%	20%
A message with unpleasant name-calling	46%	44%	31%
A message with unwanted sexual suggestions, jokes or threats	40%	32%	14%
A message with insults because of disability	31%	33%	7%

Learners with special needs, as we saw above, require a wrap-around support package that delivers safeguarding with adapted e-safety education, targeted to their abilities and understanding. They may not realise they are being targeted, bullied or manipulated, especially when playing a 'game', and they do not always report it.

A whole-school approach

A whole-school approach to reducing bullying should include peer supporters or mentors trained to help other students. Consultation and review of the school's policy and strategy should make reasonable adjustments to obtain the views and participation of all pupils to promote and demonstrate the culture of respect. The engagement and participation of all pupils is central to any intervention programme, but without *evidence* of inclusion and attention to equality it will fail to serve the pupils with special needs. I encourage schools to pay attention to their duties under the Equality Act 2010 and to include this in their staff training programme.

Prevention of discrimination includes tackling or paying attention to:

- negative attitudes to disability
- negative perceptions of difference
- greater difficulty in resisting bullies/manipulators and groomers because of SEN
- increased isolation as a result of SEN/disability
- difficulty in understanding that what is happening is bullying/manipulation or grooming
- problems telling people if they are bullied/manipulated or groomed.

About resilience

Here are a few answers from young people aged 10–16 to the question 'If you were cyberbullied, how did it make you feel?' (Cybersurvey, October 2013). They illustrate the wide range of reactions to being cyberbullied:

Angry

That it might have been one of my friends

I couldn't eat or sleep

I don't mind any more 'cos you can just block them

Didn't really care, I just brushed it off

Feelings of worthlessness caused depression

Took it as a joke in a way

Makes you feel like no one wants you to the point of suicide

Useless

I hated myself

They tried to make me upset but I just shrugged it off

It made me feel intimidated when I went out or when I went to school

Ignored the idiots who threatened me

Depressed, 'cos I knew what they said was true

They called me a slut and I suppose I look like one.

If we are to go in guns blazing to 'protect' everyone who has had a bad experience online, we could be undermining some people who are handling it well themselves. Equally, we have to remember that the more vulnerable people tell us that, if they do report it, this often makes things worse for them. So for them, telling someone is not guaranteed to be fruitful. We need to improve our responses.

What are our options?

- Build on strengths – explore the strengths a person has and help build on these.

- Help the young person to make decisions about what should happen next.

- Ask permission before implementing some action plan within the school.

- Teach problem-solving skills and digital responses such as reporting abuse on a website or blocking a sender.

- Provide a trained peer supporter.

- Work on self-esteem building activities.

- Review the plan of action regularly with the young person to see if it is working.

Steps that have helped in real cases

When supporting a young person who has been targeted for abuse online by another student from the school, it is vital to engage with the parents and try to encourage them to work with the school where possible. This can be very sensitive work, but by gaining their trust we have seen some very successful cases resolved. Serious cases may involve a counsellor. You should also explain that new approaches may take a little time to show success if a situation has been embedded for a long time. They should also expect progress with some intermittent setbacks! This is more realistic, so help them manage expectations and get regular feedback from them and the young person on how they think the new approach is going.

If the approach chosen is simply not working, do not persist beyond half a term. Select another tool in your armoury. Reflective practice is never afraid to say something could be working better. After a nasty incident, relationships can be very strained for a lengthy period unless some restorative work is undertaken. However, overcoming adversity is a great life lesson. These examples show that there is so much more than digital skill involved in dealing with cases where both the instigator and the target are students in the school.

The boy who could not lose face

Parents have been asked to help a student accommodate to failure. He could not accept any setbacks or failure to achieve the level of marks he thought he should attain. They had been pressurising him to achieve 100 per cent, nothing less. It seems he applied this to everything in life. If he failed to score in football he felt he was a total failure. This was also true with girls. His humourless pursuit of perfection seemed to invite others to target him, for they knew how easy it was to score a hit and to get him to feel bad about himself.

His tormentor used photos of him in humiliating circumstances which were posted on social media. Some were Photoshopped, which made things even worse. While the culprit was dealt with, the behaviour stopped and apologies were made and sanctions assigned, the humiliation for the victim was immense. Work with the whole group continued in order to get them to face up to the harm they had caused by laughing and sharing the images and to make them aware of the law and how their behaviour was totally unacceptable.

But the victim required a package of support that would enable him to rebuild his self-respect and learn some new ways to deal with failure. His online life was also explored with him and his privacy settings reset. He found it helpful to learn new ways of confronting difficult situations with humour, staying in control and not giving the other person the satisfaction of seeing him crumble as he had done before. He was helped towards witty replies he might deploy. The perpetrator made extensive efforts to sort things out with his former target, who agreed to help him with work he struggled with.

The girl who believed what her tormentors said

This girl believed that she deserved to be criticised – after all, she felt fat and ugly and in no way 'worth it'. In some way she had internalised the attacks on her and felt they were justified.

She said that other students criticised her online and called her awful words and she explained that must be because she was, or looked like, a 'fat slut'.

Work on her view of herself was a vital component of the support package. Getting to the bottom of how she came to have this view of herself was sensitive, lengthy work. But she could not go forward without it. This uncovered many concerns at home, and family counselling was added to her package of support while work with the girls who tormented her continued in parallel. She was not strong enough for a restorative justice approach. Her online life was examined and her privacy settings reset. Her friends list was 'cleaned' and the photos she posted of herself were discussed with her.

Gradually she began to feel able to talk about some of the other sites she visits online. The counsellor also broached healthy eating and SRE. Some young people feel a compulsion to place provocative questions online in a chat room or forum, so that others will confirm that, yes, you are ugly. This is complex behaviour, and when severe can be viewed as a form of self-harm. Group work involved dance and other fitness activities.

The perpetrators were traced and work was undertaken with them and their parents, then with the wider group who knew what was going on but stood by and did nothing. Individuals from the wider group were selected to form a nurture group around the victim. A local PCSO was invited in to talk to the group about trolls.

The couple whose break-up disrupted a whole year group

Damian and Jeannie were together for six months. When they broke up she felt betrayed and was certain one of her friends had 'stolen' him away from her. Jeannie not only posted rumours about this other girl all over social media but she also decided to get back at Damian and post some intimate photos of him that she had taken while they were together. With the latter she wrote some cruelly hurtful messages rating him as a useless boyfriend and worse.

Other members of the year group began to take sides in this drama and the whole thing escalated one weekend. On the Monday, three sets of parents wanted to see someone at the school about the online problems their children were experiencing. Three students did not attend school that day.

Unravelling this case, it had to be explained to all that so-called 'revenge porn' is to become an offence in law. Images had to be urgently taken down, and those who had posted them were asked to do so at once. Anyone else who had shared them was required to remove them. Some Facebook accounts were closed after reports of transgressing the terms, and conditions were made. Relationships education was needed to address the ethics of relationships.

Jeannie felt remorse a day later and came in to apologise to Damian and her friends. Damian said he did not want to be around girls for quite a while! The wider group had begun to feel they should not have taken sides and joined in and they were seen individually and asked how they planned to put things right. An action plan was put into place. It included work on e-safety and restorative justice sessions, and incorporated meetings with parents.

Everyone learned that some images could not be retrieved and there is a danger when posting and sharing that this could happen. Acting in the heat of an emotional moment can have devastating consequences. A visit from a police officer reinforced the messages about illegal possession or sharing of explicit images of anyone under the age of 18 and warned about the possibility of action being taken by the police. Group work was initiated and the whole year group was retrained in e-safety guidance in relation to private or explicit images, relationships, ethics, citizenship and supporting each other.

Scenarios for use in staff training discussions

1. A boy in your tutor group complains to you that he is being bullied by racist texts. What steps has your school put into place to deal with this complaint and what, if any, action would be taken against the bully? What will be done to confront prejudice more widely? How do you monitor this?

2. After a lesson you have delivered, a pupil approaches you and says that they are being pestered by someone via instant messaging who keeps asking to meet them. What steps should you take and how could you reassure the pupil?

3. A parent alerts you to a Facebook page where a group of parents are saying nasty things about a teacher, including false information and statements. What action would you take and who is responsible for dealing with this in your school?

4. A pupil with special needs is found to have stolen cigarettes from a newsagent. He reveals that he has been forced to do this by other pupils using texts and Facebook messages which threaten him if he does not do what they say.

5. There are rumours that a girl has posed nude and her photo is being circulated online. You investigate. It turns out that her ex-boyfriend has shared intimate photos of her with his friend and they have been shared with all the boys in the class and beyond. She is being 'slut-shamed'. What steps do you need to take and which agencies, if any, do you need to work with?

6. A boy of 13 reports being homophobically bullied. He does not want his parents to know. Messages and rumours are circulating online. He is too embarrassed to show you the images he was sent, but asks for help. He has never thought about his sexuality as an issue before. How would you proceed?

7. A young person anonymously contacts you saying they are being bullied because of the music they like (emo) and they are desperate. 'Life is not worth living' are the words used. They have worried all summer about going back to school. (In this case the message came via text to voice on a landline.) What can you do? You do not know their name, gender, age or whereabouts.

8. A clearly terrified 14-year-old in care tells you she is having 'a drama' with someone on SNS. Her boyfriend is part of a gang and he wants her to 'be nice' to his friends. She has had many losses in her life and doesn't want to lose him. She always does what he wants. He is sharing pics of her and joking about her with his mates on publicly viewable pages saying she is available for sex. He has given her a fancy mobile phone as a gift.

9.   A girl of 14 tells you that she is being blackmailed on Facebook over some 'selfies' she took. Things have become more serious and she is terrified to tell her parents because they banned her from Facebook and insisted she close her page down and she has created a profile in her ethnic name to avoid being found out. What help would you put in place and how would you work with the family?

10. A teenage boy was duped into an online relationship with someone he thought was a teenage girl. Over many months they corresponded. He shared some intimate images with 'her' but is now being blackmailed over these – the threat is that if he does not pay over a sum of money, the perpetrator will reveal the photos to his family and friends. You discover him in a dreadful state, unable to focus or concentrate and he blurts out his story. He insists you do not tell his parents. What do you do? How do you keep him safe while you put a plan in place?

11. A boy who was bullied badly sets up a website for young people to help each other with a live unmoderated forum in which young people give each other advice. What are the risks and how would you handle this?

12. A girl who has had a lot of online abuse targeted at her has been repeatedly helped by her school to clean up her Facebook page and sort out her problem, but she continues to open new Facebook pages and interact in a high-risk way. What would you do?

Which of these cases is a matter for the police? Are there any you would report to IWF? Are there any that are appropriate for CEOP (i.e. child sexual exploitation)? When would you involve outside agencies? How would you retain evidence? How would you work with the parents/carers?

Identifying the young person's support network

For those who feel very isolated and lonely it can help to draw a diagram of a web of support to identify who they can count on for help. The student is in the centre of the spider web, with close people in the inner ring and others, further out.

In addition, offer external sources of help such as helplines, online chat or text lines to ChildLine or Samaritans so that a young person who wants to keep it confidential can talk to someone.

Creating a safe space for student discussions

When you are planning to start a group discussion on sensitive topics such as cyberbullying, it is good practice to create a safe space with agreed rules and codes of behaviour before you begin. This pre-planning can help create a safe supportive atmosphere, but more importantly the ground rules can protect children. They also protect staff as you can adequately prepare and, if necessary, take advice in advance. Think about the seating arrangement – are people sitting around comfortably as a group or stiffly in rows? Is the environment friendly and calm? Of course there will be times when a child tells you something in the most inopportune moment – and you will have to take immediate decisions on how to handle this. But for group work it is possible to plan ahead.

Ground rules and preparation

Any staff members involved should be well prepared for disclosures. Discussions that involve explorations of how we treat one another, and what is and is not acceptable behaviour, will occasionally reveal domestic violence or some other difficult or sensitive issue as the students begin to think about this.

Ensure that staff know how to report any concerns and how to support a young person if it should be required. All staff members should know and understand the school's Anti-Bullying Policy and their Safeguarding and Child Protection systems as well as the Acceptable Use of ICT Policy and E-safety Policy if they are separate. They should be able to call on a colleague to take over if they need to take a child out of the group for one-to-one support.

Take care not to single out any pupils in the class or group if you are aware someone is vulnerable or a little different – an asylum seeker or someone who is gay, badly bullied or in care, for example. Do not single out this student too often in the discussion asking for their insights, or focus too much on someone who is a newcomer from another country excessively when discussing racism. Your eagerness to involve this student may bring unwelcome attention to someone who only wants to fit in.

As adults leading group discussions we always have to be aware of our own prejudices and attitudes – could something a child says unfairly affect our attitude towards him? Professional behaviour is required now more than ever. We like the child, but we may not like an attitude, a view expressed or a behaviour.

The group should agree some ground rules. These include the following:

1. Respect the views of others.

2. Start with and keep an open mind.

3. Use no names – talk about behaviour you do not like, not a person.

4. No question is too unimportant or wrong.

5. No answer is 'wrong'.

6. Accept that some people have different views and opinions and learn.

7. Let others speak.

8. What is discussed here today remains here.

Explain that anyone can come and see you afterwards if anything has made them feel uncomfortable or they wish to ask something.

Discussing discrimination based on prejudice or stereotypes

It can help to take a 'rights-based approach'. If we start from the idea that we all have certain rights, it is easy to take the discussion into areas that look at stereotypes and prejudice. You might find the UNCRC a useful starting point, or the Equality Act 2010. Another advantage of a rights-based approach is that it underlines our common humanity at the start and again at the finish if it is used in this way.

- Expect some views to be uncomfortable.

- Learning that prejudice-based bullying is unacceptable may take quite some time for some individuals. But it is vital to air the arguments and demonstrate that it is unacceptable and will be challenged within the school and in future workplaces. It is against our law to discriminate and to incite hatred.

- If people express offensive views, challenge the discriminatory attitudes and behaviour – not the person.

- Don't ignore racist, disablist or homophobic insults, jokes or name-calling because they are difficult to challenge or because staff feel nervous. This would give the impression that you and your school support such views. Language matters.

- Just like the pupils, staff members will have their own attitudes, stereotypes and expectations. It is best not to trivialise or deny other people's concerns and feelings, but to model an inclusive style of teaching and behaviour.

- Challenge incorrect assumptions or rumours with accurate information.

- If you tell a child to 'ignore it' they might feel you are denying their pain. You want to fully support them in various ways, even if you are suggesting they do not feed the trolls or bullies. Rather, say: 'Do not reply, save evidence, and let's take the following steps…'

Explain that what will be discussed here today are situations in which these rights are overridden. Lessons to address stereotypes are in the 'Challenging Discrimination' activity in Chapter 6.

Responding to disclosures

Ensure that your staff training includes a session on how you expect staff to respond to disclosures. This includes their reaction, treatment of the student and procedures to follow.

- If a student makes a disclosure which suggests that he or she is at risk of harm, from other people or from himself or herself, action must be taken. Staff cannot promise confidentiality in this situation. A calm response and effective compassionate listening will need to be followed by the next steps in your Safeguarding or Child Protection Policy.

- First, thank the student for coming forward with this matter and assure them that you and the school will do all everything possible to support them.

- Never underestimate the enormous step it represents for a young person to have chosen you as the person they trust! This child may have agonised for weeks about what to do; they may lie awake at night racked with worry. You might have come to represent a solution in their mind.

- They may feel desperate, anxious or relieved – and usually there are a multitude of problems piling up upon them at once. Once they have settled on you as the person to tell, they may be expecting more from you than you are actually able to deliver. You will need to support them into the next steps.

- It is not uncommon for someone to present at first with only one of these multiple problems. It is likely they will be in a fragile state. Your demeanour is vital. Looking shocked or panicky is not helpful. Offer warm, non-judgemental support. Ask gentle questions. Use effective listening techniques. Gradually the situation will be revealed.

- You will need to refer the case to the designated Safeguarding or Child Protection lead in your school. This person will liaise with the local authority designated officer as required. You should try to get the student to agree to this, even though you will be obliged to do it anyway. Then offer to consult the student on next steps and work together to try to resolve the situation wherever possible. You may be able to act discreetly and not tell the whole class, for example.

- Listen carefully and write down what the pupil has told you and check back with him/her that you have got this right. Make any evidence safe (screengrabs, texts saved). Do not download evidence onto your own phone or laptop.

- It would be useful to explain that things may take a while to resolve. It can take a little time to get the support from a range of agencies into place, for example.

- Report wrongdoing to a website to get material removed if necessary or report to the police.

- Check whether the parents know and offer to support the student when they are to be informed. A student may ask that his parents are not told, but you cannot promise this. On the other hand it may be possible to provide help via the school counsellor or another skilled person who can help mediate that session.

Why don't they tell anyone?

Large numbers of children never tell any adult that they are being cyberbullied or have other problems in life or online. The discussions below reveal some of the reasons children do not tell an adult. Thinking about what they say can help us to come up with ideas to enable more people to report if they need to do so.

How do you feel about getting help from an adult?

'Fine, but some people are scared because bullies threaten them.'

What do people do about it?

'Not much; people are scared that the teachers will tell them off and people will then bully them more.'

'I like to keep it to myself 'cos he says if I tell someone he will do worse.'

'Mum doesn't know… I didn't want them to get worried about me being teased at school.'

'When a person gets bullied the person doesn't tell.'

Why not?

'The person will be watching them all day so they don't tell 'cos they're scared.'

'They keep going on and on and the people don't tell the teacher or their mum and dad 'cos they're too scared.'

'I never told anyone 'cos he told me it was secret and if I told he would hurt my mum.'

'I didn't want to say anything 'cos my mum has so many troubles already.'

'In my culture you can't tell your parents you are bullied 'cos some kids think you are gay. They would be more angry with me than them.'

'My dad always says I should stand up for myself so I can't tell him things are going badly wrong and I can't handle it.'

"Cos of how I look and dress, they call me a slag and a slut. They make my life hell. I can't tell my parents I am getting bullied about this, they already hate the way I dress. And anyway maybe I am a slag if that's what I look like.'

'My parents struggled to come to this country so we could get educated. I can't tell them I am being bullied. It would be too bad for them after everything. But it's online and maybe they won't find out.'

'They bully me 'cos I posted this photo of myself. It seemed a joke at the time but now they all send me insults, they tweet about me and talk in WhatsApp all the time saying horrible stuff about me. I can't tell my parents – they will be furious at what I did.'

Solutions to being too scared to tell

Young people called for other people to be responsible for finding out and reporting bullying rather than solely relying on the victim. They wanted teachers to watch out for signs and suggested that turning to friends to tell a teacher on your behalf was a good idea:

'You could have systems, you could write something anonymously and then put an announcement out about punishment. You could set a patrol of people to help, like older pupils to patrol school.'

'People could look and see, look out for people, or the teachers could tell you to look out for people.'

Peer support schemes not only help those who actually do come forward but they reassure others that, if they needed to, there would be someone they could talk to.

Monitoring

Monitoring the case after the intervention is essential. Did the problem actually cease? Was the reporting student successfully reintegrated into friendship groups? Was online behaviour subsequently safer? If a school has a high rate of reports this does not necessarily mean that they are ineffective, but it does suggest a level of pupil trust in the school. If cases are not successfully resolved in most situations, fewer will come forward – then the school may indeed be ineffective.

Some cases appear to be simple low-level events at first but upon monitoring or better listening their complexity emerges.

- If a case needs to be referred to the police or an outside agency this is done by the designated lead member of staff for Safeguarding or Child Protection, whichever is the most appropriate. In some schools the same person holds both responsibilities.

- Cases of grooming, sexual exploitation and coercion are matters for the police.

- Report either via your local police service or direct to CEOP with evidence.

- Provide support for the pupil concerned and their family where this is required.

Challenging prejudice

Old prejudices die hard. Young people have always targeted anyone who is weaker or more vulnerable, unless taught other ways to behave. And now they have new tools for communication which even allow anonymity and disappearing messages or photos! This is a gift for those who want to bully, threaten or otherwise intimidate someone else.

Cyberbullying and all forms of online or mobile phone aggression can be directed at someone deemed weaker or more vulnerable for no reason at all other than the perpetrator wanting to look big in front of an audience. But it is common for bullying to be focused on difference. This difference could be because one person likes different types of music or wears different clothing. It can be based on any form of prejudice or stereotypes, but too often it is linked to:

- race, religion or culture

- special needs and disabilities

- sexual orientation

- gender

- aspects of family life such as if a child is in care, or acts as a young carer

- a perceived difference that may or may not be true

- social or economic disadvantage.

It may also be directed at pupils who join the school in mid-year, those who are newly arrived and those who have changed school many times.

But every pupil has the right to be safe and respected. Our laws and our work in schools should ensure this. The Equality Act 2010 puts general and specific duties on schools and public services.

If a coherent whole-school approach is in place it is possible to achieve real progress, as you can see in the discussion on evaluation below.

Be aware of remarks teachers make without thinking

> I heard him say, 'These girls are so bitchy.'
> He doesn't understand.

> My teacher said she hates teaching in a single-sex school.
> You wouldn't go to her with your situation, would you?

Be aware of local gangs and neighbourhood territorial wars

> I was a member of a gang; in a way it was comforting. It was an all-boy gang;
> some would help you if you were in trouble. There were olders and youngers in it.
> They controlled us all by mobiles and told us what to do and where to be.

> Our school is next door to two others, there were loads of hostilities between
> them. People punched at the bus stop for no reason and that. Then they made
> hate pages about us online and posted photos of the fights.'

> I think bullying is getting more dangerous.
> They've got knives now and they threaten me on my mobile.

Personal and professional conduct

A teacher is expected to demonstrate consistently high standards of personal and professional conduct. The following statements define the behaviour and attitudes which set the required standard for conduct throughout a teacher's career.

- Teachers uphold public trust in the profession and maintain high standards of ethics and behaviour, within and outside school, by:

  o treating pupils with dignity, building relationships rooted in mutual respect, and at all times observing proper boundaries appropriate to a teacher's professional position

  o having regard for the need to safeguard pupils' wellbeing, in accordance with statutory provisions

  o showing tolerance of and respect for the rights of others

  o not undermining fundamental British values, including democracy, the rule of law, individual liberty and mutual respect, and tolerance of those with different faiths and beliefs

  o ensuring that personal beliefs are not expressed in ways which exploit pupils' vulnerability or might lead them to break the law.

- Teachers must have proper and professional regard for the ethos, policies and practices of the school in which they teach, and maintain high standards in their own attendance and punctuality.

- Teachers must have an understanding of, and always act within, the statutory frameworks which set out their professional duties and responsibilities.

(DFE-00066-2011 Teachers' Standards. Guidance for School Leaders, School Staff and Governing Bodies. Updated June 2013)

Regularly reinforce the code of conduct and the professional version of your Acceptable Use of ICT Policy. Check whether systems are in place, encryption is being used and data security is in place. Ensure that supply teachers and new staff members are fully aware of your school's policies.

- Set up a route through which staff can ask an ICT manager urgent questions, or call for help in preserving evidence or locking down a computer.

- Consider creating a 'Frequently Asked Questions' guide for staff.

- Include staff training sessions co-delivered by the ICT manager and designated safeguarding lead.

Evaluate often!

Every intervention has a cost in terms of staff input. This includes the time it takes to train staff, agree procedures and implement the first time. There is the communications strategy and effort needed in getting buy-in from young people and parents. Then you will want to monitor how onerous it is for staff to actually fill out the incident forms and how sustainable your systems are. Very often it is more productive to introduce something less complex but flexible and sustainable, rather than start with a huge blitz and then see it fade away. A good test is to consider each incident and think about how effective your policies and systems were in this case. Did they work? Did they actually help you? Do they need a tweak? Do they cater for this type of case? If staff resent the system or it is simply not keeping up with the type of case you encounter, it will not succeed.

Monitoring is essential. Don't leave the data gathering dust on a shelf or in some long-forgotten computer file. There might be messages in your data about what is actually going on each Thursday afternoon in a particular part of your school. You might be able to identify one year group where the trouble is frequently found. Searching the data to check whether any particular groups of people are being singled out for discrimination is essential. By doing this and returning to check a new set of data after implementing any new approach, you will know whether or not your efforts are working.

There is no point in persisting with a strategy that is not working well. That is one of the reasons behind the recommendation to consult staff, parents and pupils when your policies are due for review. Apart from the fact that they will feel that they are consulted and are participating in the school's efforts, this helps 'buy-in' from all parts of the school community and strengthens your strategy. But it is so important to remember that they may contribute a new perspective to your review or tell you something you were not aware of.

Many schools do consult parents and pupils when anti-bullying policies are due for renewal and they report that it contributes to a sense of community and dialogue. Conversely, others retain a 'command and control' approach, fearing that if they consult parents it will bring a 'hornets' nest' of problems. I believe that if there are dissatisfactions brewing, it is far better to know of them early and act to address them than wait for an angry parent to trigger off a serious situation. That is why I think it is useful to consult over Acceptable Use of ICT and E-Safety policies too. 'It is too time-consuming!' you may be thinking. But it can avoid a lot of problems later.

Whatever extra time it takes to consult can be balanced against a reduction in incidents and an improvement in handling incidents once your new improved version is in place.

What does effective practice look like and what impact can we expect to have?

In a recent survey for the BIG Award, over 10,000 students rated how effective their schools were at dealing with all forms of bullying. We compared the effective and ineffective schools: the schools rated as effective were three times more likely to 'get the bullying to stop if it happens'. In the ineffective schools bullying 'remained the same' or 'got worse' for more than half of those young people who had reported it and got 'help'.

So much hinges on a successful resolution of at least most cases. Clumsy interventions are worse than none. Where a case cannot be successfully resolved, all parties have to agree to live side by side and leave one another alone. Some new agreement must be reached – an accommodation of sorts with the involvement of peer mentors and monitoring.

In order to look at the responses from pupil surveys in schools that victimised students rated as effective, I considered the answers from among the over 10,000 respondents. I divided the sample by grouping those who said 'My school deals with bullying very well', and compared them with those who said 'My school does not deal with bullying at all well'. Put aside were those who were neutral. Within these two groups, I selected all those who said they had been bullied 'a lot', so it is their experience we focus on here.

In the effective schools we see that prejudice-driven bullying was less likely:

Effective schools		Ineffective schools
12%	Sexist bullying	30%
14%	Homophobia	35%
29%	Racist bullying	35%
7%	Bullying re: long-term illness	21%

There was evidence of less staff time wasted with endless conflict. But we can see that, with the national discourse focusing heavily on immigration, racist bullying was less amenable to change than other types of prejudice-driven bullying. One year before, racist bullying was down. This might be an illustration of the changing attitudes and public and media discussions.

There were also further reductions and cyberbullying was halved:

I have been bullied 'a lot'	7% vs 29%
I've been bullied in cyberspace	12% vs 24%
I told nobody	15% vs 22%
Rumour-spreading	27% vs 35%

What were the effective schools doing that the ineffective schools were not doing?

Students said that effective schools:

- use peer support schemes

- engage pupils in policy reviews (consult everyone)

- are twice as likely to teach pupils to 'respect people who are different'

- teach pupils to be safe online

- give pupils safe routes to report problems

- are more than three times as likely to get bullying to stop if it occurs.

Ineffective schools were doing less consulting and more telling. They were less likely to train pupils to support each other and were less active on e-safety. They tended to rely heavily on assemblies and lessons – in all the activities beyond these, they were weaker than effective schools. Most markedly of all, the problem was more likely to worsen after a student reported it in these schools.

The teacher handout gives a quick safeguarding checker to help you create an overview of your practice.

Do your procedures tick these boxes?

Children feel safe and are safe. ☐	Children know how to complain or report problems ☐
Adults provide a robust response ☐	Adults recognise indicators that suggest a child is suffering harm ☐
Adults know the procedures ☐	

There is a named safeguarding lead person ☐

Children can identify a trusted adult with whom they can talk about any concerns ☐

Records are written in a timely way ☐	Records are held securely ☐	Records are shared appropriately ☐	Consent is sought to share, where necessary ☐	CP or Safeguarding concerns are promptly shared with LA ☐

Referral records are retained ☐	Referrals are followed up and action taken ☐	Steps to make child safe are taken promptly ☐	Children are supported, protected and informed ☐	Parents are made aware & consent sought unless risk suggests otherwise ☐

A written plan is in place + agreed procedures ☐	Plan identifies help to be given to the child ☐	Plan identifies actions to be taken if further concerns or information emerge ☐

Children are protected and help to keep themselves safe from bullying, homophobic behaviour, racism, sexism and other forms of discrimination. This behaviour is challenged and children supported to treat others with respect ☐

Adults understand risks posed by adults online to bully, groom or abuse children and have well developed strategies in place to support and keep children safe ☐

Leaders oversee the safe use of electronic and social media when children are on site and act immediately if concerned about bullying or risky behaviours. ☐

Governing bodies and proprietors comply with their safeguarding duties. Safe systems are in place re ICT. Training is regularly given to all staff. ☐

Safeguarding related to internet safety, bullying and risky behaviour

What inspectors expect to see

8

The More Serious Cases

In Chapter 7 you will find useful information on handling disclosures, how to challenge prejudice and a discussion on why teenagers find it so hard to report the problems they are having. This is discussed with some ideas on how to make it more likely that they will report and how you can handle these situations.

In this chapter we are looking at incidents or situations where there is some concern that there might be something serious going on.

It begins with procedures. They might seem dull, but it is only through having good records that the case can be assessed or referred, action plans can be developed, next steps taken and evidence saved. Via these records you can also do some periodic monitoring of the types of case being reported, who is mainly reporting cases and note whether there is any pattern of discrimination taking place.

So below is a sample form for taking down a record of an incident. It is so important not to ask leading questions or put words into the mouths of those reporting incidents. Carefully reflect back to the student what you have understood and make sure you have got the facts right.

This is followed by a step-by-step flowchart to offer you a route to take when assessing a situation. It is not the only way of setting out these steps, and I strongly advise each school/college or service to develop their own so that it suits your setting.

Online Safety Incident Form

Name of person reporting the incident/ongoing situation	
Name of staff member recording incident	
Anonymous, via (record method)	
Date of report	
Name of victim/target	

Class/form/age		Year group/house	

Name of perpetrator(s) if known	1)
	2)
	3)

Class/form/age		Year group/house	

Date(s) of incidents	Day	Month		Year	
Approximate time(s)	Before school	am	pm	After school	Weekend

Type of cyberbullying or other incident (please tick all that apply)

Via mobile phone		Involves Internet	
Involves chat room/s		Involves social media	
Other			
Involves photographs**		Friendship feud?	
Persistent teasing/sarcastic remarks		Demanding money/valuables	
Name-calling		Ridicule/humiliation	
Threats		Coercion	
Spreading rumours		Encouraging others to join in	
Unpleasant/hurtful email/texts/web posts combined		Provocative/sexist taunts	
Plans to isolate someone		Linked to bullying in school?	
Is a student self-harming?		Other causes for concern about wellbeing of student?	
Is there a concern about anorexia?		Is there a concern about suicidal thoughts?	

Other. *Please explain if you have concerns that might involve child sexual exploitation or other high-risk scenarios such as radicalisation.*

Cyber-aggression

Racist*		Cyberbullying associated with offline bullying in school	
Homophobic		Due to disability	
Sexual		Student is in care	

If racist, report it to your local authority if they are collecting this information.

How long has this being going on?	
Has any intervention been tried?	
If abusive, illegal, hate speech or involving explicit material, has this been reported to the service provider or website?	
**Does this case require the Serious Incident Protocol to be activated? Has the CEOP report abuse button been used?	
Do the police need to be informed?	
Does another agency need to be brought in? For example, mental health professionals	
Does a device need to be confiscated or a computer isolated as evidence?	
Does material need to be taken down?	
Have parents been alerted?	
Who has taken responsibility for the above steps?	

**If you have triggered the Serious Incident Protocol, that will take precedence over anything in this document. Report it to your designated Child Protection or Safeguarding lead person.*

If you are not sure what steps to take, talk to your e-safety lead in school or within the local authority. The school has the powers to search and confiscate a phone. (EIA 2006)

Follow-up	
Has the cyberbullying or abusive behaviour stopped? Does the student (target) feel safe?	
Is further action required?	
If the perpetrators are in your school: have those involved changed their behaviour/acknowledged the harm caused?	
Have the target's privacy settings been checked, passwords changed and friends' list been cleaned?	
Has the case contributed to the learning of the class/year group in some way?	
Any further recommendations or next steps?	

Signed.. Date ....

Further notes, such as the impact of this incident or recommendations

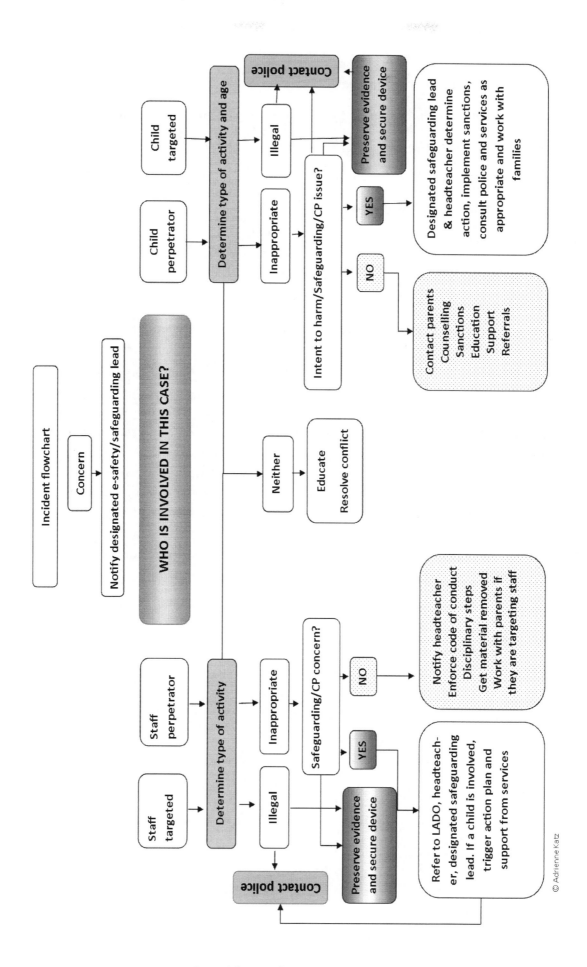

Incident flowchart

Concern

Notify designated e-safety/safeguarding lead

WHO IS INVOLVED IN THIS CASE?

Child perpetrator / Child targeted → Determine type of activity and age

Inappropriate → Intent to harm/Safeguarding/CP issue?

Illegal → Contact police

Preserve evidence and secure device

YES → Designated safeguarding lead & headteacher determine action, implement sanctions, consult police and services as appropriate and work with families

NO → Contact parents / Counselling / Sanctions / Education / Support / Referrals

Neither → Educate / Resolve conflict

Staff perpetrator / Staff targeted → Determine type of activity

Inappropriate / Illegal → Safeguarding/CP concern?

Illegal → Contact police

Preserve evidence and secure device

NO → Notify headteacher / Enforce code of conduct / Disciplinary steps / Get material removed / Work with parents if they are targeting staff

YES → Refer to LADO, headteacher, designated safeguarding lead. If a child is involved, trigger action plan and support from services

© Adrienne Katz

How to act: Is it illegal activity?

Illegal means something against the law, such as:

- downloading child pornography

- passing onto others images or video containing child pornography

- possessing explicit images of children

- inciting racial or religious hatred

- extreme cases of cyberbullying

- promoting illegal acts

- malicious communications

- threats of violence and rape.

You are also likely to come across cases where there was no intent to harm but nevertheless the images could be misused in the wrong hands or they are humiliating or hurtful. They may be of young siblings in the bathtub and were taken with no harmful motive, but they are questionable if shared.

However, if any adult is acting with intent to harm and is involved with images of children under 18 that are explicit, you will need to escalate the case immediately to the highest level of action.

Teachers themselves have recently reported very abusive behaviour towards them by parents involving rape threats and other malicious communications. These are a matter for the police. In your role as a teacher you will of course be protecting children and will always be alert for any suspicious activity involving images of young children. To help when deciding to escalate a case, the following flowchart is offered. You can adapt this according to your setting.

Images: Does the incident involve illegal activity?

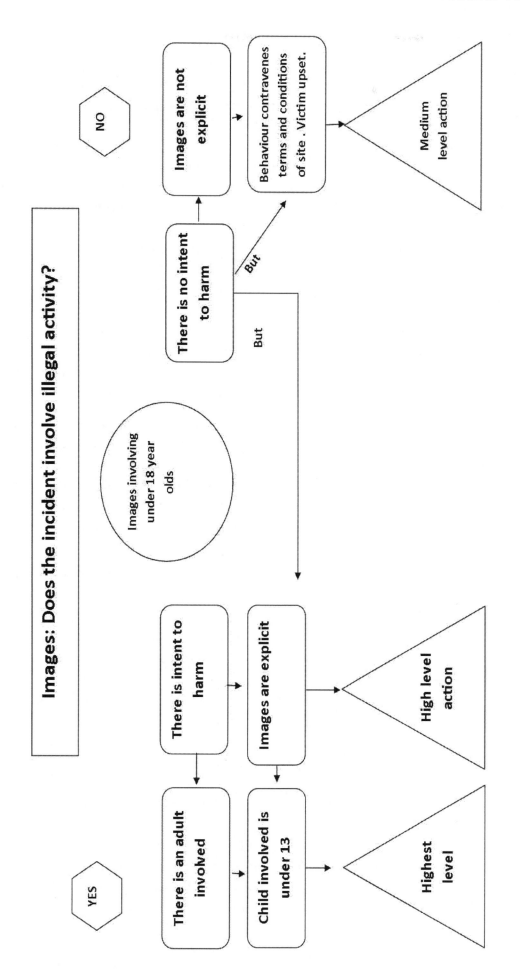

NO

Images are not explicit → Behaviour contravenes terms and conditions of site. Victim upset. → Medium level action

There is no intent to harm

But

But

Images involving under 18 year olds

YES

There is intent to harm → Images are explicit → High level action

There is an adult involved → Child involved is under 13 → Highest level

Keep up-to-date with trends in child protection

There appear to be changing patterns of abuser behaviour. The ease with which offenders can find and 'harvest' images of children and young people online could have led to a drop in physical contact. Peter Davies, chief executive at CEOP, said: 'For a growing proportion of grooming cases reported to us, online abuse is an end in itself.'

The number of children targeted online by sex offenders with a view to meeting them in person fell last year, according to a report by the University of Birmingham and the Child Exploitation and Online Protection Centre. (It is easier to manipulate, threaten and blackmail a young person into sending images than it is to groom someone for six months and then try to get them to meet up.)

The report also suggests, in line with other research, that some children are more at risk from online abuse than others. Factors such as parental or carer involvement in a child's online life, as well as personal issues such as low self-esteem, loneliness or confusion about their sexuality, can all play a crucial role in a child's online protection.

A role for parents was clearly identified: 'Children whose Internet activities are monitored and who have an open dialogue with their parents about what they do or see online are better protected from offenders and more resilient to the techniques they use.'

The behaviour patterns of the teenagers played a role:

Adolescents who take risks online by having sexualised chats or exchanging sexual images are particularly prone to the increasingly sophisticated and coercive tactics of online predators.

Children may be targeted because of their vulnerability, but any child can be a victim. What is apparent is that parents and carers can make that vital difference whether or not a child becomes a victim of these ruthless predators online.

The rise in smartphone usage raised particular concern, with six out of ten 12–15-year-olds now owning one – an increase of 21 per cent in the last year (the report was published in 2013).

But built-in cameras and a new generation of messaging apps are giving children the ability to easily communicate and share images with strangers online.

The study found that instant messaging was used to make contact with children in around one third of reports of inappropriate sexual contact and that more than two thirds of parents of 12–15-year-olds with a phone that can be used to go online do not have parental controls or 'filters'.[81]

Different concerns could be current at any one time. For example, as I write, the major issues at the top of the current agenda involve protecting children from child sexual exploitation and from being radicalised or recruited via social media on behalf of Islamic extremist groups to go to Syria. New issues may come to the fore at any time and it is vital to remain well informed and refresh training regularly. But there is a danger in focusing on one type of risk to the detriment of others. The gaze might be so focused in one direction that it is possible to overlook other serious problems. For example, numerically there may be more young people visiting sites that encourage suicide and self-harm than the number who are sexually exploited via the Internet. There are certainly more who are desperately miserable because of cyberbullying; and to overlook this is a mistake, because those are often the very people who are vulnerable to other online risks and grooming as they seek love and validation through online contact.

Preparation: Before delivering an e-safety session on child sexual exploitation

- Are you familiar with your school's Safeguarding Policy?

- Is the designated person for safeguarding aware that you are planning to deliver this lesson?

- Are you working in line with your school/college policy for delivering SRE?

- Are you familiar with the legal background?

- Have you checked that there is no current case of which you are aware within this class that is similar to the scenarios in a film you plan to show?

- Have you planned to set some 'contract' agreement or ground rules with the group before you start? These could include the following:

  o What is said in the room stays in the room. The only exception is if there is a risk to a child's safety, or disclosure of a criminal act, in which case the facilitator will report this.

  o Choose your words carefully. Use language that will not offend or upset anyone. When you give an opinion, try to explain your reasons. Listen to the views of others, and show respect.

  o Don't put anyone on the spot. If you disagree, comment on what was said, not the person who said it.

  o If you're worried about something that has happened to you or a friend, don't share it with the whole group, but do make sure you talk to [*session leader*] at the end of the session.

  o If you feel upset or anxious at any point, raise your hand at any time and ask for 'time out'.

Managing disclosure

- Have the school/college serious incident protocol accessible.

- Make the young person feel safe and guide them to a private space.

- Set this up so that you are sitting not too far apart, nor too close, and slightly at an angle rather than opposite or across a desk.

- Thank them for coming forward.

- Employ effective listening techniques.

- Confirm you have understood what the student has told you.

- Do not put words into their mouth or ask leading questions.

- Make evidence safe.

- Take a device out of use if necessary.
- Discuss confidentiality with them, explaining that you do have to report it if you believe they or anyone else is in danger.

Further advice on best practice for managing disclosure is available from the NSPCC (www. nspcc.org.uk) and the Safe Network (www.safenetwork.org.uk).

Develop and follow a serious incident flowchart like the one earlier in the chapter.

Definition of child sexual abuse

Online child sexual abuse is the use of technology to manipulate, coerce or intimidate a child to engage in sexual activity that is abusive and/or degrading in nature. Online child sexual abuse is characterised by an imbalance of power and lack of choice resulting from physical, emotional and/or social vulnerabilities.

As with other forms of sexual abuse, online abuse can be misunderstood by the child and others as being consensual – it might seem to the child that they are singled out as a favourite and must reciprocate. Bear in mind that no child or young person below the age of 18 can consent to being abused or exploited.

Behaviour may take place without the child's immediate recognition or understanding of abusive or exploitative conduct; this does not indicate consent. The NSPCC definition of online child sexual abuse is:

> Online child sexual abuse includes, but is not limited to, the grooming of children for sexual purposes, including sexual acts online, and the production, distribution or possession of indecent images of children. Online child sexual abuse takes different forms and can lead to or be preceded by contact abuse. Financial gain can be a feature of online child sexual abuse and it can involve serious organised crime.[82]

Electronic self-harm

Is it possible that some online behaviour is actually a form of self-harm?

We ask this question because of the tragic case of Hannah Smith in 2013, in which the police found that several of the 'bullying' posts appeared to come from her IP address. Of course it is possible that someone else using that IP address posted these, but this case triggered much reflection and discussion. Some experts suggest that there is some online behaviour that can be seen as a form of compulsive self-harm.

A study carried out by the Massachusetts Aggression Reduction Center (MARC) discovered that, out of 617 young people that were interviewed, 9 per cent had actually 'cyber-bullied themselves' online.[83]

It seems that a very few young people might send awful messages to themselves. This is thought to be a form of self-trolling that might be intended to reinforce their view of themselves as 'unworthy' or to strengthen self-hatred. On the other hand it may be to provoke others into being sympathetic.

Some troubled young people will deliberately ask provocative questions such as 'How do I look?' that repeatedly prompt replies with abusive remarks. This in some sense is thought to justify their low self-worth. A young person may return again and again to the site where this happens, repeating the experience rather than simply shutting down that account and moving away from a forum.

Another pattern that has been reported is that they may set up several different profiles and send multiple abusive messages to themselves saying 'You are a slag', 'You don't deserve to live', and so on.

Self-harm can be a coping mechanism to distract from emotional pain. Like cutting one's body, the immediate pain is some form of release from the other, bigger pain.

'Cyberpain' is said to possibly replace or provide release from other emotional pain in a similar way. This type of behaviour, which may be noticed first as 'cyberbullying', should be treated with extreme sensitivity and I recommend contacting professionals at once. It can be very hard for a young person to seek help, so staff should be alert to this possibility and provide non-judgemental support before working to help the young person develop more positive feelings.

This is a high-risk situation and every effort should be made to reduce the chance of escalation. If their computer or phone is examined by police, it might be evident that they are visiting websites that encourage suicide.

Further reading

For further information about self-harm, here are some references:

- Step Up! International at http://stepup-international.co.uk has support for professionals and parents to help deal with this issue.
- Steve Gresty (July 2014) *Cyber Self-harm – Methods and Motives*: www.e-safetysupport.com/stories/131/cyber-self-harm-methods-and-motives#.U-OGVfldVHU.
- Alexandra Topping (2014) *Self-harm Sites and Cyberbullying: The Threat to Children from Web's Dark Side*: www.theguardian.com/society/2014/mar/10/self-harm-sites-cyberbullying-suicide-web.
- BBC News (12 February 2014) *Cyberbullying Suicide: Italy Shocked by Amnesia Ask.fm Case*: www.bbc.co.uk/news/world-europe-26151425.
- Fisher, H.L., Moffitt, T.E., Houts, R.M., Belsky, D.W., Arseneault, L., and Caspi, A. (2012) 'Bullying victimisation and risk of self harm in early adolescence: longitudinal cohort study.' *BMJ 344*, e2683.

The complexity of these cases suggests that professional help should be sought as early as possible and multi-agency work might be needed.

A study in the *British Medical Journal* found that:

Compared with bullied children who did not self-harm, bullied children who self-harmed were distinguished by a family history of attempted/completed suicide, concurrent mental health problems, and a history of physical maltreatment by an adult.[84]

Among the conclusions of this study, the researchers suggested the following:

Conclusions. Prevention of non-suicidal self-injury in young adolescents should focus on helping bullied children to cope more appropriately with their distress. Programmes should target children who have additional mental health problems, have a family history of attempted/completed suicide, or have been maltreated by an adult.[85]

Other factors in their lives

We learned that those students who were involved in sexting also reported high levels of online risky or needy behaviour and they were more likely to have also experienced abusive aggressive actions from other people towards them. We learned that young people in care and those who are young carers were disproportionately more likely to be in this group and we also found that people who needed help with English were likely to need greater help. Those who have mental health difficulties were at very high risk, often visiting websites urging people to take their lives or harm themselves.

We would all wish to help a young person before things developed into a serious situation if we could – but how does one do so without asking intrusive or personal questions? There are opportunities when a student reports a problem that may be on a lesser scale such as being hacked or cyberbullied – then you can explore their wider online experiences and consider the factors in the table om p. 250 to get a bigger picture and assess their situation. They may decide to trust you with the true picture once you offer help with their e-safety.

Based on the responses of young people who are already involved in sexting,[86] the table shows common aspects of their lives which came up disproportionately in their answers compared with their peers who were not involved in sexting. To create a picture of the whole person and to provide appropriate support, this tool may help you to decide to take steps at an early preventative stage. It may also help you to identify a young person who could be at risk of serious harm via sexting, because they have come to you with another problem which is perhaps easier to report. You may be able to prevent them drifting into this high-risk behaviour.

Look at the whole person

In the table we can see the responses of young people aged 10–16 who are involved in sexting. Here is a portrait of their experiences on a number of fronts as well as their personal circumstances and home situation. We can see how they are targeted online in so many ways – they report aggression and racism or homophobia directed at them, but they also tend to visit sites encouraging illegal or high-risk behaviour. They visit pro-anorexia and self-harm sites 'often' and they are more likely to have had their personal details hacked, bought fake goods, been tricked into buying goods they did not want, and more. Here we see that 68 per cent of those involved in sexting also report being cyberbullied. They might well come forward for this reason, giving you an opportunity to assess their situation more broadly. How many 'friends' do they have in their friends list? Have they ever had their SNS page hacked or altered? Begin with mild and non-intrusive questions.

It helps not to be blinkered when assessing the situation of a student who is reporting these types of incident. Don't look at the one incident in isolation. If their lives are considered in a more holistic way, it is possible to work to make changes in their online lives before they get into a more serious 'drama', to use their own description.

Screening tool for secondary schools – online high risk behaviours

Young people may at first present with a 'problem' that is not at first glance extremely serious in terms of safeguarding. They may tell you they are being cyberbullied or that their social media page has been hacked. It may seem that this can be solved within school between students. It may not be the whole story. Our research has flagged up the issues below because they happened more frequently and disproportionately to certain young people who turned out to be extremely vulnerable online, or were involved with sharing explicit images, being severely pressured or coerced or blackmailed and several other situations that led to concern. If someone you know to be vulnerable in other ways tells you that they are experiencing the types of behaviour listed in the table, then it is useful to be able to ask some further non-intrusive questions that may elicit a clearer picture of their online life. If you are able to help with the presenting issues, trust may be built up so that you are able to ensure that other more private parts of their online life are conducted safely. The young person may disclose other worries. You may even head off risky behaviour before it happens. But above all we all have a safeguarding duty. The steps below are intended to alert you when there is a case that needs further support or escalation immediately, even though it was not clear from the description of the problem the young person first gave.

Following this table which illustrates some evidence for our designation of these groups of young people as 'vulnerable', you will find a suggested screening tool. By asking questions in these different domains it is possible to build a bigger picture of the young person's safety and respond appropriately. In some categories you may already know enough about your student, such as the home circumstances of the student for example or whether there is a mental health concern, so there is no need to ask this again.

The groups found to be most vulnerable are: Young carers, those in care or leaving care, those who need help with English, those with SEN, those with mental health difficulties, young people involved in sexting and those who are cyberbullied.

Please always use your own judgement rather than any scale suggested here as a guide.

Vulnerable groups and their online lives.

Support is needed across a range of online activities and experiences. All were cyberbullied considerably more than their peers with no difficulties.

BOLD: This group is markedly more likely than peers to experience this.

The presence of several factors combine to produce high risk

It is essential to consider many facets of a young person's online life. Any one factor could be the presenting problem.

	I am a carer	I am in or leaving care	I have a longstanding illness	I have learning difficulties	I need help with English	I have special educational needs	I have mental health difficulties	I have none of these difficulties	Young people involved in sexting
	64 people	61 people	64 people	170 people	224 people	91 people	156 people	1658	113
I often visit gambling sites	17%	18%	17%	16%	18%	13%	18%	5%	
I often visit pages meant for adults	28%	31%	27%	22%	20%	21%	23%	9%	
I have had my social media account hacked	36%	38%	25%	21%	21%	21%	35%	15%	
I often try to get round blocks/filters	19%	23%	17%	18%	14%	15%	20%	7%	
I have had personal details hacked/ stolen	22%	30%	19%	12%	15%	16%	17%	4%	
I have had credit card details stolen	14%	8% *	8% *	5%	4%	8%	6%	1%	
I've been tricked into paying for items I did not want	22%	25%	22%	12%	12%	13%	15%	3%	
I've been tricked into buying fake goods	14%	16%	11%	8%	8%	10%	10%	3%	
I've experienced online aggression including racism and homophobia	34%	36%	27%	19%	20%	24%	44%	17%	
I often visit websites urging you to be very thin	33%	39%	36%	24%	28%	24%	44%	17%	
I often visit websites encouraging self-harm or suicide	31%	36%	31%	23%	28%	26%	44%	17%	
I often encounter very violent images or videos I did not want to see	37%	30%	25%	25%	25%	24%	35%	16%	
I often see websites promoting hatred or racist views	20%	20%	30%	18%	17%	18%	26%	10%	
I have often seen websites giving advice that is dangerous	34%	26%	22%	28%	19%	26%	27%	13%	
I often use chatrooms and forums	33%	43%	33%	36%	25%	22%	29%	18%	
I often see websites trying to sell you stuff that might be illegal	36%	25%	25%	30%	21%	30%	24%	12%	
Sexting: it happened to me	13%	11%	6% *	8%	10%	9%	14%	3%	
I have been cyberbullied	58%	48%	39%	36%	33%	32%	47%	25%	
I spend more than 5 hrs a day online	50%	41%	45%	38%	38%	35%	54%	27%	
I post about what I am doing	36%	43%	30%	24%	29%	30%	37%	28%	
I post photos	52%	52%	42%	37%	40%	38%	51%	44%	

Assessing risk in young people's online lives. Intensive support required.

NB Scoring is a suggestion only. Please do not ignore your own concerns or judgements. The accumulation of evidence may lead you to trigger support or escalate a case. This is a guide to what you might ask about when assessing a situation. Support is needed across all aspects.

Presenting problem/incident involves:		Duration		Specific group		Social situation		Emotional health and wellbeing		Online life	
'Sexting' problem has developed Involves a young person 10 involves adult 12	10	Multiple times	8	Young carers	7	Homeless or unaccompanied arrival	7	Suicidal or attempts made	10	Further blackmail or pressure to post or share images/videos	10
Credit card details stolen	10	Recent	5	LAC	7	Known to services	10	Severe paranoia	10	Stolen card used	10
SNS page hacked	7	3+ months	8	SEN	7	Insecure or inadequate	7	Hallucinations/voices	10	Online 5 + hrs a day	7
Humiliating photo mis-used	7	Recurring at intervals	5	Home difficulties	7	Parental neglect	10	Extreme weight loss	10	Gaming: meeting players in real life	10
Cyberbullied	7	Last three weeks	5	Requires help with English or poor communication skills	5	Poor attendance	7	Self-harm	10	(Flashy) phone provided by someone unexpected, i.e. 'boyfriend'	7
Rumours circulated about me	4	More than one year	10	Gay or questioning	7	At risk of exclusion	7	Bouts of depression	7	Visits pro- anorexia websites	10
Homophobic bullying	7	Had stopped but begun again	5	Age below 13	7	At risk of suspension	7	Anxiety	7	Friends or followers exceed 500	5
Relational aggression/friendship issue	4	A while ago	4	Age 13-16	5	Parent/carer unemployed	4	Sleep problems	4	Active in chat rooms	5
Other prejudice-driven behaviour/racism/disablism	7	Just started	5	Learning difficulties	7	Online life unsupervised; no filter in place	5	Cannot concentrate	4	Using dating apps adults use	7
Extortion/blackmail	10	Happens sometimes	4	Minority ethnic group	5	New to the school	4	Low self-esteem	7	Visits pro-self-harm or suicide-encouraging websites	10

	Risk = 1 (4 and under)	Risk = 2 (5–7 YELLOW)	Risk = 3 (7–10 AMBER)	Risk = 4 (10+ RED)
Presenting incident/ issue	4 and under, e.g. friendship issue. Risk = 1. Monitor regularly and support. Update e-safety advice. Use peer mentors. Alert carers and other teachers. Check filter on phone is on.	5–7 YELLOW. Risk = 2. Intervene, support and re-visit e-safety basics, do a follow-up check. Monitor. Explore other factors outlined here. Filter on phone? Alert Safeguarding officer.	7–10 AMBER. Risk = 3. Involve other agencies, teach e-safety intensely, preserve evidence, provide targeted support. Action Safeguarding Policy.	10+ RED. Risk = 4. Involve local authority social care. Intensive support and e-safety 'service'. May be a matter for police. Use Child Protection Policy. Urgent action may be required. Preserve evidence. CAF likely.
Duration	4 and under, e.g. happened once or twice. Risk = 1. Monitor regularly and support. Update e-safety advice. Use peer mentors. Alert carers and other teachers. Check filter on phone is on.	5–7 YELLOW. Risk = 2. Intervene, support and re-visit e-safety basics, do a follow-up check. Monitor. Explore other possibilities outlined here. Alert Safeguarding officer.	7–10 AMBER. Risk = 3. Involve other agencies, teach e-safety intensely, preserve evidence, provide targeted support. Action Safeguarding Policy.	10+ RED. Risk = 4. Involve local authority social care. Intensive support and e-safety 'service'. May be a matter for police. Use Child Protection Policy. Urgent action may be required. Preserve evidence.
Specific group	4 and under, e.g. simply belonging to a particular group does not imply risk itself. Risk = 1. Monitor regularly and support. Update e-safety advice. Use peer mentors. Alert carers and other teachers. Check filter on phone is on.	5–7 YELLOW. Risk = 2. Intervene, support and re-visit e-safety basics, do a follow-up check. Monitor. Explore other possibilities outlined here. Alert Safeguarding officer.	7–10 AMBER. Risk = 3. Involve other agencies, teach e-safety intensely, preserve evidence, provide targeted support. Action Safeguarding Policy.	10+ RED. Risk = 4. Involve local authority social care. Intensive support and e-safety 'service'. May be a matter for police. Use Child Protection Policy. Urgent action may be required. Preserve evidence. Consider Equality Act 2010.
Social situation	4 and under, e.g. sudden change in social situation. Risk = 1. Monitor regularly and support. Update e-safety advice. Use peer mentors. Alert carers and other teachers. Check filter on phone is on.	5–7 YELLOW. Risk = 2. Intervene, support and re-visit e-safety basics, do a follow-up check. Monitor. Explore other possibilities outlined here. Alert Safeguarding officer.	7–10 AMBER. Risk = 3. Involve other agencies, teach e-safety intensely, preserve evidence, provide targeted support. Action Safeguarding Policy.	10+ RED. Risk = 4. Involve local authority social care. Intensive support and e-safety 'service'. Preserve evidence. May be a matter for police. Use Child Protection Policy. CAF likely. Temporary foster care or other arrangements may be needed.
Emotional health	4 and under, e.g. seems unhappy. Risk = 1. Monitor regularly and support. Update e-safety advice. Use peer mentors. Alert carers and other teachers. Check filter on phone is on.	5–7 YELLOW. Risk = 2. Intervene, support and re-visit e-safety basics, do a follow-up check. Monitor. Explore other possibilities outlined here. Alert Safeguarding officer.	7–10 AMBER. Risk = 3. Involve other agencies, teach e-safety intensely, preserve evidence, provide targeted support. Action Safeguarding Policy.	10+ RED. Risk = 4. Involve local authority social care. Intensive support and e-safety 'service'. May be a matter for police. Use Child Protection Policy. Respond to professional advice. Collaborate with agencies and professionals. CAF likely.
Online life	4 and under, e.g. risk taker. Risk = 1. Monitor regularly and support. Update e-safety advice. Alert carers and other teachers. Teach how to save evidence and keep a diary. Check filter on phone is on.	5–7 YELLOW. Risk = 2. Intervene, support and re-visit e-safety basics, do a follow-up check. Monitor. Explore other possible behaviours outlined here. Alert Safeguarding officer.	7–10 AMBER. Risk = 3. Involve other agencies, teach e-safety intensely, preserve evidence, provide targeted support. Action Safeguarding Policy.	10+ RED. Risk = 4. Involve local authority social care. Intensive support and e-safety advice. May be a matter for police. Use Child Protection Policy. Record all actions taken. Preserve evidence. Respond to professional advice. ICT manager to assist. CAF likely.

Look beyond the immediate facts
Case of two 12-year-olds and adult manipulation

Two 12-year-olds were an 'item' for a few weeks. During this time the boy persuaded the girl to share a revealing intimate image with him. Nothing happened immediately after this. For six months there were no repercussions, although their relationship had ended. The image remained on the boy's phone.

After six months the boy showed a friend this image. The friend then dared him to share it among a group of their friends. He took up the dare and in one click the image was shared among a group of pupils in the school. It soon became known to the girl and her parents as students sniggered and whispered about it and the parents alerted the school.

The school was working with all the pupils involved and their families. The parents of the girl decided they would like to go to the police and informed the school of their decision. The police took possession of the boy's mobile phone which had already been confiscated by the school. Upon searching this phone, it was found that the initiator of the idea to ask the girl for a photo was an adult relative of the boy. This of course escalated the case into an entirely different category.

Discussion

- What are the issues here? How does this discovery change the way the case is now categorised?

- Is there a risk the involvement of the adult might never have been discovered?

- How could you avoid that happening in any future case?

- What should happen now? How would you work with all the recipients of this image?

- What is the position in law of the boy who dared his friend to share the image?

- What is the position in law of the boy who possessed and shared the image?

- What is the position in law of the friends who received this unsolicited image? What should they have done upon receiving it? What should they be sure to do now?

- If the police wish to interview all the boys in the friendship group, what procedures would you put in place when you call them in for this interview?

- Are there some pupils you might treat differently from others and, if so, why?

- What message would you send to all parents of pupils in your school as a result of this case?

- If you were reviewing your school's procedures as a result of a case like this, are there changes you feel are or might be necessary?

- Considering your Safeguarding Policy and practice, your Acceptable Use of ICT Policy and your e-safety education curriculum, how well have they served you in this case and do you need to adjust, change or rewrite them?

What is the Prevent strategy?

Prevent is one part of the government's CONTEST strategy which aims to target the threat of terrorism and extremism. The programme is focused on non-criminal activity, and is intended to 'safeguard vulnerable people from being exploited by violent and extreme ideologies'.

At the same time, the government has been promoting the concept of 'fundamental British values' and this is to be incorporated into school inspections. There is some controversy over the definition of these values and indeed over the success of this programme itself. Many countries will be struggling to find effective ways of presenting a counter-ideology to the threat of terrorism and extremism and it is likely that this will be a debate for some time.

The Prevent strategy:

- responds to the ideological challenge we face from terrorism and aspects of extremism, and the threat we face from those who promote these views

- provides practical help to prevent people from being drawn into terrorism and ensure they are given appropriate advice and support

- works with a wide range of sectors (including education, criminal justice, faith, charities, online and health) where there are risks of radicalisation that we need to deal with.[87]

The strategy covers all forms of terrorism. This can include both far right extremism and some aspects of non-violent extremism. The fact is that the Internet is being used to engage, persuade and recruit young people. Messages frequently glorify violence and promote extreme views. Some young people cannot detect the bias in certain messages, while others are susceptible to these messages and can become excited or shocked by images of extreme violence.

The Home Office works on this initiative with the police, local authorities, a wide range of government departments, and community organisations. The programme can support community-based campaigns which attempt to rebut propaganda and offer 'alternative views' to target audiences.

At the time of writing there is tremendous concern about the way in which many young people, often academically successful and apparently happy, are lured into secretly travelling to Syria to join IS. The role of social media and online communications is considered crucial in cases of this kind.

British citizens who have made this choice are often used to recruit others, and the online conversations that are taking place between recruiters and local young people appear to be well concealed from families and schools.

Where people are identified as being at risk of being drawn into terrorism activity, the Channel process, which aims to provide support to such individuals, can involve multi-agency work to provide support and alternative activities.[88]

- If you have a concern about a child in relation to extremism and the support options of the Prevent strategy are not available locally, your Local Safeguarding Children Board (LSCB) police representative will be able to discuss support options.

- To report suspected online terrorist content go to www.gov.uk/report-terrorism.

- You can also refer content of concern directly to social media platforms to have accounts blocked or material taken down.

Advice to LSCBs on radicalisation is available from the UK Safer Internet Centre: www. saferInternet.org.uk/Content/Childnet/SafterInternetCentre/downloads/Online_ Safety_-_LSCB_bulletin_-_Radicalisation.pdf.

9

Inspection and Self-review

What are the e-safety goals?

E-safety is concerned with ensuring that students use electronic resources safely and legally. The aims are to:

- protect and educate pupils and staff in their use of technology

- have appropriate mechanisms to intervene and support any incident where appropriate

- help students understand and manage risk

- train staff to improve their knowledge and expertise in the safe and appropriate use of technology.

E-safety encompasses a wide array of concepts and issues, including:

1. **Copyright awareness**

   Many students and staff show little consideration for intellectual property and ownership.

   This includes film, music or images. Many will happily download music without thinking of the need of the musician to sell it. More than a third of young people aged 10–16 said they download films and music without having to pay for it. Eighty-seven per cent watch films and TV online.

   Creative Commons is a non-profit organisation that enables the sharing and use of creativity and knowledge through free legal tools. Its website (http://creativecommons.org/about) contains information and detailed examples to explain the different Creative Commons copyright licences that content owners can apply to their digital creations.

2. **Cyberbullying**

   o   bullying using technology including computers and mobile phones

   o   identity theft

   o   hijacking control of social network profile pages or accounts in games o misuse or malicious sharing of images.

3. **Privacy**

  o disclosure of personal information

  o digital footprint

  o online reputation

  o safe social networking and digital communication.

4. **Risks of harm for children and young people**

  o inappropriate content

  o online pornography

  o ignoring age ratings in games

  o exposure to violence

  o racist language

  o pro-anorexia websites

  o self-harm websites

  o suicide websites

  o hate sites

  o content validation (making sure that the content is accurate and authentic)

  o the risk of being persuaded to adopt a belief or cause that is dangerous.

E-safety within the Ofsted School Inspection Framework

A new inspection programme launched in 2015 will use a Common Inspection Framework to inspect different phases of education. Non-association independent schools will now be brought under this umbrella too, alongside maintained schools and academies and further education and skills colleges.

Inspectors will make judgements on the following four areas:

- effectiveness of leadership and management
- teaching learning and assessment
- personal development, behaviour and welfare
- outcomes for children and learners.

The three main documents issued in Summer 2015 are the following:

1. *The Common Inspection Framework*: education, skills and early years.

2. *Inspecting Safeguarding in Early Years Education and Skills Settings*, June 2015.

3. *School Inspection Handbook*, Section 8.

Since September 2015, Ofsted inspects good schools and further education and skills providers once every three years under a new short inspection model and a new Common Inspection Framework.

Inspectors will start from a premise that the school or provider is still good and focus on ensuring that those standards are being maintained. They will check that leaders have identified key areas of concern and that they have the capacity to address them. They will make judgements on whether the school remains good and the safeguarding is effective.

But safeguarding has, if anything, a stronger focus than before, being described as 'central to every inspection'.[89]

Inspectors will always make a written judgement in the section on leadership and management about the effectiveness of the arrangements for safeguarding pupils.

Short inspections of good schools will *always* report on the effectiveness of safeguarding. If safeguarding is not effective, HMI will always convert the short inspection to a fuller Section 5 inspection.

Safeguarding

In relation to children and young people, safeguarding and promoting their welfare is defined in *Working Together to Safeguard Children* (March 2015) as:

- protecting children from maltreatment

- preventing impairment of children's health or development

- ensuring that children are growing up in circumstances consistent with the provision of safe and effective care – taking action to enable all children have the best outcomes.

The definition of safeguarding in *Working Together to Safeguard Children* refers clearly to online safety (paras 10 and 11). Safeguarding action may be needed to protect children and learners from:

- bullying, including online bullying and prejudice-based bullying

- the impact of new technologies on sexual behaviour, for example sexting.

Safeguarding is seen as not just about protecting children, learners and vulnerable adults from deliberate harm, neglect and failure to act. It relates to broader aspects of care and education, including online safety and associated issues. The term 'online safety' reflects a widening range of issues associated with technology and a user's access to content, contact with others and behavioural issues.

The signs of successful safeguarding arrangements

In settings that have effective safeguarding arrangements, there will be evidence of the following:

- Adults understand the risks posed by those who use technology, including the Internet, to bully, groom, radicalise or abuse children or learners. They have well-developed strategies in place to keep children and learners safe and to support them to develop their own understanding of these risks and in learning how to keep themselves and others safe.

- Leaders oversee the safe use of technology when children and learners are in their care and take action immediately if they are concerned about bullying or children's wellbeing. Leaders of early years settings implement the required policies with regard to the safe use of mobile phones and cameras in settings.

Inspecting how effectively leaders and governors create a safeguarding culture in the setting

Inspectors will want to consider evidence that:

- staff, leaders and managers understand the risks posed by adults or young people who use the Internet to bully, groom or abuse children, young people and vulnerable adults

- there are well-developed strategies in place to keep learners safe

- staff, leaders and managers oversee the safe use of electronic and social media by staff and learners and take action immediately if they are concerned about bullying or risky behaviours.

Inspectors will make a judgement on the personal development, behaviour and welfare of children and learners by evaluating, where applicable, the extent to which the provision is successfully promoting and supporting children's and learners' safety.

Arriving at judgements about safeguarding arrangements

In order to make this judgement, inspectors will consider, among other things, the extent to which children and learners understand how to keep themselves safe from relevant risks such as exploitation and extremism, including when using the Internet and social media.

Inspectors are instructed to include online safety in their discussions with pupils and learners (covering topics such as online bullying and safe use of the Internet and social media).

Inspectors will also investigate what the school or FE provider does to educate pupils in online safety and how the provider or school deals with issues when they arise.

Bullying intervention will be inspected under the new heading 'Personal Development Behaviour and Welfare'. Inspectors will ask students about bullying in school and outside it.

When reporting on personal development, welfare and behaviour, inspectors must make a clear written judgement about behaviour and a separate clear written judgement about personal development and welfare. Where the judgements differ, the lower of the two will determine the overall judgement for personal development, behaviour and welfare and is recorded in the report.

For the institution to be judged outstanding, inspectors will need to find the following:

- Pupils work hard with the school to prevent all forms of bullying, including online bullying and prejudice-based bullying.

- Staff and pupils deal effectively with the very rare instances of bullying behaviour and/or use of derogatory or aggressive language.

- The school's open culture actively promotes all aspects of pupils' welfare. Pupils are safe and feel safe at all times. They understand how to keep themselves and others safe in different situations and settings. They trust leaders to take rapid and appropriate action to resolve any concerns they have.

- Pupils can explain accurately and confidently how to keep themselves healthy. They make informed choices about healthy eating, fitness and their emotional and mental wellbeing. They have an age-appropriate understanding of healthy relationships and are confident in staying safe from abuse and exploitation.

- Pupils have an excellent understanding of how to stay safe online, the dangers of inappropriate use of mobile technology and social networking sites.

An institution will be judged inadequate when the following occurs:

- Incidents of bullying or prejudiced and discriminatory behaviour, both direct and indirect, are frequent. Pupils have little confidence in the school's ability to tackle bullying successfully.

- Pupils or particular groups of pupils are not safe or do not feel safe at school and/or at alternative placements.

Keeping Children Safe in Education outlines a range of e-safety topics that schools must consider and address under 'specific safeguarding concerns', which include child sexual exploitation, bullying (including cyberbullying), radicalisation and sexting.

Schools (specifically leaders, managers, governing bodies and proprietors) should therefore ensure that e-safety messages are embedded throughout the school's curriculum to ensure that pupils are prepared for life in modern Britain and the wider world.

Before inspection

Before inspection and at all times, schools can demonstrate that they take e-safety seriously and address it competently as part of their safeguarding responsibilities by ensuring that their school website has up-to-date and appropriate information and guidance offered for parents/carers and children about online safety both at school and at home. This may include sharing the school's own policies and procedures, guidance for children and parents, links to both internal and external content, plus links to further help such as Think U Know (www.thinkuknow.co.uk), CEOP (http://ceop.police.uk), Childnet (www.childnet.com), ChildLine (www.childline.org.uk), the Internet Watch Foundation (www.iwf.org.uk), Internet Matters (www.internetmatters.org), Get Safe Online (www.getsafeonline.org) and the UK Safer Internet Centre (www.saferinternet.org.uk).

It is good practice to alert students and families to how they might report any online concerns either via the designated lead in school, your local police or children's social care teams, and nationally (CEOP, IWF, ChildLine, NSPCC).

Inspectors may request the results of any self-evaluation by the school and will look at responses from parents via the Ofsted ParentView survey. They will ask the school to have available, among other items:

- records and analysis of exclusions, pupils taken off roll and incidents of poor behaviour, any use of internal isolation and racist incidents

- records and analysis of bullying, discriminatory and prejudicial behaviour, either directly or indirectly, including racist, disability and homophobic bullying, use of derogatory language and racist incidents

- a list of referrals made to the designated person for safeguarding in the school and those that were subsequently referred to the local authority, along with brief details of the resolution

- a list of all pupils who are open cases to children's services/social care and for whom there is a multi-agency plan

- up-to-date attendance analysis for all groups of pupils.

Online reputation?

Schools, like individuals, can develop an online reputation! How do you look from the outside? Inspectors will undertake a search before inspection using the provider information portal and the Internet to be aware of any live or historic safeguarding concerns, complaints or related issues, and this may include accessing publicly available content about the school. The school's digital footprint, in other words, will be revealed in a search of this type.

A search may uncover stories from local or national press as well as material (or grumbles) posted by parents, staff or pupils on unofficial sites and forums, or on social media, which mention the school name. Whether this content has been shared or posted intentionally or accidentally, it could include content which can be misread or misinterpreted. On the other hand it could also highlight positive practice and celebrations and show how the school uses technology to engage with the wider community, locally and globally.

How much do you know about your school's online reputation? It is essential to check your school's 'digital reputation' at regular intervals via public search engines or other tools such as reputation alert systems so that the school can respond (e.g. request removal of content, speak with those involved or share good news).

Staff awareness

Schools should address professional conduct with staff as part of induction and ensure that this is reinforced through regular staff training. Parents/carers and pupils should also be made aware of online safety and digital reputation as part of the home–school agreement and be encouraged to consider how they can act positively online to safeguard themselves and the school community. Schools should of course include appropriate use of technology and social media in the school Acceptable Use of ICT Policy which must be regularly reviewed to make certain that it remains appropriate and up-to-date. Schools need to be able to demonstrate that the AUP is effective, understood and actively adhered to by all members of the school community. Preferably everyone should sign it to show they are aware of updates from time to time.

During the inspection, inspectors will request that certain information is made available, such as self-evaluation and the school improvement plan. They may also wish to see incident logs, including actions taken, as well as identifying a designated person who is responsible for e-safety concerns in the school. The inspectors will also gather evidence from pupils about cyberbullying and online safety education and behaviour in school.

Across all aspects of school management

When inspectors are considering and evaluating the effectiveness of safeguarding within schools and settings, many strands will include e-safety practice. They may include:

- effectiveness of safeguarding arrangements

- leadership and management

- personal development, behaviour and welfare.

Online safety should therefore be embedded throughout school safeguarding practice and be clearly identified as an issue for leaders and managers to consider and address.

Online safety is an essential element of schools' safeguarding responsibilities and should also be considered to be a key priority for all members of staff.

The e-safety agenda and consensus has shifted towards enabling children to manage risk, rather than filtering/blocking, and therefore requires a comprehensive and embedded curriculum which is adapted specifically to the needs and requirements of pupils and the technology to which they are exposed.

Leadership and management

Inspectors will consider how well leaders and management ensure that pupils receive a broad and balanced curriculum which prepares pupils for the opportunities, responsibilities and experiences of later life in modern Britain. The online world is undoubtedly an important part of modern British life, so this should be addressed by leaders. The curriculum should also include a rounded assemblies programme which promotes pupils' spiritual, moral, social and cultural development and provides clear guidance on what is right and wrong, which will include online actions and consequences as well as understanding the online world in relation to British civil and criminal law.

Whole school consistent approach	All teaching and non-teaching staff recognise and are aware of and prioritise e-safety issues. High priority is given to staff training in e-safety. The contribution of the wider school community is valued and integrated.
There are robust and integrated reporting routines	School-based reporting routes (including Report Abuse buttons that are clearly understood, respected and used by the whole school.
Policies	Policies are rigorous, contributed to by the whole school and integrated with other relevant policies, such as behaviour, safeguarding and anti-bullying.
Education	An age-appropriate e-safety curriculum teaches pupils how to stay safe and take responsibility for their own and others' safety. Uses positive rewards and peer mentoring programmes.
Infrastructure	Recognised Internet Service Provider (ISP) or Regional Broadband Consortium together with age-related filtering that is actively monitored.
Monitoring and evaluation	Risk assessment taken seriously and used to good effect in promoting e-safety.
Management of personal data	The impact level of personal data is understood and data is managed securely and in accordance with the Data Protection Act 1998.

Figure 9.1 Key features of e-safe schools

Essential documents on safeguarding

- *Working Together to Safeguard Children* (DfE, March 2015)

- *Keeping Children Safe in Education for Schools and Colleges* (DfE, July 2015)

- *Inspecting Safeguarding in Early Years Education and Skills Settings* (Ofsted, June 2015)

Policy and practice review

This is a reflective activity for the senior leadership team and governors to consider whether the school has the right strategies, education and training, policy and procedures in place on e-safety.

What indicators reveal that your school is not adequately addressing e-safety?

- Personal data is often unsecured and/or leaves school site without encryption.

- Security of passwords is ineffective; for example, passwords are shared or common with all but the youngest children.

- Policies are generic and not regularly updated.

- There is no progressive, planned e-safety education across the curriculum; for example, there is only an assembly held annually.

- Infrastructure is weak. There is no Internet filtering or monitoring.

- There is no evidence of regular staff training on e-safety.

- Children are not aware of how to report a problem.

(From Ofsted Inspecting E-safety Briefing for Section 5 Inspection)

What would be considered outstanding practice?

The advice below was developed from the former Section 5 e-safety inspection briefing by Ofsted which has now been withdrawn from public access in the move to the new Common Inspection Framework. Only three documents are now online: The *Common Inspection Framework*, the *Inspectors' Handbook* and *Working Together to Safeguard Children*. But this briefing on inspecting e-safety is thought by many working in the field to be essential. It outlines best practice in e-safety in considerable detail and forms the basis of training for inspectors. The advice outlines vital elements in a school's armoury when considering what is required for an e-safe school. Even if you are not due for an inspection, it is necessary to stay up-to-date and alert to all online risk.

This is what is needed:

- There is a consistent whole-school approach and all staff, both teaching and non-teaching, are trained and aware of e-safety issues and how to respond. The contribution of pupils, parents and the wider school community is valued and integrated.

- There are robust integrated reporting routines that everyone understands and uses – such as online anonymous reporting mechanisms. Easily recognised buttons for reporting abuse are signposted and there are pathways to report to key staff members. Peer mentoring and support schemes are effectively used.

INSPECTION AND SELF-REVIEW

- Staff training is regular and up-to-date. One or more staff members have a higher level of expertise and clearly defined responsibilities.

- There are rigorous e-safety policies and procedures, written in plain English, to which the whole school has contributed. These are updated regularly and ratified by governors. The policy on Acceptable Use of ICT should be integrated with other relevant policies such as behaviour, safeguarding and anti-bullying. The E-safety Policy, which outlines your school's approach to teaching e-safety, should work alongside an Acceptable Use Policy that is understood and respected by pupils, staff and parents.

- An age-appropriate e-safety curriculum is being taught. This is flexible, relevant and engages pupils' interest. It is used to promote e-safety through teaching pupils how to be safe, how to protect themselves from harm and how to take responsibility for their own and others' safety. Positive rewards are used to cultivate positive and responsible use.

- There are peer mentoring programmes in place.

- Regarding infrastructure: there is a recognised Internet Service Provider or Regional Broadband Consortium together with age-related filtering that is actively monitored.

- Risk assessment is taken seriously and used to good effect in promoting e-safety. The school uses data effectively to assess the impact of their e-safety practice and inform strategy.

- There is secure management of personal data in accordance with the statutory requirements of the Data Protection Act 1998.

- Professional communication between school and pupils/students, their families or external agencies via technology should:

  o take place within clear and explicit professional boundaries

  o be transparent and open to scrutiny

  o not share any personal information with a child or young person.

Adapted from: Ofsted Inspecting E-safety in Maintained Schools and Academies Briefing for Section 5 Inspection (September 2014)

To help you check that you have everything in place, a few audit tools are given here – some quick, others in greater depth. Use them informally to check your progress.

What does outstanding look like?

A whole-school consistent approach

Robust integrated reporting routines are in place

Staff training regular and updated

Staff responsibilities well understood

Policies are rigorous and integrated

E-safety education is age-appropriate and flexible

Infrastructure is excellent

Monitoring and evaluation taking place

Safe management of personal data

What does inadequate look like?

Personal data is often unsecured

Security of passwords is ineffective

Policies are generic and not updated

There is no progressive, planned e-safety education across the curriculum but only an annual assembly

There is no Internet filtering or monitoring

There is no evidence of good staff training

Children are not aware of how to report a problem

SELF-REVIEW: HOW WOULD YOUR SCHOOL ANSWER THESE QUESTIONS?

SECURITY Describe how personal data is secured. Describe rules or protocols for situations in which data leaves the school site, i.e. on teachers' laptops or USB sticks or in emails. How often are passwords changed? How is traffic filtered and monitored in your school?	
ACCEPTABLE USE POLICY FOR ICT When was your AUP last reviewed and updated? Do staff and students sign it? Was it created specifically in and for your school or setting? Is it available for students in child-friendly language? How well does the entire school community understand this policy and how do you know this? (Surveys, lesson assessments, staff training needs assessed.) How well does it perform when incidents occur?	

TRAINING

How often is the staff trained in the AUP and in school protocols on e-safety?

Who attends? Is this for teaching and non-teaching staff?

What training have the staff had in understanding and addressing cyberbullying and safeguarding students from risks linked to the Internet or mobile phones?

Has training included recognising CSE and radicalisation?

Are staff given training that addresses mental health concerns online?

E-SAFETY EDUCATION

Do you have a planned e-safety teaching programme that becomes more sophisticated as the students move up the school?

How do you educate students with special needs or other vulnerabilities in e-safety in your school?

If outside guests come in to deliver e-safety sessions, what support is in place for students after they leave?

What follow-up is planned?

How do you ensure students have understood the guest session? Is it evaluated?

REPORTING SYSTEMS

Do students and parents/carers know how they can report any concerns?

What is the internal system for a member of staff who wishes to report a concern about a student or a staff member?

Are all staff well trained in this internal system?

Are whistleblowers encouraged to come forward?

Questions for staff	Red	Amber	Green
Have you had any training that shows the risks to your own and your pupils' online safety?			
Are there policies in place that clearly demonstrate good and safe Internet practice for staff and pupils?			
Are there sanctions in place to enforce the above policies?			
Do all staff understand what is meant by the term cyberbullying and the effect it can have on themselves and pupils?			
Are there clear reporting mechanisms with a set of actions in place for staff or pupils who feel they are being bullied online?			
Does the school have any plans for an event on Safer Internet Day?			

Strengths, Weakness, Threats and Opportunities – The SWOT Diagram

Could this diagram help trigger regular reviews of your system and training?

Could you develop this concept further? Will it help you keep on top on things?

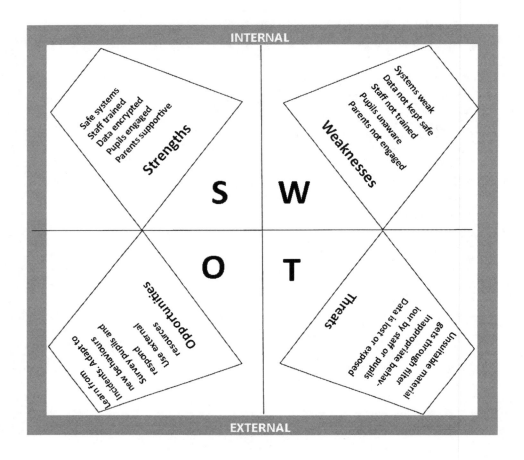

10

How Can I Get the Behaviour to Change?

Can I bore you into behaving well? I don't really believe that if I go on repeating our position the offensive behaviour will miraculously change if it has not responded so far. And yet so often schools are stuck in a rut with the strategies 'we always use' to enforce good behaviour.

Do you actually know whether or not these strategies are working? These seem such obvious questions but too many people are too busy and rushed to step back and get some perspective on the whole question of handling behaviour. Yet one of the reasons they are probably so busy is because managing behaviour and conflict is eating up their time!

Behaviour management techniques vary from one setting to another. The approach of the whole institution plays a vital role. So if the whole school favours a restorative approach, that tends to be the approach teachers reach for. But while it is remarkably successful in some cases, it is not suitable for every case – especially if the target pupil is not feeling strong enough to take their part.

Punitive approaches alone are not likely to succeed in bullying cases, let alone online harassment or victimisation cases. They tend to drive it underground to an even more secretive level or online and into anonymity. Punishment alone seldom changes entrenched prejudice that is all too often reinforced at home. Indeed, some pupils revel in being the 'bad boy or girl' and even come to see their punishment as some sort of heroic status symbol among their henchmen. Some adopt the dignity of becoming a victim of your punishing regime! In other words, if they and their parents believe that the behaviour was justified, perhaps because they are all racist, or they believe the victim 'deserved it' in some way, then the punishment you impose will be resisted to the core by both parent and pupil.

Another scenario is when clever ringleaders manipulate others to do their 'dirty work' for them. This is particularly easy to do via social media where girls bestow or withhold approval numerous times each day. You may apprehend and punish the workers but not the Queen Bee, when you really need to dismantle her power over the group. By punishing them and not her, you are reinforcing her power over them. Now they are caught between fear of her disapproval and your punishment. They are unlikely to move forward until you unlock this jam.

So a combination of thoughtful responses needs to be selected from a menu of options, to fit the case as appropriate.

Some form of sanction is useful alongside new steps to challenge the behaviour and thinking. But do not continue using a strategy which is patently not working.

Can you assess the tools you are using and refresh them? Consider the following:

- Are we tending to use rigid behaviour management tools like yellow and red cards because they are mandated, without fitting the tool to the case?

- Do some tactics work better with boys than with girls?

- Have our management tools lost their impact?

- Does the student actually stop and think about what has happened or mechanically go through the motions?

- Do they change their behaviour as a result?

- Do our management tools create more work for staff with onerous systems?

- Do pupils behave more secretively or target different people?

Author Dave Stott, a former teacher, explains that not all strategies have the intended outcome. He cites a school using detentions as a strategy. When asked if they used this form of disciplinary action, teachers enthusiastically said they did so. In fact Stott reports that in one week one individual teacher issued as many as 17 detentions to several different pupils. All detentions were logged and parents informed. Then rooms were allocated and staff were scheduled for the duty of supervising those on detention. But by the end of the following week it appears that only five of the pupils had turned up for their detentions. The school then took the next step in their strategy, eating up more staff time, and there was still no change in the named students' behaviour patterns. Stott points out that the message got through that some pupils had not turned up for the detentions and this in turn had a negative impact on the behaviour of other students. He comments:

> 'Detention is a perfectly acceptable response to some behaviours, but if it is failing to change behaviour and is causing stress and more work for staff, it's time to review, modify or dispense with this approach.'

> Dave Stott Behaviour Masterclass (www.youtube.com/watch?v=qLBajv4Ndko)

The same is true in cyberbullying cases. If the approach you are using has not reduced online aggression and/or cyberbullying over a couple of terms – change it! Monitor the incident reports and the anonymous pupil surveys to tweak your approach in a flexible, responsive way.

I have had cases brought to me that have run on for a long time – in one case, 18 months! This surely tells you that whatever is being tried is not working! It is time to change tack and try another approach. The first thing to do with a case that has gone on for such a long time is to create a timeline – look at what has happened and what interventions have been tried (and failed).

When we create this timeline it suddenly becomes easier to see where the weaknesses lie. If all the entries to the timeline are letters from the victim's parents reporting the problem again and again, where are the action plans and school responses? How has the case been escalated? Who is co-ordinating the school's response to this case and are all staff members aware of the approach currently being tried so that they can sing from the same song sheet?

Then consider the students' perspective. What do the students involved suggest? This can be fascinating. One boy explained that the boy he tormented online and who irritated him endlessly in return 'is always just asking for a fight, so I give it to him and he is weak 'cos he's got asthma. But if the teacher just sat us down to talk about it, I think it would be better.' You can hear that he cannot see a way of resolving their rivalrous hurtful behaviour without losing face, so it needs to be re-framed in some new manner. Both boys need to walk away feeling that their honour and reputation are intact and that they have graciously agreed to grow up and be more mature in their behaviour from now on. (It was ended in two days and the offensive material taken down when a negotiated approach was tried.)

Detention rarely helps a young person think about their prejudices and change them. A visit to a special school might instead help some people change their views about targeting people with special needs. Pick what suits the case. You might challenge racism by putting an older peer mentor in charge of this pupil with racist views. Pick an older mentor of a different background who is confident and assured. Prepare the mentor beforehand and explain that you are challenging prejudice. Ask the trained mentor to get to know this pupil, build a rapport and try and explore why he or she is discriminating against others. Look at their online profile and ask what sites they visit. People tend to hang around with like-minded individuals on sites promoting hate and racism. This leads them to think everyone agrees with them. They need to be carefully handled to broaden their horizon and change.

Think about your body language when addressing a pupil about an aggressive online incident. Is your message threatening, bullying even? Aim for a calm and assertive approach. Stand or sit at a slight angle to the pupil. When perpetrators are backed into a corner, they tend to come out fighting or deny everything. (Then their parents arrive and deny their child could have done this.) Leave a route by which they can exit and maintain face.

Avoid arguing. Repeat your point with authority; if you cannot get to where you would like to be in this discussion (the student understands the harm they have caused and is sorry), ask the student to think about this very serious situation and come back tomorrow to tell you what next steps he or she proposes to take to make amends. Meanwhile preserve evidence, have offending material taken down and report abuse. Make it clear that some of this behaviour might be against the law, such as incitement to hatred.

Keep your voice calm – you are aiming for behaviour change.

Ensure the victim is made safe while you work to change the perpetrator's behaviour. Retaliation is always a possibility. Your actions should not make this more likely.

'So where do the sanctions come in then?' I hear you ask. Well, it is often necessary to get the behaviour change *and* apply the sanction. So people who bully others would be denied a school trip or outing until they can show they can behave and get on well with others, collaborate in class and in teamwork and also demonstrate some positive prosocial behaviour. This could be through earning positive points until a certain number are achieved which will then gain them access to the event. You want to link the sanction to your desired outcome, which is behaviour change. I believe it is also good to link it to earning positive points for better behaviour towards others.

In the restorative approach, which works well in certain cases, the idea of recognising the harm caused and then finding a way to make amends is in itself quite difficult to go through for the perpetrator. In some formats other family members are asked to attend as well. They can take some responsibility for seeing that the problem is addressed.

It may be necessary to impose a sanction on a whole group – or even a whole class – because their behaviour has fallen far short of your expectations. Instead of investigating endlessly if a large group of students have been involved in cyberbullying and sharing messages or images, it might be worth putting the whole class under sanction. Nobody stopped it or spoke out against what was going on – therefore all are in the same boat. Nothing unites them like a group sanction.

On the other hand, if you do not manage this well they can unite against your rules, claiming injustice. That is why you will need to work on why it was so wrong, what the principles are, what was agreed by everyone in the AUP in ICT and the anti-bullying work of the school such as pledges, agreements or manifestos. Reinforce the fact that they will soon be out of school and working – bullying in the workplace is a sackable offence and some online behaviour is against the law. Ask for suggestions from the whole group on how people can be reconciled, involve your peer mentors, and if suitable invite your PCSO into school to address the group sternly.

Encourage self-review:

- How has my behaviour hurt/harmed others?
- Who has been hurt by this?
- What steps can I take to put this right?

What schools can do about sexting
What do we mean by this term?

> Images or videos generated…
> BY young people under the age of 18, or OF young people under the age of 18 that are sexual or indecent. These are often willingly shared between young people or posted by the generator via a mobile phone or other hand-held device.

There are many different types of sexting, and we are building experience in different types of cases, but this is a relatively new behaviour made easy by smartphones and webcams. Young people often share an image in what they understand to be an intimate personal relationship. But these images are often obtained by others and shared online. In some cases an adult may be soliciting the images by pretending to be a teen. In others the couple believe their relationship will last forever and everything they share will be private. Sadly this is rarely so.

While the original intention might in some cases have been fairly harmless, the end destination of these images is certainly not harmless. Around 88 per cent are thought to end up on parasite sites as they are 'harvested' and then misused (Internet Watch Foundation).

Ensure your e-safety education covers this behaviour with scenarios that illustrate how to say no to requests for these images and allow students to discuss the options available to them. They will need to consider why this idea has become socially acceptable when it causes so much distress. Emphasise that no matter what the behaviour has been, if someone is in difficulty they can safely come to the staff who will help without judgement. Encourage parents to deliver the same message. All too often a young person is terrified to confide in parents precisely because they have forbidden them to share explicit photos. Facing them now is too hard. Others fear the shame it will bring upon their family, with cultural pressures and family honour playing an understandable role.

Sharing indecent images of people under 18 years of age is illegal. However, the Association of Chief Police Officers (ACPO) has said it does not intend to criminalise young people but instead takes a proportionate stance where this is possible.

Your school serious incident protocols should outline what staff should do if a pupil discloses problems due to this behaviour.

Some questions to consider are:

1. Is it potentially illegal or inappropriate?
2. Was there an intention to harm or was it 'experimental'?
3. Is an adult involved in soliciting the images? If so, trigger action for an illegal incident.
4. Were the images produced with consent or produced without consent?
5. Will this case trigger child protection and safeguarding protocols?
6. How widely has the picture been shared? Who has the original device?
7. Is it a school device or on the school system, or is it on a personal device?
8. Was there malicious intent, for example through grooming?
9. Does the student need immediate support and protection?
10. Does the student know where the image has been shared?

Images are rarely on one device – they are usually rapidly shared and passed around. They can also be hacked and obtained by people the subject does not know. A picture could be uploaded to websites in various locations – so acting fast can be vital. Schools have powers to confiscate a device and search it (Education Act 2011).

The device can be examined, confiscated or securely stored if there is reason to believe it contains indecent images or pornography. But there are a number of conditions that apply.

Make certain that the action you take is in line with the school's CP and Safeguarding Policies.

The search should be conducted by the headteacher or someone authorised by them. A member of the safeguarding team or the designated person for safeguarding should be present. The search should be conducted by a person of the same gender.

If illegal images are found you must inform the police. See the ACPO advice in this regard.

Distinguish between an incident involving 'aggravated' sharing of images and 'experimental' conduct that may be proportionately dealt with without referral, particularly where a child shares images of themselves in a romantic relationship and these are accidentally shared.

Record in writing the reasons for not referring the case to the police and record any steps taken.

AVOID...

- searching the device if this is likely to cause additional distress to the young person UNLESS there is evidence to suggest that there is an immediate problem
- printing out material for evidence
- moving or sending material from one device to another
- keeping it in your possession.

- Inform the Child Protection Officer.

- Record the incident.

- Act in line with the school or institution's safeguarding and child protection policies and procedures.

- Inform relevant colleagues, i.e. senior management, before searching a device or give it to the designated person to search.

Dealing with the image or images

- Confiscate and secure the device if that was the vehicle for sharing the image.

- Do not view the image unless there is a clear reason to do so.

- Do not send, share or save it anywhere unless the designated safeguarding lead decides to save it onto a school device with the agreement of the headteacher. Write down the date, time and action taken to preserve this evidence.

- Do not share with any students even if you suspect they sent the image.

- If the image was shared across a school network, block access to the network for all users and isolate the image.

- Never print the image.

- Never view the image outside of the protocols in your safeguarding and child protection policies.

Pupils will very often disclose to a trusted adult within the school. Are all your staff trained in what to do? Whoever receives the disclosure must act in line with the school's safeguarding and child protection procedures and report to the designated person for safeguarding. They must involve senior management and act to protect the child's interests. The student could be under extreme stress, may have been pressured into these actions or may be blackmailed or threatened. They may be fearful of what their parents will do or say and terrified of the consequences. Skilled counselling help is likely to be needed for students and parents.

The senior designated safeguarding lead should decide whether or not to involve the police. Either way the incident should be recorded. Remember to store the device securely.

Make a referral if needed after making a risk assessment in relation to the young person. Inform parents/carers about the incident and how it is being dealt with.

Cases can be assessed using a booklet: *Sexting in Schools: Advice and Support Around Self-generated Images. What to Do and How to Handle It.*[90]

If the child is under 13 or has a vulnerability, contact Children's Social Care, who will refer to the police.

Teachers can use UKCCIS' professional helpline (tel: 08443814772) for getting material removed.

It is a matter for the police:

- if it involves porn images of under-age children (18 years)
- if an adult is involved
- if there is intent to harm
- if the images have been distributed.

Report to CEOP or the Internet Watch Foundation:

The Internet Watch Foundation is the UK Internet Hotline for anyone to report their exposure to online child sexual abuse imagery hosted anywhere in the world, and non-photographic child sexual abuse images and criminally obscene adult content hosted in the UK.

IWF was established in 1996 by the UK Internet industry and works in partnership with the wider online industry, law enforcement, government, the education sector, charities, international partners and the public to minimise the availability of content within its remit. As a result of this self-regulatory approach, less than 1 per cent of online child sexual abuse content has been hosted in the UK since 2003, down from 18 per cent in 1997.

For more information or to report a website, visit www.iwf.org.uk.

Handling incidents

1. Employ effective listening techniques.

2. Stay calm and exude calm.

3. Keep everything in proportion.

4. Make a record of the incident.

5. Ask or help the victim to preserve evidence.

6. Speak to witnesses and bystanders.

7. Ascertain the hoped-for outcome – restore friendship group? Justice.

8. Removal of harmful material from cyberspace.

9. Consider restorative practices where appropriate.

The key questions in restorative approaches

The use of restorative practices can, in the right cases, help to:

- reduce violence and/or bullying

- improve human behaviour

- strengthen the civil ethos of the school

- provide effective leadership

- restore relationships

- repair harm.

When there is an extreme imbalance of power between the two parties, or when the incident is still very recent and feelings are too raw to bring the parties face to face without harm being caused to the victim, it may not be appropriate. Both parties need to agree to this.

You may need to do some work with each side in advance.

Confused about restorative practice and restorative justice?

- **Restorative Practices (RP)** can intervene early – to be proactive before something has gone badly wrong. RP aims to build relationships and a sense of community in order to prevent conflict and bullying.

- **Restorative Justice (RJ)** is usually taken to mean a practice method used after the incident. Both of these are based on similar principles.

- **Restorative Conferences** are slightly more formal, often used by police and when there is crime in the community, but used in educational settings too.

This restorative approach is in direct contrast to the punitive approach that starts with motives such as: 'We won't tolerate this, I must get to the bottom of this, the perpetrator must be identified and punished.'

The punitive approach will focus on investigating, fact finding, allocating blame and punishment with intent to deter. It can take a lot of teacher time. But bullying is a very complex behaviour, and very often we find that victims also bully others and bullies may have been bullied or very punitively parented in their turn. Cases do not present as clear-cut evil and angel!

Some cases involve children who are so entwined, magnetically drawn towards each other and constantly driving each other crazy – it is hard to determine fault because both are implicated like squabbling siblings. In addition, bullying can be very secretive and onlookers can be cowed into silence. Precious time might in certain circumstances be wasted in 'investigating', if the case does not present a simple and clear narrative of victim and perpetrator.

By contrast, a restorative approach is often described as 'positive discipline' or a 'responsive classroom'.

This can challenge the way a victim of bullying has been made to feel, which is usually helpless, powerless and unable to act. Restorative approaches encourage the target to take a role – to give their suggestions and permissions for next steps to happen. They are helped to find ways forward. Their views are listened to rather than adults taking over and leaving them prey to retaliatory bullying when it emerges that they have reported it. They may be taught skills to use.

The perpetrator/s will be encouraged to play a role too. First they need to recognise the harm they have caused and the wider circle of people who are affected by their behaviour. Then they are asked to offer suggestions to make amends. This approach does not push them into a corner, nor label them with hated labels such as 'bully'. It aims to separate the young person from the behaviour and appeal to their better character to help solve the problem.

Over-reliance on punishment to stop bullying is problematic because it can seem like bullying in itself, just when you want to model the behaviour you want the students to use!

By shaming and labelling perpetrators, they can become proud to be wrongdoers, the tough guys or the baddies; it is a type of status, or it can fail to change their behaviour because a loss of face would be involved – especially if they are the leader of a group who look up to them because they are hard. The restorative approach does not involve losing status – it can reintegrate the perpetrator/s and reduce reoffending. But as said above, it should only be used when the parties both agree and are ready. There are some cases where it would not be appropriate.

Restorative questions for challenging behaviour

- What happened?

- What were you thinking about at the time?

- What have you thought about since?

- Who has been affected by what you've done?

- In what way have they been affected?

- What do you need to do to make things right?

You will notice that these questions put the onus on the offending person to do something about the problem – rather than the teacher saying, 'I will take the following actions against you.' While you may indeed have to take some actions, such as excluding this student from a class outing, your aim is to get this person to change their behaviour. You cannot give the perpetrator any assurance that the victim will accept their proposals to put things right. Allow some time for this to hang in the air unanswered. The victim should answer for themselves.

Restorative questions to help those affected

- What did you think when you realised what had happened?

- What impact has this incident had on you and others?

- What has been the hardest thing for you?

- What do you think needs to happen to make things right?

- How do you want things to be in the long run?

To parents

- What happened?

- How do you think your child has been affected?

- If it is something illegal or the child is at risk/in danger, refer to your serious incident protocol. If not, continue...

- If it is cyberbullying or cyber-abuse, save the evidence and put the device out of use if necessary. Continue...

- How does your child handle friendships and fallouts?

- What changes have you noticed in your child?

- Is there anything we should know? For example, self-harm, depression, refusal to come to school.

- What would help your child most in handling situations like this?

- What does your child want in the longer term? For example, to be accepted in the friendship group.

- Are you willing to work with us as we implement an action plan?

- What are the best ways for us to be in touch regularly while we try to change things for your child?

Take notes of the meeting and what was agreed. Confirm in writing to the parents as soon as possible. Agree a follow-up or report-back date. Make it clear that sometimes friendship fallouts and feuds can be intractable. Also explain that any action plan put in place might take time to bear fruit; however, you will act as fast as possible to get offensive material or images taken down from a website or service if that is necessary.

Capturing and preserving evidence

It is important to capture evidence of cyberbullying before the perpetrator alters or takes it down. Cyberbullying on social networks can be deleted when it is known that you are investigating and then the evidence is lost. In other cases a perpetrator might choose to use a live chat service where the dialogue is not saved or a self-destruct service where a message disappears after a few seconds. An offensive photo can be Photoshopped to look better or it might be taken down once it is clear that the case is being investigated.

In all cases of bullying, evidence is that vital component that proves what the victim alleges. Even to get something taken down or to report it to a website, the victim may have to produce the evidence.

Bullying may get worse, in which case having evidence of how long it has gone on will be helpful.

So how can this be achieved? Of course you can print out any emails, but few young people use email today. Here's how.

Capturing and preserving the evidence on a computer
1. Capture a screenshot or screengrab

A screenshot is essentially a photo of what you can see on your computer screen. It captures everything just as it looks in the original context, such as a Facebook page or the full email. This gives it more credibility than if only the message is copied and pasted.

How to capture a screenshot:

- In the top right-hand side of your keyboard is a key that says 'PRTSC' on it. This is short for 'print screen' and is the one you need to press to capture everything you can currently see on your computer screen. Once you click it, it copies your screen, even though you will see no message.

- Open 'Paint', which you will find by going to your programs and looking under 'Accessories'.

- Click on the 'Edit' button, which will give you an option to paste. Click on this and the screenshot should appear.

2. Store the image

Once you have the screenshot on the screen in Paint, you need to save it as an image. To do this:

- Click on the 'File' button followed by the 'Save as' button. This will open a list of folders on your computer and there should be one named 'Pictures' or 'My Pictures'.

- Click on the folder to open it. The screen will ask you for a name to save the file as and will also ask for the file type. Choose JPEG. Type in a name for the image such as Cyberevidence1 and label subsequent ones as Cyberevidence2, Cyberevidence3, etc..

- It might help to open a sub-folder inside your My Pictures file called Evidence. Do this by opening My Pictures, right-clicking the mouse and clicking on 'New' and then 'Folder'. A folder icon will appear and you can type in the name you want to give it.

- Select JPEG as the file format.

- You can also do this using Microsoft Word or, better still, Microsoft Publisher – simply paste the screenshot into a blank page and go to 'Save as', where you select a name and type as above.

- On some software you will need to press the Microsoft key and the print screen key together to achieve this.

3. Find the stored screenshot

When you need your evidence, you will easily find it by looking in My Pictures and then in the Evidence folder. The images can then be printed, emailed or saved onto your camera's SD card.

It can help to create a timeline or diary, noting the date each time there is another incident.

4. Email the screenshot

You might be required to send your screenshots to the police, lawyers or other people who are involved in your case such as a designated safeguarding lead or the provider:

- Open the saved Evidence folder and decide which images you want to send by email.

- If your email goes through Outlook Express or Windows Live Mail, select the images by holding down the 'Control' key and clicking on them. The computer will highlight them for you.

- Right-click on one of the pictures and a list of options will appear. Select 'Send to' and the computer will open a new email with the pictures attached. All you need to do is type in the email address who you want to send them to.

- If using Gmail or Hotmail, open a new email. Find the 'Attach' or 'Insert' file command, then click on it. It will open a list of folders. Find your Pictures folder and inside it will be your Evidence folder. Once you open it you can select which pieces of evidence you want to attach to your mail. Hold down the 'Control' key and click on the images you wish to send.

Note: In cases which involve nude or explicit images of young people under 18 it is not advisable to look at them, nor to download any onto your own devices. Lock the device into a drawer until the designated person within your school or the police are able to look at it. Ask the victim to save the evidence first.

Capturing and preserving the evidence on mobiles and tablets

The victim can place the phone onto a photocopier or take a photo with another phone. Screenshots can be saved. You can also take a photo of a computer or tablet screen with a phone.

It is advisable to keep a record of the abusive or aggressive incident. Note down the date and time; the content of the message(s); and where possible a sender's ID (e.g. username, email, mobile phone number) or the web address of the SNS page or the content. Even better, keep an accurate copy of the whole web-page address, as this will help the service provider to find the content you wish to complain about.

Keeping the evidence will help in any investigation into the cyberbullying by the service provider, but it can also be useful in showing what has happened to those who may need to know, including parents, teachers, pastoral care staff and the police.

It is always useful to keep a written record, but it is better to save evidence of bullying on the device itself:

- For mobiles, ask the young person being bullied to keep or save any messages, whether voice, image or text. Do not have them forward the message to your staff phone. This could cause the vital information from the original message to be lost. If using an iPhone, press and hold the 'home' button at the bottom of your phone. While you're doing that, press the top 'sleep' button. The screen will flash white for a moment, and the image will be ready to text, email, upload or view in your camera uploads.

- For Android phones or tablets, hold down the 'power' key, and press the volume down button. The screen will flash white, and you can access the image in your gallery. But this can vary from phone to phone, so you might want to use a free Google app such as aScreenshot, which lets you take a screenshot by shaking the device or pressing whatever button you have chosen to trigger it (https://play.google.com/store/apps/details?id=com.enlightment.screenshot&hl=en).

- For Instant Messenger, some services allow the user to record all conversations. The user could also copy and paste, save and print these. If you think about it, it is obvious that if evidence is kept via a copy and paste method it might appear less genuine, as it could have been altered. This is why, when reporting a case to the service provider or the police, authentic evidence made from saved evidence is more convincing, so conversations recorded/archived by the instant messaging service are better for evidence here. Conversations can also be printed out in hard copy or sections can be saved as a screengrab.

- For SNS, video-hosting sites or other websites, copy and save the site link, print the page or take a screengrab of the page and save it. Instructions are given above. You can also take a photo of the entire screen using a mobile. Aim for a high-resolution image.

- Some versions of Messenger offer the option to archive conversations. Check your Messenger toolbar for your preferences and privacy options and switch on the archive setting.

- If this case involves one that does not offer this option, either copy and save the conversation or use one of the ideas above such as a photo of it or a screengrab.

- For chat rooms, print the page or produce a screengrab of the page.

- For email, ask the person being bullied to print it; forward the message on to the staff member investigating the incident; and encourage them to continue to forward and save any subsequent messages. Preserving the whole message, and not just the text, is more useful, as this will contain 'headers' (information about where the message has come from). They can also print out the emails and keep a folder.

A note about images: If images are involved in the cyberbullying, it is important to find out if these might be illegal or raise child protection concerns. Indecent or sexual images of children (people under the age of 18) are illegal to produce, circulate or possess in the UK. These include images that children have taken of themselves or their friends, using their mobile phone for example.

In cases which involve nude or explicit images of young people under 18 it is not advisable to look at them nor to download any on to your own devices. Lock the device in a drawer until the designated person within your school or the police are able to look at it. Ask the victim to save the evidence first.

Contact: Involve the Internet Watch Foundation if the images are Internet content or the local police if illegal images have been taken of a child and circulated. Similarly if the case involves an assault on another young person or some other crime, contact the local police. If it is a safeguarding matter, trigger your school's safeguarding procedures. If the case involves child sexual exploitation, contact CEOP.

Less serious situations: If the case involves images that are not illegal you may prefer to try to contain the incident within the school. Some cases benefit from the utmost discretion and it is not always necessary to tell the whole school about the case. However, cases should trigger useful work across a year group, for example, to counter any prejudice that has emerged or to teach them a new aspect of staying safe. Cases may trigger letters home to all parents about particular sites or warnings about new behaviours that are coming to light.

Identifying the young person who is doing the bullying

In cases where you do not know the identity of the bullying student, you can often find out the IP address of the device used – but it is wise to remember that someone else might have used that device, even using someone's identity or SNS account. Many young people do lots of social networking with friends who can memorise their password, or someone may know that their friend's phone is always linked to their Facebook page so they could use it when their friend goes out of the room for a moment. Siblings often know or can guess the password their brother or sister is using. Evidence of an IP address is just that – nothing more is proven.

But there may be witnesses who visited that page, school logs and service provider data. The police would have to request an action from a service provider if it involved someone else. If the bullying person withheld their number, then the date and time of the call or message should help the provider identify the caller to the police.

Schools can often have a number identified because they have a list of students' mobile numbers or other pupils can recognise the number. But there are situations in which it is more difficult. When the phones are using local Wi-Fi to communicate, the call does not process through the provider's network; texts sent from a website to a phone are also difficult to trace.

Where a crime has been committed

In cases where a crime has been committed and reported to the police, they have protocols for working with service providers if they wish to request information.

Investigating allegations against staff

Allegations against staff are a safeguarding and possibly child protection matter. Devices should be put out of use and safely stored. All evidence should be saved.

Parents

We also see cases where parents or pupils attack staff members online. Parents should use the school's complaints procedure rather than go online and encourage other parents to comment on or defame a teacher. Staff can gain advice from their union or the professionals' helpline. The behaviour may involve defamation or damage to a teacher's professional reputation. Governing bodies should invite the parent instigators to a meeting in the first instance, with written notes taken.

How do I preserve evidence in Snapchat?

Preserving evidence presents a challenge when the problem is Snapchat – designed so that all the images and messages vanish after a few seconds. Users do not view their exchanges as permanent, but a threat can hang in the air long after it is off the screen. In some cases it may be essential to capture what is sent via Snapchat in order to investigate. In other cases it is exactly this ability to capture what the sender thought would vanish that gives a cyberbully the ammunition to use against the sender. If a screenshot is taken, the sender is notified, so a number of apps have sprung up that do not notify the sender and images can be taken without their knowing.

These apps should be used with great care and only if it is essential to capture evidence. Seek permission from your designated safeguarding lead before doing so. Apps are available on the app store for capturing Snapchat photos and videos, such as the free Snapkeep which allows you to save the images to your camera roll if saved before viewing in Snapchat. However, you should never save any of these images to your own phone but only to a designated one the school or the police agree should be used.

In October 2014 hackers threatened to release thousands of nude images from Snapchat, taken by senders who thought they would disappear in seconds. While Snapchat denied any hacking took place on their servers, it seemed that popular third-party apps used to save the images had been hacked. This threat shows that nothing disappears in the electronic world. Many people had sleepless nights worrying about whether or not their snaps would be released or posted on boards.

Reputation damage? What can you do?
Online reputation check

Remove any images or posts that you can trace – first any that the young person has posted themselves or shared with a friend, then via a wider group: this includes the young person's friends, classmates and immediate relatives who may have seen one somewhere. Enlist their help to tell you where they have seen the image and to remove it if they have shared it.

Contact the service provider where possible and ask for help to have the image removed.

The counterblast

Help the targeted student to increase the number of positive posts about themselves in an effort to 'drown out' the negative ones. Explain that the aim is to create a new digital footprint with a more positive image. You are hoping through this that you can help push further down the list of search results those that throw up negative messages about this young person.

What steps can help achieve this?

- Support good causes or do sponsored charitable activities via online webpages.

- Volunteer and write a blog about it.

- Create an interesting YouTube channel with positive content.

- Visit social networks and leave comments or posts that are useful, kind or thoughtful.

- Get mentioned by other friends in a positive way.

11

Supporting Parents

The items in this chapter can be used by schools at different times when resources are required or in a programme of mailings to parents. The first is a handout or email content for advice to parents.

PARENTS: DON'T BE FOOLED, GET TOOLED UP!

Confused? Get to grips with all the new devices that can connect to the Internet. Understand how your child is living in a connected world with multiple platforms. You'll find it's not that difficult! Visit the UK Safer Internet Centre's *Parents' Guide to Technology* at www.saferInternet.org.uk/advice-and-resources/parents-and-carers/parents-guide-to-technology.

Hold on to your parenting role. It is easy to feel out of your depth as your child guides you through games and apps at high speed. But you are first and foremost a parent and your instincts are honed by now. Not everything is appropriate for her to view, upload or play. Just as you protected her from unsuitable movies when she was little, so now you need to protect her from some risks and guide her towards being a responsible citizen online. Have you set parental controls at home and on any devices she uses? Have you talked about who she hangs out with online just as you talk about people she hangs out with in the real world? Try to delay social networking until your child is aged 13 if you can and talk about what they post or share online.

Try the free Vodafone Digital Parenting magazine on how to use and set parental controls, safe search or setting ground rules: www.vodafone.com/content/parents.html. Set boundaries early before they get a new game or console.

See The Parentzone for useful factsheets: www.theparentzone.co.uk/factsheets/3836.

What's in it? Is that game suitable for your year 7 child? Does he join in Grand Theft Auto with his older brothers or dad? He might be playing it when he is alone at home. If you want to know what's in the game, try a useful guide from Common Sense Media on what is in a game, book, TV show, film or app: www.commonsensemedia.org/game-reviews. Content really matters.

Heard about PEGI? You can access this information wherever you are with a simple app on your mobile. Available for iPhone or Android, download the Pan European Gaming Information app.

Parent forums. There are parents out there chatting about whether a game, TV series or film is suitable for different age groups. You can join in on the *Hunger Games* for example at www.amazon.co.uk/Age-enjoy-appreciate-Hunger-Games/forum/Fx10U2Z20CPKBVS/Tx2FSMEZD5T5E17/1?_encoding=UTF8&asin=0439023483 or on www.mumsnet.com where you can start a discussion thread yourself.

Safe or unsafe? True or false? Questions for parents in a parents' evening on e-safety

Keep it light and friendly with parents – too often it's all about dire warnings on what can happen and what they must do. This quiz is to use as an ice breaker.

Get everyone to stand up. Designate one corner of the room as True and the other False; if you draw a line between the two, the centre represents 'unsure'.

As you read out the quiz questions, people take up a position on the line in a spot that represents what they think. A few judicious questions about why people took the positions they did will often help you find an opportunity to explain some nugget of e-safety and will let parents hear what others are saying or worrying about.

Questions to read out:

1. Thank goodness I don't really have to teach my child about e-safety until he or she is about 12 or 13. True or false? Safe or unsafe?

2. My child will come and tell me if there is anything worrying him or her. Is this always true? What about the children who say they are scared to tell their parents about a problem online?

3. It will all be OK if I set filters on the home PC and on my child's phone too. Is this safe or unsafe?

4. There is nothing I can do if my child is cyberbullied. True or false?

5. I always know what my child does on Facebook because I am a friend. True or false?

6. I share my Facebook page with my child so we are OK. Is this safe or unsafe?

7. My child helps me buy things online with my credit card 'cos he knows more about it than I do. Safe or unsafe, or safe in some circumstances?

8. I worry about my daughter online but my son seems really good at tech stuff so I don't need to worry about him. True?

9. My son just plays games so he isn't really likely to get cyberbullied. True or false?

10. My child is 14 and a half and he/she knows about staying safe online so I don't have to worry any more. Safe or unsafe?

11. I work hard and hardly get to spend time with my child but I text her all the time. It seems to be enough, don't you think? Safe or unsafe?

12. I love Facebook because parents get together and it's where we can safely discuss problems we have with teachers at the school. Good idea? Safe or unsafe?

Below are advice sheets that can be given to parents, emailed in regular updates, or placed on the school's website in an area for parents about e-safety. Staff may need to help parents with advice on problems as they arise. The advice below may be used in some of these situations as needed.

GENERAL ADVICE FOR PARENTS

- Talk to your child's school about their anti-bullying approach – know what it is and remain involved. Know what the route is if you need to report any concerns. Be aware of what the school recommends and stay up-to-date.

- Be alert. If your child changes their normal routine and habits suddenly, is not sleeping or eating, doesn't want to go to school or changes their route to school, is not seeing friends – act.

- If your child appears to be bullied:

  o Do not show how upset you are – stay calm and try to work with your child to hammer out a plan of action: next steps – people who love you – we understand – support is here, together we can get over this. A helpless or over-upset parent makes matters worse.

  o Keep evidence – save messages or screengrabs, but block the sender where possible.

  o Report abuse to the website itself, or to the police if appropriate. Hate crime, harassment or sexual exploitation can be a criminal offence. In these cases report to CEOP if a child is involved.

- Clean friends list on SNS – help your child to remove anyone they do not know in the offline world. Having 4000 friends is not a sign of true popularity!

- Check photos are correctly tagged and privacy settings are all in place, including old photos put up ages ago. Talk to your child about inappropriate images that will still be out there years from now. While everyone posts photos that they believe show them as humorous, popular and attractive, every photo should be thought about carefully before posting online. What does it say about you? How could it be viewed? How could it be misused? What are you giving away about your identity?

- Encourage them to avoid sites that are anonymous – like Ask.fm.

- Do not allow them onto Facebook if they are too young. Be aware they may set up pages in an alternative name. Remind them that they can always leave a chat room.

- Make clear that you are not judgemental – they can tell you anything. For this to be true, you will have had to show an open mind beforehand. Young people can be blackmailed over something they have done, such as once posting a sexy photo, because they are scared their parents will find out. It is surely better to have made a mistake and to learn from it and be safe than to be forced into inappropriate behaviour over the initial mistake through fear.

- If vulnerable or isolated in the offline world, young people often seek intimacy and relationships online. These young people need extra e-safety advice and support.

- If a young person is being bullied face-to-face in school, the addition of cyberbullying sets up a devastating environment in which there is no respite. Bullying can occur multiple times a day and targeted young people need immediate support and intervention:

  o Keep a copy of the abusive messages or images.

  o Record the date and time – there will be a trail.

  o Block the sender where possible. Don't reply.

  o Get friends to post supportive messages and 'drown' out the negative messages.

  o Show them how to keep personal details private. Report abuse.

  o ChildLine and the Samaritans can be contacted in multiple ways. They are trained to help.

TIPS FOR PARENTS ABOUT CYBERBULLYING

- **You are a parent first and foremost** – use your parenting skills if you are less skilled on the Internet.

- **Discover the Internet together.** Ask your child to show you what they can do – games they can play, places they can visit. Pupils tell us that e-safety education should start at eight years old.

- Teach them that if you have used **your credit card** to buy something online together and they have helped you do it they must never use your card without your permission – many children as young as six remember passwords and pin numbers. Check that sites are safe before paying.

- If your child comes across **unsuitable images or sites** – it is not always your child's fault. Don't be too judgemental as they will be unlikely to come to you if they have a problem for fear you will be angry.

- **Be positive.** The Internet is one of the most momentous leaps forward in communication and learning and your child will need to be skilled in using it for their learning and for their future personal life and career. Teach your child what they can do if something goes wrong.

- When they get **their first mobile** teach them to be safe. They shouldn't leave the phone on at a website with their password logged in – anyone can grab it and pretend to be them. If they feel forced to give their password to someone, tell your child to immediately change it and show them how. Ten-year-olds complain of chain letters containing threats – talk to them in advance about this and explain what to do: Come and tell you – and do not fear the threat. Block the sender and keep the evidence. If it continues you may need this evidence to get help. Set parental controls on your child's phone.

- Learn to recognise a **Report Abuse button** in case you or your child might need it.

- Bullying in general diminishes as children get older, but cyberbullying is an exception. **It peaks at age 14–15** with the arrival of sexual jealousy and more digital skills among young people.

- **Mid-teens** are least likely to tell their parents when things go wrong – they might be bullied due to a photo they uploaded thinking it was private or within a personal relationship. They may feel worried that you will blame them for doing so in the first place. This type of bullying gets out of hand fast and a young person without support can become extremely desperate or depressed. Keep talking. Offer various routes to help if they want to keep something private. Find out how to get it removed.

- Other forms of bullying can be based on **prejudice or identity** – this can lead to hate crime and could become serious. Homophobic or racist bullying or bullying to do with religion or culture can be especially distressing. Every child has a right to be safe and not to be discriminated against. Pave the way for your child to be able to come and talk to you about the most awkward or embarrassing situations. Teach them to treat others well and respect people. They can expect the same.

- If your child is **depressed or withdrawn**, be alert and take steps to find out if they are being bullied or harassed by others or influenced by websites urging them to do something. To do this, try to avoid questions where the answer is either 'yes' or 'no'. Frame the question in a more open way: 'How are things among your mates these days?'; 'Have you seen Joe lately? I haven't seen him around.'

Filters at home – why parents are not using them

Parents are offered filters on their home Wi-Fi systems by the providers, but in fact the take-up is extremely low.

Here are the reasons parents gave for not activating parental controls. In parents' evenings on e-safety these reasons can be discussed, particularly in relation to year 7.

Reasons parents did not make use of parental controls

- Idea that they are complex to install
- Not understood
- Lapsed and out of date
- New device bought and not re-installed
- Switch to new ISP and forgot
- Risks not a major worry for parent right now
- Not got around to it
- More inclined to worry their child spent too long online/gaming than risk
- Lack of awareness
- Rules not strictly followed – busy life – path of least resistance
- Forgetting to install if Parental Controls stopped working for some reason
- Think you have to know a lot to choose or research it
- Feel ill-equipped to intervene due to own lack of digital competence
- Child learns about this at school
- Child is always supervised
- Trust child to be sensible

Ofcom, January 2014

Gaming and public Wi-Fi

Gaming is very popular in Britain. But it seems we are not always able to separate play from parenting. Most parents have never heard or thought about the PEGI ratings on games. While they would not take their child to an 18-rated movie, they think nothing of letting them play games that are extremely violent or rated over 18.

It seems there are some chats to have and some thinking to do. It is possible to limit or shape the play to suit family groups, but first non-gamers and gamers need to show a little mutual understanding.

When parents want to have useful chats with their children about online games, non-gaming parents do not understand the fun and thrill the games offer. It might be worth acknowledging this so that your advice is more meaningful to the young person. After all, research in the UK by the Internet Advertising Bureau in 2014 suggests that 70 per cent of the UK population played a computer game in the last six months and women now account for 52 per cent of that audience. Mum, is that you?

The study revealed all those people over age 44 as ardent gamers! They account for 27 per cent of all players, while children and teenagers represent 22 per cent of the gaming audience. This surge in gamers in new age groups is thought to be linked to smartphones making games available in the pocket or palm of your hand without consoles or desktop PCs. Think long, boring train commutes!

So what should schools' advice to parents be?

1. Respect their enthusiasm, skills and speed.

2. Play together. Don't let them lock themselves away in their rooms to play on desktop computers, laptops and TV-based console games.

3. Instil Internet safety basics, remain available to help out, but don't be a helicopter parent.

4. Read and understand the ratings on games.

5. Games do not trump schoolwork.

6. Limit time on games. Parental control settings allow you to choose blocks of time that an account is and is not accessible for play.

7. Show them how to customise and opt out of Real ID where this is offered, but check their screen names – are they appropriate? Ask Urban Dictionary, or Google it.

8. Recognise signs of addictive or overlong play.

9. Turn off chat channels for younger players to limit their interaction with other players and rule that any downloads, add-ons, modifications or patches must be agreed to by you first.

10. Read together and agree to play by the rules of the game.

> Agree rules. NO real names, addresses, suburbs, postcodes or local areas, sports clubs, school names, phone numbers, email addresses and AIM or Twitter handles or passwords and accounts to be shared with any other player.

Parents need to help children if problems crop up. If your child is bullied by someone online, the answer is not to take away their smartphone or ban or deactivate their account in the game. Report the player if they have contravened the terms and conditions. Help your child understand that they might have problems with other players from time to time but to save the evidence and discuss it with you. Avoid an angry reply. Activate the Ignore button. Turn off chat channels when necessary or block voice chat. Help kids set up guilds, teams or chat channels with their genuine real-life friends. (The bullying may come from someone they know, of course – so the usual responses to cyberbullying come into play.)

Parents should be reminded of the need for global security within their home system, as well as on devices. When did they last check their Internet protection systems? Are they updated regularly? The firewalls, routers and virus protection software should be reconsidered each time there are changes to service providers, new devices or phones. Passwords need to be strong and varied – how about changing them every so often? Two-step security adds another layer.

What can parents do?

Examine with young people the idea that everything we say, do or post stays on the Internet leaving a trail or a digital footprint and that also means inside games (see the related activity in Chapter 6).

Lots of companies make their money by using details about us and our online habits to sell to advertisers. There is no real privacy. Even if we delete something, other people or players might take screenshots or save the chats. Some children will grow up to find that their childhood misdemeanours are still out there haunting them when they apply to university or for a job.

Encourage young people to play with their real-life friends. It is just the same when parents let their children play out in the park or go out – they usually want to be sure they are with friends for safety. In the gaming world, 'griefers' may prey on vulnerable, lone players, so it is better to be in a group of friends.

There are features within games that allow players to ignore trolls. Retaliating and revealing how upset you are gives bullies and trolls just the reaction they hoped for. But keep a record and report it. Telling young people to 'ignore' it does not make them feel you are sympathetic – what you are trying to tell them is that they should take lots of assertive action but not let the troll or bully see that they are upset.

Some advice for families of gamers can be found on engadget.com: *MMO Family: 17 Internet Safety Tactics for Gaming Families* (www.engadget.com/2009/10/09/mmo-family-17-Internet-safety-tactics-for-gaming-families).

If families are playing *WOW* or *World of Warcraft* then they can refer to *A Parent's Guide to World of Warcraft for Kids* (www.engadget.com/2011/04/27/a-parents-guide-to-world-of-warcraft-for-kids) for advice on making it family-friendly.

How can parents deal with sexting?

This is advice a school can use with parents.

So your teen, like many others, has shared a photo or video of themselves that is explicit or inappropriate, to use the formal language. These self-generated photos are causing a great deal of worry and are providing pornographers with easy ways to harvest images by simply searching the net rather than having to produce these images in the first place. The Internet Watch Foundation estimates that around 88 per cent of these photos actually end up on porn sites. That is only the half of it. Many teenagers don't actually care what the far-off distant world thinks about their image, but care desperately if people they know get to see the photo. But they are shocked when strange people start contacting them because they have seen their photo on some sleazy website. This can cause enormous harm, as we have seen in recent tragic suicides of young people linked with self-generated photos.

There are generally three types of scenario in which these photos are created.

Romantic escapees

Too often intimate photos 'escape' from romantic relationships when young couples have a spat or split up. Created in a loving relationship, perhaps with some pressure from the boy, but frequently willingly, they are often shown by the recipient to his best friend and, like shampoo draining out of the bottle on the floor of the shower, they are gone, never to be squeezed back into the bottle.

The emotions of pride ('Look at that!') or revenge ('I will make her sorry') are often driving the behaviour and rational thoughts simply vanish. Girls will also circulate photos of boys with killer captions about his prowess, or lack of it, if relationships break up.

Pressurised pics

Another scenario is the making of images under pressure. Some teens are pressured or blackmailed into making and sending these photos because someone says they already have some photos of them and will send them to the victim's parents, or post on a website all their friends will see. This can lead into extortion as requests for money are made – 'If you don't put money into this bank account I will send the photos to your family!'

Trying out my new me

The third scenario is simply experimental. Teenagers are exploring their identities and their sexuality. All around them on billboards, magazines and screens are sexy explicit images. They want to try it out. They want to test their new sexual power and see people say how hot they are.

What not to do

High-profile cases and media stories can make every parent worry and feel tempted to ban their teen from all sorts of sites or take away their mobile phone. None of this will achieve parents' aims to increase their child's safety. If you strictly forbid something it is very difficult for that child to come to you when things have gone wrong, and they need a parent more than ever. Even without their phone – every other teen has a phone, some without safety filters; so if they are pressured, unhappy or insecure and dying to be accepted, they can take a photo on someone else's phone in only a moment to please a boyfriend or girlfriend. The partner probably has a phone, a webcam and more. Your son or daughter may feel unable to say no. Fear of your anger can stop them coming to you in the biggest crisis of their young lives. Your greatest challenge is to keep a door always open. Even if you are not an expert on the Internet, you need to summon all your parenting skills!

So how worried should we be and is there anything parents can do to help?

Don't panic! Let's get this into perspective. Acknowledge that there are really serious risks involved but also that around two thirds of the teens who did share or post photos like this say that nothing happened as a result. In two quite separate surveys in different local areas, each of over 1000 students aged 10–16, we found that around 4 per cent of teenagers told us they had made and shared photos that were explicit or nude. That means most teens are *not* doing this!

Of those who did:

- 7 said they had been threatened or bullied because of a selfie like this that they uploaded or sent someone

- 24 said nothing happened to them as a result of the photo

- 3 said they were not prepared for what happened after they posted the photo

- 8 said they were blackmailed and told that if they did not send more photos or videos the person would send them to their family and friends

- 8 said: 'I have had a lot of drama over sexy selfies.'

So for those who do this, while some are lucky, the risks are high and the fallout can be not only cruel but incredibly dangerous and risky. This is because adults often become involved, even posing as a young person interested in your child, or other teens have an intent to harm and there are aggravated circumstances which require police involvement. Each and every case like these is serious and requires skilled support at once.

It is of course against the law to share photos of this nature of anyone under the age of 18, so they are breaking the law; and anyone who passes one on, saves it or shares it is doing so too. There are other laws in relation to malicious communications or harassment.

Step 1

Try to give an impression of calm and plan your next steps. Contain your anxiety – it can deeply affect your child's state of mind.

Your first priority must be to keep your child safe. If they are desperately depressed, anxious or sad, seek professional help at once. If there is any history of self-harm, seek professional help at once.

Tell your child you are glad he or she came to you with this problem and you are going to try to help.

Explore the facts carefully with them – they may not know where the photo has been shared.

- If it involves an adult, or there is intent to harm, call the local police.
- If it involves child sexual exploitation, report to CEOP.
- If the case has become criminal, report to the IWF.

Step 2

Establish who they shared it with in the first place (or where they posted it).

If you know the person, it may be possible to contact them or their parents immediately and get it taken down.

Your child may be very upset at having to disclose this information. If it is a former boyfriend or girlfriend it can seem like a double betrayal.

Step 3

If it is on a website or social network, try and get the provider to remove it by reporting it at once on their report button.

If it was shared on a mobile, this makes it harder to retrieve it, but you can trace who it was sent to and you can contact the provider to change the mobile number so that your child does not receive any unsolicited contact.

Step 4

Inform the authorities. It is a matter for the police if you think your child was coerced into making and sharing one or more images, your child's image is being exploited or there are threats, blackmail or extortion. Contact: www.ceop.police.uk.

But if your child willingly made and shared a photo or several of this type and it was part of a romantic relationship, you may not want the police involved. Having a criminal record can blight a young person's life and your own child has actually broken the law by sharing this photo. How well do you know the other young person's family? Can you find other ways to resolve this?

Sometimes the local Community Safety Officer will give the young people a talk about the law and it frightens them a bit but they are not charged. Use your judgement here. These two young people may yet get back together again. Your priority must be to control the sharing and circulation of any photos or videos.

If your child simply made what he or she thought were cool or funny photos for fun or to experiment, it is not a matter for the police unless an adult has become involved, perhaps blackmailing your child.

Step 5

Inform their school or college.

Usually the photos are circulating within the school – there could be 200 phones with this image on them. The school can help control this.

If there has been a history of bullying of your child or someone in school has been pressuring your child to make and share these images, the school has powers to deal with it. They will follow their child protection and safeguarding policies and will support you as things develop.

Step 6

Even if you do not understand what led your child to do this – after all you have warned them about – now is the moment to be a loving, caring parent. Later you will go through their e-safety advice and online privacy settings with them once more and ensure they are set up as safely as possible. Consider too that many young people who are lonely or unhappy in real life seek friendship and intimacy online. Think about why your child felt the need to do this. Can you provide some genuine support for their innermost insecurities? A photo can be sent in a momentary click when a young person has barely thought it through – regrets are too late. The shampoo cannot be put back into the bottle.

Parents online criticising the school

Parents may discuss teachers or the school online with others. This can escalate into a campaign in which teachers feel defamed. The school will be monitoring its profile on the Internet and will want to take protective steps. Clearly it is advisable to agree with parents when they join the school that there is an agreed complaints procedure and that this is the manner in which any concerns should be dealt with.

The next handout is a list of actions you may need to take in such a case.

'She's a dreadful teacher'

Parents/carers as instigators of abusive, defamatory material aimed at staff

1. Contact parent/s or lead instigator and invite them into school.

2. Explain that you are aware of some discussions between parents taking place online/on Facebook concerning the school/key teachers or governors.

3. Remind them that you have an open door policy/a parents' complaints procedure/a parents' survey, so you are disappointed that they did not contact the school in the first instance via one of these, as agreed in the Home/School agreement.

4. This agreement also clearly states that parents will support the school to uphold standards of equality, openness and anti-bullying approaches.

5. If parents at your school sign a Home/School agreement, remind them they have signed this.

6. Make clear that defamatory material targeted at a professional is damaging to their career and the person concerned may wish to take legal action.

7. If the remarks are sexual, racist or otherwise contravene the Equality Act 2010, it may be a matter for the police.

8. Request the offending material be removed.

If this does not solve the problem:

1. Report the case to the Chair of Governors. Use the screengrab you have saved.

2. Contact the professional helpline to get it removed.

3. If, however, there is evidence of wrongdoing by a member of staff, do not hesitate to investigate. In such a case, inform the parent and set a date when you will report back to them. In the interim, offensive material must be taken down.

4. Note down what has been agreed with the parent/s. Write to them confirming the agreed actions at this meeting. Re-confirm what they are taking down. Include any steps you have agreed to take to look into what may lie behind this frustration.

5. For example: does this member of staff need support with a difficult class?

Screengrab the evidence and save it

Contact the Professionals' Helpline for advice or to have material removed faster: 0844 381 4772

Unions can advise individual staff members

Home/School agreements can be useful in these cases

Give parents several ways to report concerns

Write to all parents reminding them of complaints procedures and unacceptable actions

12

How the Law Can Apply to Online Behaviour

Every school must have measures in place to prevent all forms of bullying. This includes academies and independent schools. Note that while many of the government documents mentioned in this chapter and elsewhere relate to England, the principles are broadly the same for the rest of the UK.

Definitions of bullying

The Anti-Bullying Alliance define bullying as:

> The repetitive, intentional hurting of one person or a group by another person/group; where the relationship involves an imbalance of power. Bullying can be physical, verbal or psychological. It can take place face to face, indirectly or in cyberspace. It can involve prejudice towards an individual or group of people.

The DfE guidance *Preventing and Tackling Bullying* (2014) defines it as:

> …behaviour by an individual or group, repeated over time, that intentionally hurts another individual or group either physically or emotionally. Bullying can take many forms (for instance, cyberbullying via text messages or the Internet), and is often motivated by prejudice against particular groups, for example on grounds of race, religion, gender, sexual orientation, or because a child is adopted or has caring responsibilities. It might be motivated by actual differences between children, or perceived differences. Stopping violence and ensuring immediate physical safety is obviously a school's first priority but emotional bullying can be more damaging than physical; teachers and schools have to make their own judgements about each specific case.

> Many experts say that bullying involves an imbalance of power between the perpetrator and the victim. This could involve perpetrators of bullying having control over the relationship which makes it difficult for those they bully to defend themselves. The imbalance of power can manifest itself in several ways: it may be physical, psychological (knowing what upsets someone), derive from an intellectual imbalance, or by having access to the support of a group, or the capacity to socially isolate. It can result in the intimidation of a person or persons through the threat of violence or by isolating them either physically or online.

There is currently no legal definition of bullying.

Schools' duties

The school has a duty of care to protect all its members and provide a safe, healthy environment, and these obligations are highlighted in law and in guidance detailed below.

The Department for Education has produced guidance for all schools, including academies and free schools, which outlines duties to prevent and tackle bullying in schools: www.gov.uk/government/publications/preventing-and-tackling-bullying.

Bullying and child protection

Some incidents of bullying or cyberbullying may also be considered as a child protection matter. These cases should be considered as a child protection issue when there is reasonable cause to suspect that a child is suffering, or is likely to suffer, significant harm. These concerns must be reported to the local authority's children's social services.

New guidance on safeguarding (2015)

Keeping Children Safe in Education 2015 statutory guidance for schools and colleges applies to all schools and colleges. It includes new guidance and legislation introduced since the earlier 2014 version and covers preventing radicalisation under the Counter Terrorism and Security Act 2015.

The DfE has published a shorter explanatory document: *Keeping Children Safe in Education: Information for All School and College Staff.* Former local authority designated officers are now referred to as designated officers. Staff are encouraged to speak directly to children's social care services in emergencies. The guidance covers what staff should do if they have concerns about another staff member, including whistleblowing procedures. This document has been updated to clarify relationships and communications between staff and pupils, especially using social media. There is an emphasis on keeping looked-after children safe, including requiring academies to appoint a designated teacher to promote the education and safety of these children.

Education and Inspections Act 2006, Section 89

Headteachers, with the advice and guidance of governors and the assistance of school staff, must identify and implement measures to promote good behaviour, respect for others and self-discipline among learners, and to prevent all forms of bullying. This includes the prevention of cyberbullying. These measures must be communicated to all pupils, school staff and parents. This information can be in a separate Anti-Bullying Policy or sit within a policy on behaviour.

The headteacher must follow through and adopt the policy, and all students, parents and teachers should be notified of it once it has been adopted.

Pupils should be involved in both the drafting of their Anti-Bullying Policy and its monitoring by being encouraged to discuss the policy and its effectiveness. Involving pupils in this way is compatible with young people's rights to participate under Article 12 of the UN Convention on the Rights of the Child 1989, to which the UK is signed up.

(I recommend that any policy relating to bullying should interact closely with the school's policies on Equality; E-safety; Acceptable Use of ICT; Behaviour; and Safeguarding, Child Protection and Inclusion.)

The Education Act 2006 also outlines some legal powers which relate quite directly to cyberbullying:

- Headteachers have the power 'to such extent as is reasonable' to regulate the conduct of learners when they are off-site or not under the control or charge of a member of staff. This is of particular significance to cyberbullying, which is often likely to take place out of school but which can impact very strongly on the school life of those learners involved.

- The DfE guidance clarifies this further in *Behaviour and Discipline in Schools: Advice for Headteachers and School Staff*.

Education Act 2011

The Education Act 2011, Section 85, Clause 3a, gives additional powers to schools – on screening, searching and confiscation, including of electronic devices, where they believe that 'there is a risk that serious harm will be caused to a person if the search is not carried out as a matter of urgency'. There is DfE advice: *Screening, Searching and Confiscation: Advice for Headteachers, Staff and Governing Bodies*. This includes the power to delete certain content within certain conditions.

This Act will 'increase the authority of teachers to discipline pupils':

- Teachers have increased powers to search pupils for objects which could be dangerous or cause harm.

- Pornography and mobile phones have been added to the list of items schools can search for.

- Schools are told they can search for anything they have banned.

- Teachers are given the right to anonymity if they are accused by pupils to protect them from false accusations.

Academies, free schools and independent schools

The Independent School Standards Regulations 2010 state that the proprietor of an academy or other independent school is required to ensure that an effective anti-bullying strategy is drawn up and implemented.

The Equality Act 2010

This Act replaces previous separate Acts addressing discrimination and brings them into a single Act. Schools must follow the Equality Act 2010. Staff must act to prevent discrimination, harassment and victimisation within the school. Under the Act, schools have duties to:

- eliminate discrimination

- advance equality of opportunity

- foster good relations.

There are specific protected characteristics spelled out under this Act:

The specific duties require public bodies to prepare and publish one or more specific and measurable equality objectives which will help them to further the three aims of the Equality Duty. All public bodies subject to the specific duties must publish their first equality objectives by 6 April 2012. Subsequent objectives must be published at least every four years.

See:

www.equalityhumanrights.com/uploaded_files/EqualityAct/PSED/public_sector_
    equality_duty_guidance_for_schools_in_england_final.pdf

www.pfc.org.uk/pdf/specific-duties%20Nov%202011%20(2).pdf

A hate crime is any occurrence as perceived by the victim or any other person to be one of the following: racist; homophobic; transphobic; because of religion; beliefs; gender identity; or disability.

Hate crime includes name-calling, violence, property attacks such as graffiti, verbal attacks and abusive messages either by phone or mail or via the Internet. Contact the police if hate crime occurs.

The Education Act 2002

Maintained schools have obligations under Section 78 of the Education Act (2002) which requires schools, as part of a broad and balanced curriculum, to promote the spiritual, moral, cultural, mental and physical development of pupils at the school and of society. The DfE guidance issued in November 2014, *Promoting Fundamental British Values as Part of SMSC in Schools*, relates specifically to the requirements to actively promote fundamental British values in schools and explains how this can be met through the general requirement in the 2002 Act:

Pupils must be encouraged to regard people of all faiths, races and cultures with respect and tolerance.

It is expected that pupils should understand that while different people may hold different views about what is 'right' and 'wrong', all people living in England are subject to its law.

The school's ethos and teaching, which schools should make parents aware of, should support the rule of English civil and criminal law and schools should not teach anything that undermines it. If schools teach about religious law, particular care should be taken to explore the relationship between state and religious law.

Pupils should be made aware of the difference between the law of the land and religious law.

Sexting – advice on dealing with cases

The section on sexting in the Useful Resources and Websites at the end of the book is useful here.

See also *Cyberbullying and E-safety: What Educators and Other Professionals Need to Know* (Adrienne Katz, 2012, Jessica Kingsley Publishers).

Criminal and civil law relating to cyberbullying
Protection from Harassment Act 1997

This Act is relevant for incidents that have happened repeatedly (i.e. on more than two occasions):

- Section 1 prohibits behaviour amounting to harassment of another.

- Section 2 provides a criminal offence.

- Section 3 provides a civil remedy for breach of the prohibition on harassment in Section 1.

- Section 4 provides a more serious offence of someone causing another person to fear, on at least two occasions, that violence will be used against them.

A civil court may grant an injunction to restrain a person from conduct which amounts to harassment and, following conviction of an offence under Sections 2 or 4, restraining orders are available to protect the victim of the offence.

Communications Act 2003

Section 127 covers all forms of public communications, and subsection (1) defines an offence of sending a 'grossly offensive…obscene, indecent or menacing' communication.

Subsection (2) defines a separate offence where, for the purposes of causing annoyance, inconvenience or needless anxiety, a person sends a message which that person knows to be false (or causes it to be sent) or persistently makes use of a public communications system.

Malicious Communications Act 1988

Section 1 makes it an offence to send an indecent, grossly offensive or threatening letter, electronic communication or other article to another person with the intention that it should cause them distress or anxiety.

Public Order Act 1986

Section 5 makes it an offence to use threatening, abusive or insulting words, behaviour, writing, signs or other visual representation within the sight or hearing of a person likely to be caused harassment, alarm or distress. This offence may apply where a mobile phone is used as a camera or video rather than where speech writing or images are transmitted.

Obscene Publications Act 1959

It is an offence under this Act to publish an obscene article. Publishing includes circulating, showing, playing or projecting the article or transmitting that data, for example over a school intranet. An obscene article is one whose effect is such as to tend to deprave and corrupt persons who are likely to read, see or hear the matter contained or embodied in it.

Computer Misuse Act 1990

When cyberbullying takes the form of hacking into someone else's account, then other criminal laws will come into play, such as the Computer Misuse Act 1990, in addition to civil laws on confidentiality and privacy.

Crime and Disorder Act 1998

An Antisocial Behaviour Order (ASBO), subsequently changed to a Criminal Behaviour Order, could be used for cyberbullying. This is a civil order which prohibits an individual from engaging in specific antisocial acts. One can be made against any person, aged ten or over, where there is evidence that their behaviour caused, or is likely to cause, harassment, alarm or distress to others, and where an order is needed to protect a person or persons from further antisocial acts.

Whether a course of conduct is antisocial in nature is primarily measured by the consequences and the effect it has, or is likely to have, on a member or members of the community within which it is taking place.

Such an order can be used in conjunction with other measures as part of a tiered approach to tackling antisocial behaviour. Prohibitions should be precise, targeted at the specific behaviour complained of, and proportionate to the legitimate aim of protecting the community from further abuse. This can be an effective first step to prevent escalation to criminal behaviour. Breach of an Order is a criminal offence and criminal penalties apply.

Defamation

Defamation is a civil 'common law' tort in respect of which the Defamation Acts of 1952 and 1996 provide certain defences. It applies to any published material that damages the reputation of an individual or an organisation, and it includes material published on the Internet. A civil action for defamation can be brought by an individual or a company, but not by a public authority. It is up to the claimant to prove that the material is defamatory. However, the claimant does not have to prove that the material is false – the burden of proof on that point lies with the author/publisher, who has to prove that what they have written is true.

Where defamatory material is posted on a website, the person affected can inform the host of its contents and ask the host to remove it. Once the host knows that the material is there and that it may be defamatory, it can no longer rely on the defence of innocent dissemination in the Defamation Act 1996. This means that the person affected could (if the material has been published in the jurisdiction, i.e. in Wales and England) obtain a court order (an injunction) to require removal of the material, and could sue either the host or the person who posted the material for defamation.

Note from Ministry of Justice: People who maliciously share sexually explicit pictures of former partners will face prosecution under new laws.

Sending images of this kind may, depending on the circumstances, be an offence under the Communications Act 2003 or the Malicious Communications Act 1988. If repeated, this may also amount to an offence of harassment under the Protection from Harassment Act 1997.

Specific legislation also applies to the making, dissemination or possession of indecent photographs of children under the age of 18.

The maximum penalty for possession of indecent photographs of children is five years in prison.

The creation and distribution of such photographs carries a maximum penalty of ten years.

If anyone has been a victim of this kind they should go to the police.

'Revenge porn' became a specific offence in the Criminal Justice and Courts Bill 2015.

It is an offence for a person to disclose a private sexual photograph or film if the disclosure is made:

- without the consent of an individual who appears in the photograph or film

- with the intention of causing that individual distress.

Useful Resources and Websites

Weblinks change frequently but if you find a weblink is no longer live, very often a quick search for the item will produce it on another page or new website. The best resources are often archived on various sites by charities and training organisations.

General

- Safer Internet Day packs are issued each year: www.saferinternet.org.uk

- www.Childnet.org for initiatives around e-safety such as Safer Internet Day and resources.

- www.swgfl.org.uk for self evaluation of your school strategy and more.

- BIG Award issues resource packs for Anti-Bullying Week every year for members and include cyberbullying and other e-safety advice regularly in news and newsletters www.bullyinginterventiongroup.co.uk

- www.esafetyforschools.com for updates and useful information on e-safety teaching, training, inspection and resources.

- Google offers education on safe searching: https://sites.google.com/site/gwebsearcheducation/lessonplans

- The UK Safer Internet Centre: resources for parents and teachers www.saferinternet.org.uk

- The UK Council for Child Internet Safety: www.gov.uk/government/groups/uk-council-for-child-internet-safety-ukccis for national advice

- Internet Service Providers offer parental controls.

- Parental controls are available in Windows 10 with individual accounts per child set to appropriate levels.

- Restrictions can be selected on Apple products to increase safety of young children.

Cyberbullying

- Thinkuknow – cyberbullying: www.thinkuknow.co.uk/11_16/control/cyberbullying

- BIG Award: www.bullyinginterventiongroup.co.uk/bighelp.php

For advice on Twitter, SNS, Mobiles, Snapchat etc., and general advice on bullying for young people with a separate page for parents:

- ChildLine www.childline.org.uk offers many ways to communicate and get help.

- NSPCC www.nspcc.org.uk offers help to young people and plenty of resources

Safety

- Google family safety information: www.google.co.uk/familysafety

- Yahoo safety information: http://safely.yahoo.com

- The Google family safety channel: www.youtube.com/user/googlefamilysafety

- YouTube safety resource page – short film clip and advice: www.google.com/support/youtube/bin/request.py?contact_type=abuse

- YouTube Educators' resource page: www.google.com/support/youtube/bin/answer.py?answer=157105

- YouTube film clip on how to turn on safety mode: www.youtube.com/watch?v=gkI3e0P3S5E

- Thinkuknow: www.thinkuknow.co.uk for extensive resources and training for CEOP ambassadors

- Internet Matters: www.Internetmatters.org a website supported by internet service providers with a growing library of resources.

- CEOP: www.ceop.police.uk keep an eye on any messages from CEOP and their reports on trends.

- Childnet International: www.childnet.com for advice on online safety

- Digizen: www.digizen.org run by Childnet this is a site with resources for young people

- UK Council for Child Internet Safety ran a Click Clever, Click Safe campaign you might find useful for younger pupils. www.iwf.org.uk/about-iwf/news/post/282-uk-internet-safety-campaign-click-clever-click-safe-launched

- www.knowthenet.org.uk offer various tests to check your knowledge of threats. These may change from time to time. They are fun to do and an easy way to learn.

- Connect Safely: www.connectsafely.org

In Ireland

- www.watchyourspace.ie/about/ Watch this space is an e-safety initiative in Ireland targeting teenagers, by Webwise, www.webwise.ie They also have resources on connecting with respect:

- www.webwise.ie/teachers/connect-with-respect-programme-2

Websites to help keep informed on all things 'Facebook'

- Facebook safety centre www.facebook.com/safety

- Facebook Developers blog: http://developers.facebook.com/blog

- Facebook – controlling what information you share: www.facebook.com/privacy/explanation.php

- Facebook Help Centre: www.facebook.com/help

- While it is noticeable that many young people are moving to other social network sites, it is still the case that many maintain a page on Facebook alongside this. Please note most social networking sites will have a safety page or advice on privacy settings. This is often well hidden but repays a search.

Sexting

- Advice from NSPCC to help parents: www.nspcc.org.uk/preventing-abuse/keeping-children-safe/sexting

- ChildLine is now able to help get explicit images removed by working with IWF. Young people will need to verify their age. They also provide an app called Zippit which offers some useful images to send back if asked to send an intimate photo. Tel. 08001111. www.childline.org.uk/explore/onlinesafety/pages/sexting.aspx?utm_source=google&utm_medium=cpc&utm_campaign=NSPCC_Sexting&utm_term=advice_on_sexting

- NSPCC offers a booklet for young people 'So you got naked online': www.nspcc.org.uk

- Resources for both parents and teachers on how to address sexting are available from the UK Safer Internet Centre:

- www.saferinternet.org.uk/advice-and-resources/parents-and-carers

- www.saferinternet.org.uk/advice-and-resources/teachers-and-professionals

- Vital resources for training staff on dealing with sexting cases: www.naace.co.uk/esafety/sexting

- What view do the police take? Read a position paper. http://ceop.police.uk/Documents/ceopdocs/externaldocs/ACPO_Lead_position_on_Self_Taken_Images.pdf

The Digital Literacy Curriculum

- Resources available from South West Grid for Learning include resources on Digital Literacy: www.digital-literacy.org.uk/Home.aspx

- The Creative Commons website contains information and detailed examples to explain the different Creative Commons copyright that content owners can apply to their digital creations: http://creativecommons.org/about

Safe searching

- Google Search Literacy lesson plans: https://sites.google.com/site/gwebsearcheducation/lessonplans

- Commonsense Media: www.commonsensemedia.org/educators/lesson/strategic-searching-6-8

- South West Grid for Learning 'Strategic Searching': www.digital-literacy.com

Security

- A broad range of e-safety topics are covered by CEOP's Thinkuknow website: www.thinkuknow.co.uk

- www.knowthenet.org.uk offer various tests to check your knowledge of threats. These may change from time to time. They are fun to do and an easy way to learn.

- 'Perfect Passwords' is a lesson from Childnet's Know it All Lower Secondary Toolkit: www.childnet.com/resources/know-it-all-secondary-toolkits/lower-secondary-toolkit

- Childnet also offers an Online Reputation Checklist to help young people manage their online reputation: www.childnet.com/resources/online-reputation-checklist

- Get Safe Online offers information and advice for protecting devices and security on line, including topics on viruses, passwords, malware and other considerations related to online security: http://getsafeonline.org

Stay safe

- The Australian Communications and Media Authority has some excellent resources on the Cybersmart website. Interactive games and lesson plans for staying safe online: https://esafety.gov.au/?from=cybersmart

- 'Accidental outlaw' is an interactive test created by Knowthenet that provides practical information and tips for what constitutes illegal behaviour online: http://accidentaloutlaw.knowthenet.org.uk

- CEOP's Thinkuknow website contains a number of films, activities and lesson plans for KS3. The 'First to a Million' resource can be used to discuss the consequences of sharing content online, the need for respecting others and how content can impact on online reputation. The 'Exploited' films and supporting activities can be used with KS3 to discuss contact with strangers on line, risks of sexual exploitation and the importance of protecting personal information. Note that free sign-up is required in order to download Thinkuknow resources: www.thinkuknow.co.uk/teachers

- Childnet International's award-winning film Let's Fight It Together highlights cyberbullying. There are also character interviews and question sheets that can be used to examine the story and characters in more detail. www.childnet.com/resources/lets-fight-it-together

- Many other resources are provided on the Childnet International site.

Safe viewing

The BBC created Internet-themed Horrible Histories clips for Safer Internet Day in 2012.

- 'Lady Jane Grey – Beware What You Download' is an enjoyable way to explore the consequences of accepting downloads from untrustworthy sites: www.bbc.co.uk/cbbc/clips/p01g2ppl

- 'Prudish Victorian – Don't Lie About Your Age Online' highlights the risks involved in seeing content intended for a different audience: www.bbc.co.uk/cbbc/clips/p00nxznx

- 'Saxon Monk – Internet Videos Are Forever' is a humorous way of exploring the consequences of sharing and exhibiting questionable behaviours online: www.bbc.co.uk/cbbc/clips/p01g2pg0

Prejudice and hate crime – Racism and Homophobia

- EqualiTeach provides materials for support and training to meet your Equality Act duties. Audits, educational materials and policy development. www.equaliteach.co.uk

- Prejudice-driven behaviour – cyberhomophobia. The Reach resource by charity EACH contains lesson plans and film clips: www.each.education

- Kick it out, football's answer to racism: www.kickitout.org

- Show Racism the Red Card a site challenging racism produces new resources regularly: www.srtrc.org

- The Crown Prosecution Service has produced a series of guidance documents in its Schools Project. These consist of lesson activities, PowerPoints and a Guidance document.

- Disability: www.cps.gov.uk/publications/prosecution/disability.html

- Hate crime: www.cps.gov.uk/northwest/get_involved/hate_crime/schools_project___lgbt_hate_crime

- Religious, race and hate crime: www.cps.gov.uk/northwest/get_involved/hate_crime/schools_project___racist_and_religious_hate_crime

- And their general 'Guidelines on prosecuting cases involving communications and social media': www.cps.gov.uk/legal/a_to_c/communications_sent_via_social_media/index.html

- For advice to schools on all things related to equality and diversity: www.insted.co.uk

- To help parents deal with racism and bullying in schools: www.bteg.co.uk/content/help-parents-dealing-racism-and-bullying-school

- Homophobia

- www.each.education A wealth of resources and knowledge, training and films to assist schools to be sensitive and imaginative when addressing homophobia.

- www.stonewall.org.uk for materials on addressing homophobia.

Resources for this book will be posted on www.esafetyforschools.com

Notes

1. The Child Internet Safety Summit, July 2015. Talk by Ofsted's David Brown, HMI: *Online Safety and Inspection*. Available at www.slideshare.net/ Ofstednews/childinternetsafetysummitonline safetyinspection, accessed on 7 October 2015.

2. The Cybersurvey, Autumn 2014.

3. The Cybersurvey, January 2014.

4. Finkelhor, D. (2014) 'Commentary: Cause for alarm? Youth and Internet risk research – a commentary on Livingstone and Smith (2014).' *Journal of Child Psychology and Psychiatry 55*, 655–658.

5. Josie Gurney-Read, *Telegraph Online*, 29 September 2014.

6. Dieter Wolke, *The Long Shadow of Bullying*. Evidence to the APPG, Westminster, 2014.

7. Louise Arseneault *et al.*, Institute of Psychiatry, 'Childhood Trauma and Children's Emerging Psychotic Symptoms.' Talk for BIG Award conference, June 2013.

8. Lereyo, S., *et al.* (2013) 'Being bullied in childhood and the prospective pathways to self-harm in adolescence.' *Journal of the American Academy of Child and Adolescent Psychiatry 52*, 6, 608–618.

9. ChildLine Review: *Under Pressure*. Available at www. nspcc.org.uk/globalassets/documents/annual-reports/ childline-review-under-pressure.pdf, accessed on 7 October 2015.

10. Available at www.lse.ac.uk/media@lse/research/ EUKidsOnline/EU%20Kids%20III/Reports/ NCGMUKReportfinal.pdf, July 2014, accessed on 7 October 2015.

11. Available at www.hscic.gov.uk/article/3956/Statistics- on-children-admitted-to-adult-mental-health-wards- released, accessed on 7 October 2015. See also Tim Brooks-Pollock, *The Telegraph*, 10 August 2014, 'Self- harming among children surges to unprecedented levels.'

12. *Ofcom Report on Internet Safety Measures – Internet Service Providers: Network Level Filtering Measures*, 22 July 2014.

13. BASW (2013) *Social Workers Need More Support in Dealing with Online Abuse of Children*. Available at www.basw. co.uk/news/article/?id=556, accessed on 7 October 2015.

14. The Cybersurvey by Youthworks Consulting is an online service providing a survey and results to individual schools, chains and clusters of schools.

15. Spiritual, Moral, Social and Cultural Development.

16. Available at www.theguardian.com/uk-news/2014/ nov/25/breck-bednar-murder-parents-sue-police, accessed on 7 October 2015.

17. *Communications Market* report, Ofcom, 2014.

18. Inspecting E-safety in Schools refers to: *The Safe Use of New Technologies*, February 2010, which quotes a study of 35 schools. Available at http://webarchive. nationalarchives.gov.uk/20141124154759/http:// www.ofsted.gov.uk/resources/safe-use-of-new- technologies, accessed on 7 October 2015.

19. Ofsted Online Safety Survey, March 2015.

20. NASUWT poll released 2 April 2015: *Huge Rise in Teachers Being Abused on Social Media*. Available at www.nasuwt.org.uk/Whatsnew/NASUWTNews/ PressReleases/NASUWT_013930, accessed on 7 October 2015.

21. DfE: *Computing Programmes of Study, Key Stages 3 and 4*. Reference: DFE-00191-2013. Available at www. computingatschool.org.uk/data/uploads/secondary_ national_curriculum_-_computing.pdf, accessed on 7 October 2015.

22. Available at www.brook.org.uk/about-brook/single/ sre-supplementary-advice, accessed on 7 October 2015.

23. The Cybersurvey for e-Safer Suffolk, 2014.

24. Katz, A., Buchanan, A., and Bream, V. (2001) *Bullying in Britain*. East Molesey, UK: Young Voice.

25. Katz, A., Dabbous, A., and Stockdale, D. (2002) *Islington and You*. East Molesey, UK: Young Voice.

26. Available at www.webmd.com/parenting/features/ is-your-boy-a-bully-why-he-needs-help-and-fast, accessed on 8 October 2015.

27. For example, Boulton, M.J., and Smith, P.K. (1994) 'Bully/victim problems in middle-school children: stability, self-perceived competence, peer perceptions and peer acceptance.' *British Journal of Developmental Psychology 12*, 315–329.

28. Hodges, E.V.E., Malone, M.J., and Perry, D.G. (1997) *Individual Risk and Social Risk as Interactive Determinants of Victimization in the Peer Group Developmental Psychology 33*, 6, 1032–1039.

29. Kochenderfer, B.J., and Ladd, G.W. (1997) 'Victimized children's responses to peers' aggression: behaviors associated with reduced versus continued victimization.' *Development and Psychopathology 9*, 59–73.

30. Boulton, M.J., Trueman, M., Chau, C., Whitehand, C., and Amatya, K. (1999) 'Concurrent and longitudinal links between friendship and peer victimisation: implications for befriending interventions.' *Journal of Adolescence 22*, 461–466.

31. Hodges, E.V.E., Malone, M.J., and Perry, D.G. (1997) *Individual Risk and Social Risk as Interactive Determinants of Victimization in the Peer Group Developmental Psychology 33*, 6, 1032–1039.

32. Pellegrini, A.D., Bartini, M., and Brooks, F. (1999) 'School bullies, victims, and aggressive victims: factors

relating to group affiliation and victimization in early adolescence.' *Journal of Educational Psychology 91*, 2, 216–224.

33. Hodges, E.V.E., and Perry, D.G. (1999) 'Personal and interpersonal antecedents and consequences of victimization by peers.' *Journal of Personality and Social Psychology 76*, 4, 677.

34. Rigby, K. (1997) *Bullying in Schools – And What to Do About It* (British Edition). London: Jessica Kingsley Publishers.

35. Olweus, D., and Endresen, I.M. (1998) 'The importance of sex-of-stimulus object: age trends and sex differences in empathic responsiveness.' *Social Development 7*, 370–388.

36. Cowie, H. (2000) 'Bystanding or standing by: gender issues in coping with bullying in English schools.' *Aggressive Behavior 26*, 1, 85–97.

37. Naylor, P., and Cowie, H. (1999) 'The effectiveness of peer support systems in challenging school bullying: the perspectives and experiences of teachers and pupils.' *Journal of Adolescence 22*, 4, 467–479.

38. Graham, S., and Juvonen, J. (1998) 'Self-blame and peer victimization in middle school: an attributional analysis.' *Developmental Psychology 34*, 3, 587–599.

39. Smith, P.K., Talamelli, L., Cowie, H., Naylor, P., and Chauhan, P. (2004) 'Profiles of non-victims, escaped victims, continuing victims and new victims of school bullying.' *British Journal of Educational Psychology 74*, 565–581.

40. Available at www.mbro.ac.uk/home/index/collegeinfo/equalityanddiversity/eqdocs.aspx, accessed on 8 October 2015.

41. Ofsted (2010) *The Safe Use of New Technologies.* Available at http://webarchive.nationalarchives.gov.uk/20141124154759/http://www.ofsted.gov.uk/resources/safe-use-of-new-technologies, accessed on 8 October 2015.

42. Interview with Donna Bowman for A.V. Club, 17 November 2008. See www.avclub.com/article/malcolm-gladwell-14333, accessed on 12 October 2015.

43. DfE (September 2013) *National Curriculum in England: Citizenship Programmes of Study for Key Stages 3 and 4.* Available at www.gov.uk/government/publications/national-curriculum-in-england-citizenship-programmes-of-study/national-curriculum-in-england-citizenship-programmes-of-study-for-key-stages-3-and-4, accessed on 12 October 2015.

44. Available at www.un.org/en/globalissues/briefingpapers/humanrights/quotes.shtml, accessed on 12 October 2015.

45. Anderson, C.A., *et al.* (2008) 'Longitudinal effects of violent video games on aggression in Japan and the United States.' *Pediatrics 122*, 5, e1067–e1072.

46. Available at www.pamf.org/parenting-teens/general/media-web/videogames.html, accessed on 13 October 2015.

47. Gaming Revolution conducted by Populus for the Internet Advertising Bureau. Infographic at www.iabuk.net/research/library/gaming-revolution-summary-infographic, accessed on 13 October 2015.

48. *Parents Fail to Spot Their Kids Are Obese.* London School of Hygiene and Tropical Medicine, the University of Bristol, University College London and Imperial College London, funded by the National Institute for Health Research. Available at www.nhs.uk/news/2015/03March/Pages/Parents-fail-to-spot-that-their-kids-are-obese.aspx, accessed on 15 October 2015.

49. Gentile, D.A., and Anderson, C.A. (2014) 'Long-term relations among prosocial-media use, empathy, and prosocial behavior.' *Psychology Science 2*, 358–368.

50. See www.theguardian.com/technology/2014/sep/17/women-video-games-iab, accessed on 15 October 2015.

51. See www.bmj.com/content/344/bmj.e2598, accessed on 15 October 2015.

52. *How Video Gaming Can Be Beneficial for the Brain.* Available at www.mpg.de/7588840/video-games-brain, accessed on 12 October 2015.

53. Available at www.huffingtonpost.com/2013/11/07/video-games-good-for-us_n_4164723.html, accessed on 15 October 2015.

54. Przybylski, A. (2014) *A Little Video Playing Linked With Better-Adjusted Children.* Available at www.ox.ac.uk/news/2014-08-04-little-video-game-playing-linked-better-adjusted-children, accessed on 15 October 2015.

55. Available at www.apa.org/pubs/journals/special/5561402.aspx, accessed on 15 October 2015.

56. BBC, Sean Coughlan (February 2014), available at www.bbc.co.uk/news/education-26049333, accessed on 15 October 2015; Mirjana Bajovic (2012), available at http://dr.library.brocku.ca/bitstream/handle/10464/4115/Brock_%20Bajovic_Mirjana_2012.pdf, accessed on 15 October 2015.

57. Read more at www.brainyquote.com/quotes/keywords/privacy.html#d4s7DIKj2fkzMeeT.99 and www.britroyals.com/windsor.asp?id=princess_margaret, accessed on 19 October 2015.

58. Interview for *The Telegraph* with Roger Highfield, 21 October 2001. Available at www.telegraph.co.uk/news/science/science-news/4766816/Interview-with-Stephen-Hawking.html, accessed on 19 October 2015.

59. Ofsted (September 2012) *Inspecting E-safety in Schools*; and *Online Safety Survey* (March 2015), in which 39 primary and 45 secondary schools were studied.

60. Phippen, A. (2013) *Online Safety Policy and Practice*, based on feedback from 1500 UK schools via the self-evaluation tool developed by South West Grid for Learning. Available at http://swgfl.org.uk/products-services/esafety/resources/E-Safety-Research/Content/Online-Safety-Policy-and-Practice-2013, accessed on 19 October 2015.

61. South West Grid for Learning (November 2009) survey of 1100 11–16-year-olds, *Sharing Personal Images and Videos Among Young People.*

62. DfE (April 2011) *The Use and Effectiveness of Anti-bullying Strategies.*

63. These grade descriptors are taken from an Ofsted Section 5 briefing on e-safety that was current until mid-2015. Although it is no longer available online, we are told that inspectors have received training in all that is contained within it. Inspection has changed to focus on looking at radicalisation and CSE, but these basic building blocks of e-safety form the foundation required.

64. Ofsted – *The Safe Use of New Technologies*, 10 February 2010.

65. Byron 2008, *Safer Children in a Digital World.*

66. DCSF (July 2008) *Disabled Children: Numbers, Characteristics and Local Service Provision.*

67. The National Autistic Society.

68. Mencap.

69. Cybersurvey, 2013.

70. National Autstic Society, 2006, *B is for Bullied.*.

71. Mencap, 2006, *Bullying Wrecks Lives.*

72. The Cybersurvey, Autumn 2014. Report on those involved in sexting. Published 2015.

73. Mishna, F. (2003) 'Learning disabilities and bullying: double jeopardy.' *Journal of Learning Disability 36*, 4, 336–347.

74. DCSF (2008) *Safe to Learn: Bullying Involving Children With Special Needs and Disabilities.* The consultation was titled *Safe to Play* and undertaken by Youthworks in the West Midlands.

75. Bond, E. (2012) *Virtually Anorexic – Where's the Harm?* Available at www.ucs.ac.uk/Faculties-and-Centres/ Faculty-of-Arts,-Business-and-Applied-Social-Science/Department-of-Children,-Young-People-and-Education/Virtually%20Anorexic.pdf, accessed on 19 October 2015.

76. The Bullying Intervention Group runs the Big award and offers all member school a free pupil survey. This data is regularly collated and analysed in order to improve practice.

77. ChildLine survey of 400 people, 2014. See *Number of Children who are Victims of Cyberbullying Doubles in a Year*, www.theguardian.com/society/2014/nov/14/35pc-children-teenagers-victims-cyberbullying-fears-grooming-tinder-snapchat, accessed on 19 October 2015.

78. NSPCC, August 2014.

79. *The Canadian Press*, 15 December 2013. See www.macleans.ca/news/canada/link-between-cyberbullying-and-teen-suicides-oversimplified-experts-say, accessed on 19 October 2015.

80. Marie Collins Foundation (2014) *Child Victims of Online Abuse Let Down by Lack of Training.* Available at www.mariecollinsfoundation.org.uk/news/post/7-child-victims-of-online-abuse-let-down-by-lack-of-training, accessed on 19 October 2015.

81. Whittle, H., Hamilton-Giachritsis, C., Beech, A., and Collings, G. (2013) 'A review of online grooming: characteristics and concerns.' *Aggression and Violent Behavior 18*, 1, 62–70.

82. NSPCC. www.nspcc.org.uk/preventing-abuse/child-abuse-and-neglect/

83. Massachusetts Aggression Reduction Centre, 2013. www.bbc.co.uk/news/magazine-25120783

84. Fisher, H.L., Moffitt, T.E., Houts, R.M., Belsky, D.W., Arseneault, L., and Caspi, A. (2012) 'Bullying victimisation and risk of self harm in early adolescence: longitudinal cohort study.' *BMJ 344*, e2683.

85. *Ibid.*

86. The Cybersurvey for e-Safety, Suffolk, 2014.

87. The UK Government's Prevent strategy: www.gov.uk/government/publications/2010-to-2015-government-policy-counter-terrorism, accessed on 19 October 2015.

88. The Channel process: www.counterextremism.org/resources/details/id/115/channel-process, accessed on 19 October 2015.

89. Ofsted (June 2015) *The Future of Education Inspection.*

90. This guide is written by experts with police experience. Available at www.parentsprotect.co.uk/files/Sexting%20in%20Schools%20eBooklet%20FINAL%2030APR13.pdf, accessed on 20 October 2015.

Index